God Over All

Divine Aseity and the Challenge of Platonism

WILLIAM LANE CRAIG

UNIVERSITY PRESS

Great Clarendon Street, Oxford, OX2 6DP,
United Kingdom

Oxford University Press is a department of the University of Oxford.
It furthers the University's objective of excellence in research, scholarship,
and education by publishing worldwide. Oxford is a registered trade mark of
Oxford University Press in the UK and in certain other countries

© William Lane Craig 2016

The moral rights of the author have been asserted

First published 2016
First published in paperback 2018

All rights reserved. No part of this publication may be reproduced, stored in
a retrieval system, or transmitted, in any form or by any means, without the
prior permission in writing of Oxford University Press, or as expressly permitted
by law, by licence or under terms agreed with the appropriate reprographics
rights organization. Enquiries concerning reproduction outside the scope of the
above should be sent to the Rights Department, Oxford University Press, at the
address above

You must not circulate this work in any other form
and you must impose this same condition on any acquirer

Published in the United States of America by Oxford University Press
198 Madison Avenue, New York, NY 10016, United States of America

British Library Cataloguing in Publication Data
Data available

Library of Congress Cataloging in Publication Data
Data available

ISBN 978-0-19-878688-7 (Hbk.)
ISBN 978-0-19-880292-1 (Pbk.)

Links to third party websites are provided by Oxford in good faith and
for information only. Oxford disclaims any responsibility for the materials
contained in any third party website referenced in this work.

To Richard Swinburne
Thank you

Preface

This book is an expansion of my 2015 Cadbury Lectures at the University of Birmingham, England, which themselves were a distillation of a much longer study on God and abstract objects. I am grateful to Professors Yujin Nagasawa and David Cheetham and to the John Hick Centre for Philosophy of Religion for the invitation to deliver these lectures.

The invitation came just as I was wrapping up a research project on divine aseity and the challenge to it posed by contemporary Platonism that had preoccupied me for the previous dozen years or so. This happy coincidence gave me the opportunity to state my arguments succinctly and in a semi-popular form, so as to make the lectures profitable for non-specialists.

Philosophers of religion and theologians, to whom this book is primarily directed, may be unfamiliar with the debates central to our topic which are raging in the philosophy of mathematics, philosophy of language, metaphysics, and logic. To aid understanding, I have compiled a Glossary of specialist terminology offering elementary definitions or explanations of key terms. I have also included a Figure 1 as part of the front matter of the book, to which I shall have occasion to recur, in order to provide at a glance a visual taxonomy of the various alternative views discussed in this book.

Having laboured for over a dozen years to understand how best to respond to Platonism's challenge to divine aseity, I have, as one might expect, been greatly helped by the interaction of many colleagues in a wide range of fields on various questions. I wish to thank in particular for their stimulus and input: Robert Adams, Jody Azzouni, Mark Balaguer, J. T. Bridges, Jeffery Brower, Charles Chihara, Paul Copan, Thomas Crisp, Trent Dougherty, Mark Edwards, Thomas Flint, Paul Gould, Dorothy Grover, Geoffrey Hellman, Paul Horwich, Ross Inman, Peter van Inwagen, Dennis Jowers, Brian Leftow, Mary Leng, Christopher Menzel, J. P. Moreland, Thomas Morris, Kenneth Perszyck, Michael Rea, Maria Reicher-Marek, Theodore Sider, Peter Simons, Alvin Plantinga, Joshua Rasmussen, Elliott Sober, Robert Thomas, Achille Varzi, Greg Welty, Edward Wierenga, Dallas Willard, Stephen Yablo, Takashi Yagisawa, and Dean Zimmerman. I am also grateful for the comments of three anonymous referees of Oxford University Press. My research assistant Timothy Bayless deserves grateful mention for his procuring research materials, hunting down references, compiling the bibliography, and carrying out other related tasks for me. Thanks, too, to Kevin Whitehead for his proofreading the penultimate draft of the typescript! Finally, as always, I am grateful to my wife Jan, not only for her help with early portions of the typescript, but even more for her encouragement and interaction ('Honey, what do you think? Does the number 2 exist?').

As mentioned, my lectures were a condensation of a much longer, scholarly work on *God and Abstract Objects* to appear with Springer Verlag. Readers desiring a more extensive, in-depth discussion of the questions and views treated here may consult that work.

Contents

1. Introduction — 1
2. God: The Sole Ultimate Reality — 13
3. The Challenge of Platonism — 44
4. Absolute Creation — 54
5. Divine Conceptualism — 72
6. Making Ontological Commitments (1) — 96
7. Making Ontological Commitments (2) — 125
8. Useful Fictions — 144
9. Figuratively Speaking — 167
10. Make-Believe — 181
11. God Over All — 206

Glossary — 209
Works Cited — 219
General Index — 233
Index of Ancient Sources — 242

In all things God has the pre-eminence, who alone is uncreated, the first of all things, and the primary cause of the existence of all.

(Irenaeus, *Against Heresies* 4.38.3)

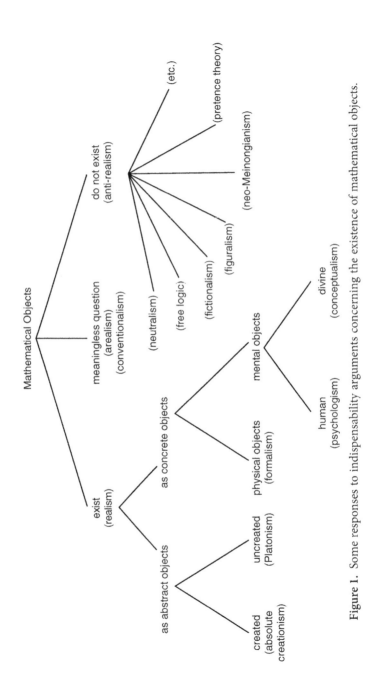

Figure 1. Some responses to indispensability arguments concerning the existence of mathematical objects.

1

Introduction

Central to the Judaeo-Christian concept of God is the notion that God is a self-existent being. That is to say, God is not dependent upon any other being for His existence; rather, He exists independently of everything else. Were everything else magically to disappear, God would still exist. God has the property or attribute of self-existence.

DIVINE ASEITY

This attribute of God is called *aseity*. The word derives from the Latin *a se*, which means *of itself* or *from itself*. God does not exist through another or from another. He just exists in and of Himself, independent of everything else. In other words, He is a self-existent being.

Protestant scholastic theologians typically distinguished between the communicable and incommunicable attributes of God. Communicable attributes are those which God shares with created things, though to different degrees. For example, knowledge and power are possessed by both God and created things, by created things to a finite degree, but by God, who is omniscient and omnipotent, to an infinite degree. Incommunicable attributes, on the other hand, are those which are unique to God. Nothing else has these attributes.

Aseity is traditionally held to be one of the incommunicable attributes of God. God alone is self-existent; everything else is dependent for its existence upon something else. Thus, the doctrine of divine aseity is closely related to the doctrine of creation. According to that doctrine, everything that exists (other than God) has been created by God. So everything that exists other than God is a created thing. Such things are therefore not self-existent, but are dependent for their existence upon God, their Creator. Even God could not create a self-existent being, for a created, self-existent being is as logically incoherent as a round triangle or a married bachelor. To be self-existent is to be uncreated. So anything apart from God is a created being and therefore not self-existent. Aseity is thus an incommunicable attribute of God.

So on the traditional conception, God is what the philosopher Brian Leftow calls 'the sole ultimate reality',[1] the pinnacle of being, so to speak. For all other beings have been created by Him and therefore depend on Him for their existence, whereas God depends upon nothing else for His existence and is the source of existence of everything else. In the next chapter, I shall say something further about the biblical and theological motivations for the traditional doctrine of divine aseity, but now I want to introduce the most formidable challenge to the coherence of the doctrine.

PLATONISM

The strongest challenge to the coherence of the traditional doctrine of divine aseity comes from the philosophy of Platonism. Plato (429–347 BC) held that there exist uncreated entities other than God. These are not part of the physical world, which God has created, but are part of a transcendent, conceptual realm comprising what Plato called Ideas or Forms. They include mathematical objects like numbers and geometrical shapes, such as the perfect circle or triangle, which are not to be found in the physical realm. Plato held that, far from being created by God, these transcendent realities served as God's model or pattern after which He fashioned the physical world.[2] Although we might be inclined to look upon such objects as having at best a ghostly sort of existence, for Plato the objects of this transcendent realm were actually more real than the objects of the physical world, which are like mere shadows of these transcendent realities.

---

[1] Brian Leftow, *God and Necessity* (Oxford: OUP, 2012), 3–5.
[2] See his dialogue *Timaeus* 3–4. It is not clear to what degree Plato took his creation story to be literally true, as opposed to mythological. What is clear is that he took these ideal objects to be uncreated.

Plato held that these transcendent, ideal objects are uncreated, necessary, and eternal. God is therefore not the sole ultimate reality. Contemporary Platonism differs vastly from classical Platonism in various respects;[3] but both views are united in holding that there exist uncreated entities—for example, mathematical objects—other than God. Contemporary Platonists call such entities 'abstract' objects in order to distinguish them from concrete objects like people, planets, and chairs. Insofar as these abstract objects are taken to be uncreated, necessary, and eternal, contemporary Platonism also comes into conflict with the traditional doctrines of divine aseity and creation.

ABSTRACT AND CONCRETE OBJECTS

How should we understand the distinction which contemporary philosophers draw between abstract and concrete objects? Although the distinction is commonplace, it remains a matter of dispute just how to draw that distinction. Many philosophers have simply given up the job of supplying a criterion to distinguish abstract from concrete objects, choosing instead simply to point to examples which serve as paradigms of each type of object. For example, physical objects are universally taken to be examples of concrete objects. On the other hand, mathematical objects like numbers, functions, and sets are regarded as paradigmatic examples of abstract objects. Only slightly more controversially, properties (universal qualities which are exemplified by particulars), propositions (the information content of sentences), and possible worlds (ways reality might have been) are taken by most philosophers to be paradigmatic abstract objects. Most philosophers would agree that, if there are such things, then they are abstract rather than concrete objects. So a discussion of the reality of abstract objects is usually able to proceed on the basis of such shared examples, even in the absence of a clearly enunciated criterion distinguishing abstract from concrete objects. Indeed, any proposed criterion will be assessed by how well it categorizes such paradigm examples.

---

[3] Principally, as we shall see, in taking abstract objects to be causally unrelated to the concrete world; neither do contemporary Platonists consider abstract objects to be more real than concrete objects. Nor do they think that concrete objects participate in some way in abstract entities, as Plato thought physical objects participate in ideal objects.

On the basis of the examples thus far considered, one might be tempted to think that the distinction between the concrete and the abstract is the same as between the material and the immaterial. But a moment's reflection shows that that cannot be correct. For if immaterial agents like souls or angels exist, they would indisputably fall in the class of concrete, not abstract, objects. Everyone recognizes that there is a world of difference between such causally active agents and things like numbers, propositions, and possible worlds. So even if, as it seems, all abstract objects are immaterial, not all immaterial objects are abstract. There could be objects which are both concrete and immaterial, so that the abstract/concrete distinction cannot be equated with the immaterial/material distinction.

One might then think that concrete objects, whether material or immaterial, are all spatiotemporal objects, while abstract objects are without exception non-spatiotemporal objects, that is, objects which transcend space and time. Is that how the distinction between abstract and concrete ought to be drawn? Again, the answer is, no. For God, if He exists, is plausibly thought to exist beyond space and time (at least sans the universe), being the free Creator of space and time. Yet, as a causal agent who has created the world, God would be a paradigmatic concrete object.

Moreover, while some abstract objects—most notably, certain mathematical objects like numbers—would seem to exist beyond space and time, if they exist at all, that is not the case for many other kinds of abstract object. Take properties, for example. Particular things are constantly changing in their properties, acquiring some and losing others at different times. Properties must therefore exist in time, if not in space, since they are constantly changing in their relation to temporal things, being exemplified by a particular object at one time and no longer exemplified by it at a later time. Such relational change is sufficient for being in time. Or consider propositions. They are even more clearly temporal, since many of them seem to change not just relationally, but intrinsically, over time. For many propositions—for example, *George Bush is the President of the United States*—are plausibly variable in their truth value, being sometimes true and sometimes false. If the propositional content of tensed sentences includes the sentences' tense, then the propositions expressed by such sentences must exist in time, since they undergo intrinsic change with respect to their truth value.

There are even more evident, if *recherché*, examples of abstract objects which, if they exist at all, exist spatiotemporally. For example, the Equator is a geometrical line which girdles the Earth and therefore exists in space. You can actually step over this abstract object! Moreover, it depends on the Earth for its existence and so exists only so long as the Earth exists. It is thus an abstract, spatiotemporal object. Or consider the centre of mass of the solar system. This is a point whose spatial location is constantly changing as the planets revolve around the Sun. You could actually enclose this abstract object in the hollow of your hand—though not for long, since it would pass right through your hand to another location! One cannot therefore equate concrete objects with spatiotemporal objects and abstract objects with non-spatiotemporal objects.

The last two examples also serve to show that the distinction between the abstract and the concrete is not equivalent to the distinction between the metaphysically necessary and the metaphysically contingent.[4] While numbers, propositions, properties, and possible worlds do seem to be metaphysically necessary, if they exist, that is not the case for all abstract objects, as the examples of the Equator and the centre of mass of the solar system show. Moreover, many contemporary Platonists think that literary and musical compositions are abstract objects, not to be identified with any particular exemplar of those works. For example, Beethoven's *Fifth Symphony* cannot plausibly be identified with some printed score, lest we be compelled to say that, if that score were destroyed, Beethoven's *Fifth Symphony* would no longer exist! But since literary and musical works are plausibly the creations of their respective authors, most Platonists hold them not to be metaphysically necessary in their existence. Moreover, in mathematics, so-called 'impure' sets, that is to say, sets which have non-sets—for example, people—as their members, do not exist necessarily, since if their members do not exist, the set does not exist either. For example, the set {Ronald Reagan, Gerald Ford} would not exist in a world in which those two men never existed. In fact, this set no longer exists if Reagan and Ford have perished.

Neither are all concrete objects metaphysically contingent, since God is usually considered to exist necessarily, if He exists at all, and

---

[4] Something is metaphysically necessary if its non-existence is impossible. Something is metaphysically contingent if it is possible for it to exist or to not exist. In the language of possible worlds, a metaphysically necessary being exists in every possible world, whereas a metaphysically contingent being exists only in some, but not all, possible worlds.

yet, as I have said, God is a paradigmatic concrete object, being a personal agent endowed with causal powers and causally active in the world, interacting with other concrete objects.

Perhaps here we have a clue as to how the distinction between abstract and concrete objects is best drawn. It is very widely held among philosophers that abstract objects, in contrast to concrete objects, are causally impotent and so are not related to other objects as causes to effects. Moreover, their causal impotence seems to be an essential feature of abstract objects. The number 2, for example, does not just *happen* to be causally effete. It seems inconceivable that 2 could possess causal powers. Abstract objects' causal impotence entails that they are immaterial, for if they were material objects, they would exist in time and space and so could come into contact with other things, thereby affecting those things. No wonder, then, that some thinkers have too hastily concluded that the abstract/concrete distinction just is the immaterial/material distinction! Perhaps the reason abstract objects are causally effete is precisely because they are neither material objects nor personal agents. Be that as it may, the criterion of essential causal impotence seems to delineate effectively abstract from concrete objects.

Fortunately, little hangs upon a successful delineation between abstract and concrete objects, for what is theologically problematic about such objects is not their abstractness, but their uncreatability, along with their necessity and eternality. Any object, whether concrete or abstract, which is uncreated will fatally compromise God's being the sole ultimate reality. The theist can happily admit the existence of created, contingent, transitory abstract objects like the Equator or Beethoven's *Fifth*. What he cannot allow is the existence of things which are as ontologically ultimate as God. The reason abstract objects are at the centre of this controversy is simply because they are the most—perhaps only—plausible candidates for uncreated, necessary, eternal objects apart from God Himself.

TERMINOLOGICAL CLARIFICATIONS

Platonism/Anti-Platonism and Realism/Anti-Realism

Before proceeding further, it will be helpful—indeed, almost crucial if we are to avoid misunderstanding—to clarify some terminology.

Platonism is the view that abstract objects exist, while *anti-Platonism* is the view that abstract objects do not exist. Sometimes these two views are equated with *realism* and *anti-realism* respectively, but this equation is misleading. For, as we shall see, there are anti-Platonists who believe in the reality of mathematical objects, propositions, and so on, but who think that these objects are concrete, not abstract. Thus, some anti-Platonists are realists and some are anti-realists about said objects. I propose, therefore, that we take *realism* to be any view according to which mathematical objects, properties, possible worlds, and so on, exist and *anti-realism* to be any view that such objects do not exist. (Obviously, someone might be a realist about some objects, say, numbers, but an anti-realist about others, for example, possible worlds.) So a realist about some such objects might be either a Platonist or an anti-Platonist; but since the anti-realist about such objects holds that they do not exist, he is obviously an anti-Platonist.

Nominalism

In the literature, both anti-Platonism and anti-realism, as I have defined them, have been called *nominalism*. Since anti-Platonism and anti-realism are two different views, this label is very confusing. Moreover, there are two further reasons to shun the use of this label. First, 'nominalism' is a term which is used in two different philosophical debates to denominate very different views.[5] The first is the age-old dispute over the existence of universals. In this debate, nominalism is the view that universals do not exist, that everything that exists is a particular. The second debate is a very recent discussion, centred in the philosophy of mathematics, that has arisen only since the publication of the German mathematician Gottlob Frege's *Foundations of Arithmetic* (1884). In this debate, the word 'nominalism' is often used as a synonym for anti-Platonism about abstract objects (abstract mathematical objects, for example, do not exist).

The problem is that a person who is a nominalist in one debate may not be a nominalist in the other debate. For example, in the old

---

[5] See the clear differentiation in Gonzalo Rodriguez-Pereyra, 'Nominalism in Metaphysics', in *The Stanford Encyclopedia of Philosophy*, 1 Apr. 2015, <http://plato.stanford.edu/entries/nominalism-metaphysics>.

dispute over universals, one type of nominalism is called class nominalism, according to which similar objects are those included in a certain class. Since classes are abstract objects akin to sets, however, such a thinker is not a nominalist in the second debate, but rather a Platonist. Similarly, a person who identifies universals as thoughts in someone's mind is a nominalist in the second debate (since thoughts are concrete, not abstract objects), but not a nominalist in the first debate (since he takes thoughts to be real and therefore universals to be real). The tendency of some philosophers to blur the lines of these two debates by use of the word 'nominalism' has therefore been a source of confusion.

The second reason I think it advisable to avoid the word 'nominalism' is because of the very negative theological connotations—such as that God is not essentially good[6]—which the term acquired as a result of the first debate. These are utterly foreign to nominalism as defined in the second debate, being a development which has had wings only since the publication of Hartry Field's groundbreaking book *Science without Numbers* (1980). It would be theologically prejudicial to call positions in this second debate nominalist.

So in this book I shall refer to the position that mathematical objects (or propositions or properties or what have you) exist as realism with respect to such objects, and the position that they do not exist as anti-realism. As Figure 1 (p. xii) illustrates, anti-realism comprises a diverse range of specific views; there are many different perspectives which count as anti-realist. Realism comprises any view that holds that things like mathematical objects exist, whether concretely or abstractly. Clearly, then, realism also comprises a diversity of specific views, some Platonist and some anti-Platonist.

Platonism

There is one more important terminological clarification that needs to be made, and that concerns the term 'Platonism' itself. For there are today two very different views on offer, both claiming the label of 'Platonism'. One is a sort of 'heavyweight' Platonism which takes abstract objects to be just as real as the physical objects which make

---

[6] On the misguided assumption that in order to be essentially good God must possess the property *goodness*.

up the world. For this sort of Platonist, numbers are just like automobiles, only more numerous, abstract, and eternal.[7] Such a comparison makes us smile; but it serves to underline the seriousness of the heavyweight Platonist's ontological commitment to abstract objects. As Michael Dummett says, 'The mathematician is, therefore, concerned, on this view, with the correct description of a special realm of reality, comparable to the physical realms described by the geographer and the astronomer.'[8] For the heavyweight Platonist, our ontological inventory of the world must include numbers, along with concrete objects.

The metaphysician Peter van Inwagen of the University of Notre Dame is doubtless the most prominent heavyweight Christian Platonist on the contemporary philosophical scene. Van Inwagen divides reality into two exclusive and exhaustive categories, the abstract and the concrete, and says that the objects belonging to each category exist in precisely the same sense.[9] He has argued specifically for the existence of abstract objects like properties, shapes, and fictional characters.[10] He rejects creationist views of such objects as well as anti-realist views, holding such objects to be, like God, uncreated things.[11] He admits that such a viewpoint makes him uncomfortable, but he feels rationally obliged to concede the existence of such uncreated objects.

By contrast, there is also a sort of 'lightweight' Platonism whose ontological commitment to abstract objects is much more obscure.

---

[7] A comparison suggested by Michael D. Resnik, *Frege and the Philosophy of Mathematics* (Ithaca, NY: Cornell University Press, 1980), 162. Never mind for the moment that some ontologists deny that automobiles exist, taking what we call automobiles to be either nothing more than fundamental particles arranged in a certain way or, alternatively, a conglomeration of metal, plastic, etc., which we see as an automobile. The illustration is too engaging to ignore merely on account of these caveats.

[8] Michael Dummett, 'Platonism', in *Truth and Other Enigmas* (Cambridge, MA: Harvard University Press, 1978), 202.

[9] Peter van Inwagen, 'Being, Existence, and Ontological Commitment', in David Chalmers et al. (eds), *Metametaphysics: New Essays on the Foundations of Ontology* (Oxford: Clarendon, 2009), 472–506.

[10] See Peter van Inwagen, 'A Theory of Properties', in Dean Zimmerman (ed.), *Oxford Studies in Metaphysics*, i (Oxford: Clarendon, 2004), 107–38; Peter van Inwagen, 'Did God Create Shapes?', *Philosophia Christi*, 17/2 (2015): 285–90; Peter van Inwagen, 'Creatures of Fiction', *American Philosophical Quarterly*, 14/4 (1977): 299–308.

[11] Peter van Inwagen, 'God and Other Uncreated Things', in Kevin Timpe (ed.), *Metaphysics and God: Essays in Honor of Eleonore Stump* (London: Routledge, 2009), 3–20.

For these thinkers, abstract objects seem to be merely semantic objects: they are what we are talking about when we use abstract terms like '3' or 'the square root of 9'. They need be no more real than grammatical objects. Something can be grammatically the direct object of a sentence without being a really existing object, as in 'The Press Secretary knew the whereabouts of the Prime Minister.' Similarly, 'the whereabouts of the Prime Minister' can be semantically a term we use to talk about his whereabouts, that is, the term refers to his whereabouts, without implying that there is some really existing object which is the Prime Minister's whereabouts.

Lest you think this a bizarre example, the Prime Minister's whereabouts is precisely one of the examples the Platonist philosopher Bob Hale uses to illustrate the abstract objects which serve as the semantic referents of certain terms. With regard to the question whether such objects exist, Hale says bluntly,

> If it is taken as invoking the everyday notion of object, the question whether there are abstract objects is devoid of philosophical interest; its answer is quite certainly that there are not, but that is trivial—a great many kinds of thing beside those whose title to be recognized as abstract objects has been taken seriously by philosophers fail to count as objects in that sense. Vague though the common notion is, it is evidently outrageous to suggest that numbers, classes, directions and shapes, say, are objects in that sense. But the same goes for hurricanes, speeches (i.e., the actual historical events) and holes in the ground.[12]

Hale's remarks are quite puzzling. He grants that abstract objects are not objects in the ordinary sense of the word and so in that sense do not exist. But he is unperturbed by this admission because many other things—such as hurricanes, speeches, and holes—do not exist in that sense either. Hale's remarks are puzzling because his examples of things that do not exist in the sense that ordinary objects exist are precisely things which many ontologists deny do exist, period.[13]

---

[12] Bob Hale, *Abstract Objects*, Philosophical Theory (Oxford: Basil Blackwell, 1987), 4; cf. the last paragraph on p. 26.

[13] E.g. Peter van Inwagen considers the postulation of events to be 'ontologically profligate'. He writes, 'There are, I would say, no events. That is to say, all statements that appear to involve quantification over events can be paraphrased as statements that involve objects, properties, and times—and the paraphrase leaves nothing out': 'God and Other Uncreated Things', 14. Theodore Sider compares talk of properties in a nominalistic understanding to talk of holes: 'We talk, for instance, as if there are such things as holes . . . But surely there aren't *really* such things as holes, are there?

Hurricanes and speeches are not things, but events, and many ontologists deny that events exist. Holes are probably the favourite illustration which ontologists use of something that we commonly talk about but which does not exist. So if numbers, classes, and other mathematical objects have no more reality than holes and hurricanes, Hale ought to count as an anti-realist, not a Platonist.

John Burgess, another prominent lightweight Platonist, considers the question of the existence of mathematical objects in a theological light:

> One very traditional sort of way to try to make sense of the question of the ultimate metaphysical existence of numbers would be to turn the ontological question into a theological question: Did it or did it not happen, on one of the days of creation, that God said, 'Let there be numbers!' and there were numbers, and God saw the numbers, that they were good? According to Dummett, and according to Nietzsche—or my perspective on Nietzsche—this is the *only* way to make sense of questions of ontological metaphysics.... I myself believe, like Russell, that analytic atheism [the thesis that theological language is meaningless] is false, and suspect, contrary to the Australians, that the Nietzsche-Dummett thesis is true. If as I believe the theological question does make sense, and if as I suspect it is the only sensible question about the italics-added *real* or capital-R Real existence of numbers, then I would answer that question in the negative; but then I would equally answer in the negative the question of the *Real* existence of just about anything.[14]

Burgess rejects what he calls 'capital-R Realism' in favour of a much weaker 'realism'.[15] This weak realism does not presume to tell us 'just what God was saying to Himself when He was creating the universe'.[16] The fact that Burgess thinks that very few things exist in the metaphysically heavy sense merely goes to show that he agrees with certain metaphysicians that composite material objects do not

---

What kind of object would a hole be? Surely what really exist are the physical objects that the holes are "in": walls, pieces of cheese, shirts, and so on. When one of these physical objects has an appropriate shape—namely, a perforated shape—we'll sometimes say that "there is a hole in it." But we don't really mean by this that there literally exists an extra entity, a hole, which is somehow made up of nothingness.' 'Introduction', in Theodore Sider et al. (eds), *Contemporary Debates in Metaphysics* (Oxford: Blackwell, 2008), 2–3.

[14] John P. Burgess, 'Mathematics and *Bleak House*', *Philosophia Mathematica*, 12/1 (2004): 30–1.
[15] Ibid., 19.   [16] Ibid.

exist.[17] For Burgess, very few kinds of things exist—perhaps only fundamental particles—and abstract objects are not among them. Like Hale, he actually seems to be an anti-realist about abstract objects.

These lightweight Platonists—who are among the most ardent defenders of Platonism today—thus seem to be committed to abstract objects only in the sense that they are semantic objects. As Burgess's statement implies, such a lightweight Platonism is not incompatible with God's being the sole ultimate reality and the Creator of everything that exists other than Himself.

The focus of our investigation is therefore heavyweight Platonism, for this is the only kind of Platonism that is in conflict with the doctrine of divine aseity. From now on, then, whenever I refer to Platonism, it is metaphysically heavyweight Platonism that I have in mind. We shall want to understand what grounds there are for affirming heavyweight Platonism and how one might respond to it. As we shall see, there is one argument in favour of Platonism that dominates the contemporary discussion. We shall then embark on a wide-ranging exploration of various responses to that argument, with a view to assessing their credibility and utility to the classical theist. I hope to show that there is a cornucopia of viable responses available to the theist, many of which contemporary Christian philosophers have scarcely begun to explore.

But before we embark on our journey, we need to examine more closely the biblical and theological foundations of the doctrine of divine aseity.

---

[17] The view that there are no composite objects is called mereological nihilism. On this view, there are at most fundamental particles arranged differently.

2

God: The Sole Ultimate Reality

In this chapter, I want to unfold the biblical and theological underpinnings of the doctrine of divine aseity. Doing so should help us to resist any temptation to accommodate ourselves to Platonism by holding that in addition to God there also exist other uncreated things. I hope to show that Platonism strikes at the very heart of biblical theism.

BIBLICAL BASIS OF DIVINE ASEITY

The biblical testimony to God's status as the sole ultimate reality is both clear and abundant. In the New Testament, both John and Paul, for example, bear witness to this doctrine. We shall look first at what John has to say and then at Paul's testimony.

John's Prologue

Undoubtedly, one of the principal texts bearing witness to God's status as the sole ultimate reality is the prologue to the Gospel of John. There John writes,

> In the beginning was the Word,
> and the Word was with God,
> and the Word was God.
> He was in the beginning with God.

> All things came into being through him,
> and without him not one thing came into being.
> What has come into being in him was life,
> and the life was the light of all people.
> The light shines in the darkness,
> and the darkness did not overcome it. (1: 1–5)

Notice that in John's view, although God and His Word (*logos* in the Greek) simply *were* in the beginning (v. 1), everything else is said to have *come into being* through Him (v. 3). The Greek word John uses in v. 3 is *ginomai*, which means 'to become' or 'to originate'. It serves to contrast everything else with God and His Word, which had no origination but were 'in the beginning' (a phrase borrowed from Gen. 1: 1). John thus implies that there are no eternal entities apart from God, for everything other than God has come into being.

The verb *ginomai* also has the meaning 'to be created' or 'to be made'. This meaning of the verb comes to the fore by John's indicating the agent who was responsible for all things' coming into being. John speaks of God's Word as the one 'through whom' all things came into being. In the Greek, the preposition *dia* ('through') + the genitive case of the noun or pronoun indicates the agency by means of which some result is produced. So John is saying that all things were created through God's Word. John thus implies not only that there are no eternal beings apart from God; there are also no uncreated beings apart from God.

At face value, then, John's prologue is pregnant with metaphysical implications, for it implies that God alone exists eternally and *a se*. There are no co-eternal, uncreated things alongside God.

Platonists who would be biblically faithful Christians must therefore say that John is not really talking about *everything* when he says 'all things', any more than we are when we say, for example, 'Everyone came to the office party' or 'There's nothing in the refrigerator'. In making such statements, we obviously don't mean that Nelson Mandela came to the office party or that the refrigerator has no shelves and no air inside! Rather, in each case we are speaking relative to a certain class of things, for example, people who work in the office or things that are good to eat.

Logicians call a statement which says something, not merely about *some* members of a class, but about *all* the members of the class, a *universally quantified* statement. Universally quantified statements may be either *affirmative*, in which case we typically use words like 'all', 'every', 'each', 'any', and so forth, or *negative*, in which case we usually employ words like 'no', 'none', 'nothing', 'no one', and so forth, with respect to the class of things we are talking about. Logicians call the relevant class of things the *domain* of quantification.

Now the third verse of John's prologue is a universally quantified statement: '*All things* came into being through him, and without him *not one thing* came into being.' The first part of v. 3 is an affirmative, universally quantified statement, while the second part of the verse is a negative, universally quantified statement. The question is: does John intend the class of things he is talking about to be unrestricted or is he talking merely about a restricted class of things? Would-be Christian Platonists must maintain that John's domain of quantification is restricted in such a way that abstract objects escape his universally quantified statements.

Now obviously the class of things John is talking about is not wholly unrestricted. For John clearly excludes God Himself and His Word from being in the class of things he is talking about, since they have already been said in v. 1 simply to exist in the beginning. God and His Word are not the subjects of temporal becoming, as are other things. They did not come into being, but simply were there 'in the beginning'. So in saying that 'all things came into being through him', John obviously does not mean to include God Himself in the domain of quantification. The Platonist must say, however, that John's domain of quantification is even more restricted than in this obvious way.

Now it is important that we understand clearly the question before us, since it is so often misunderstood. The question is *not*: did John have abstract objects explicitly in mind when he said 'all things came into being through him'? I doubt that John explicitly took abstract objects to be part of God's creation, either because he had never thought about abstract objects or else because, if he had, he did not ascribe to them extra-mental existence, as I shall explain below.

Perhaps John had never thought about abstract objects; but by the same token, neither had John thought about quarks, galaxies, and black holes; yet, he would doubtless take such things and countless other things, were he informed about them, to have been created by God and to be in the class of things he is talking about. If John would not have taken these sorts of unknown things to be uncreated, were he informed about them, why think that he would have exempted Platonic abstract objects?

Recall that for the heavyweight Platonist, abstract objects and ordinary physical objects are on an ontological par. Platonist philosopher Mark Steiner emphasizes that 'the natural numbers... are objects in the same sense that molecules are objects'.[1] As the eminent Harvard philosopher W. V. O. Quine colourfully put it, 'numbers of all sorts, functions, and much else... are as integral to the physical theory that uses them as are the atoms, the electrons, the sticks, for that matter, and the stones'.[2] Abstract entities may be even more remote from direct sense perception than micro-entities, but they are, according to Platonism, just as real, so that if subatomic entities lie in the domain of John's quantifiers, so do numbers.[3] So if abstract objects exist, as the Platonist thinks, it would seem arbitrary to exempt them from the domain of John's quantifiers.

The question, then, is not what John thought lay in the domain of his quantifiers; rather, the question is whether John intends his domain of quantification, once God is exempted, to be unrestricted. Did he think that apart from God everything else that exists has been created by God? Did he believe that God is the only uncreated reality? It is more than probable that he did. For God's status as the only eternal, uncreated being is an earmark of first-century Judaism, which is the backdrop against which the New Testament was written.

In his influential work on the character of ancient Jewish monotheism, Richard Bauckham identifies two characteristics that uniquely mark off Israel's God from all others, namely that 'he is Creator of all things and sovereign Ruler of all things'.[4] There is in the

---

[1] Mark Steiner, *Mathematical Knowledge*, Contemporary Philosophy (Ithaca, NY: Cornell University Press, 1975), 87; cf. 127.

[2] W. V. O. Quine, 'Responses', in *Theories and Things* (Cambridge, MA: Harvard University Press, 1981), 182.

[3] For the Platonist, as Quine reminds us, there is no distinction between the 'there are' of 'there are universals' and the 'there are' of 'there are unicorns', the 'there are hippopotami', and the 'there are' of '$(\exists x) (x)$' ('there are entities x such that'). W. V. O. Quine, 'Logic and the Reification of Universals', in *From a Logical Point of View* (Cambridge, MA: Harvard University Press, 1953), 105. If we are to understand Platonism, we must resist the temptation to think that abstract objects exist in some ghostly, diminished sense. Indeed, for ancient Platonists, the ideal world was actually more real than the world of concrete objects.

[4] Richard Bauckham, 'God Crucified', in *Jesus and the God of Israel* (Grand Rapids, MI: William B. Eerdmans, 2008), 8. Citing Bauckham's work, Chris Tilling reports that the majority of scholars find in early Judaism a strict monotheism that 'draws a sharp line between God and everything else'. Chris Tilling, 'Problems with Ehrman's Interpretive Categories', in Michael F. Bird (ed.), *How God Became Jesus* (Grand Rapids, MI: Zondervan, 2014), 129.

Judaism of John's day a bright dividing line which separates God ontologically from everything else, a bifurcation which Bauckham attempts to capture by the term 'transcendent uniqueness'. Bauckham observes that so-called intermediate figures in Judaism fall into one of two categories: (1) beings which are supernatural but nonetheless created, like angels, and (2) personifications of aspects of God Himself which have no independent existence, such as God's Word and God's Wisdom. God's status as the sole ultimate reality comes to practical expression in the Jewish restriction of worship as properly directed towards God alone. According to Bauckham, this restriction 'most clearly signaled the distinction between God and all other reality'.[5]

It is interesting that, like John, Bauckham makes no explicit mention of abstract objects. As a biblical scholar rather than a philosopher, he may be completely unaware of such objects. Nevertheless, it is obvious that he reads the Jewish texts he cites as unrestricted in their domain of quantification (once God is exempted). For example, he writes:

> This God of Israel is the one and only Creator of all things and sovereign Lord over all things. Among the many other things that late Second Temple period Jews said about the uniqueness of their God, these two aspects of his unique relationship to all other reality were the most commonly cited, repeatedly used to put YHWH in an absolutely unique category.[6]

Bauckham takes these Jewish texts to distinguish God from all the rest of reality, and the majority of scholars have concurred in Bauckham's exegesis of these texts.

The crucial point here is that the unrestrictedness of the domain of quantification is based, not in what kinds of objects were thought to lie in the domain, but rather in the Jewish doctrine of God as the only being which exists eternally and *a se*. It is who or what God is that requires that the domain of quantification be unrestricted, whatever beings might be discovered to lie in the domain.

---

[5] Bauckham, 'God Crucified', 11.
[6] Richard Bauckham, 'Biblical Theology and the Problems of Monotheism', in *Jesus and the God of Israel*, 83–4. YHWH is the abbreviation for the Hebrew name of God, *Yahweh*, or the LORD.

John himself identifies the Word (*logos*) alone as existing with God and being God in the beginning. The creation of everything else through the divine Logos then follows. Bauckham calls such a view 'Christological monotheism': the divine Logos is on God's side of the dividing line between God and the rest of reality. He is therefore not an additional uncreated entity existing apart from God.

So while I think that John probably did not have in mind abstract objects when he asserted that all things came into being through the Logos, there is no reason to doubt that he believed that every existing thing apart from God had come into being through the Logos. If a modern philosopher were to sit down with John and explain to him what an abstract object is supposed to be, giving him examples like numbers, propositions, and possible worlds, and tell him that many twenty-first-century Platonists believe that such things are mind-independent objects which exist just as robustly as familiar physical objects, John would doubtless have responded that, if there really are such things, then they, too, must have been created by the divine Logos. To postulate an infinite plenitude of beings as real as planets existing independently of God, so that the realm of concrete objects brought into being by God is literally infinitesimal by comparison, would be to betray Jewish monotheism and to trivialize the doctrine of creation. So I think that it is clear that John did intend his domain of quantification to include everything apart from God, whatever idea he may have had concerning what objects lay in the domain.

But was John, in fact, unaware of abstract objects, as we have assumed? This is anything but obvious. For by John's day, classical Platonism had evolved into so-called Middle Platonism, and Hellenistic Judaism bears its imprint. The doctrine of the divine creative Logos found in John's prologue, far from being original to John, was widespread in Middle Platonism. It is attested as early as Antiochus of Ascalon (125–68 BC) and Eudorus (first century BC), two of the earliest Middle Platonists. Hellenistic Jews, notably Philo of Alexandria (20 BC–AD 50), adapted the Logos doctrine to Jewish monotheism. The similarities between Philo's Logos doctrine and John's Logos doctrine are striking and numerous. In a careful review of the roles of the Logos as found in Philo and John, the German scholar Jutta Leonhardt-Balzer summarizes the most important similarities:

> both use the Logos in a way similar to that of the Wisdom literature;
> both describe the Logos as temporally prior to creation (*Op.* 17; 24; Jn

1.1–2). Insofar as they go beyond the Wisdom tradition, they call him 'God' (*Som.* 1.228-230; Jn 1.1). Both connect the operation of the Logos with the beginning of the world (*Conf.* 146; Jn 1.1-2) and see the world as created 'through' (διά) the Logos (*Cher.* 127; Jn 1.3). Both connect the Logos with light (*Som.* 1.75; *Op.* 33; *Conf.* 60–63; Jn 1.4–5, 9) and see in the Logos the way for people to become God's children (*Conf.* 145–146; Jn 1.12). Both make a clear distinction between the Logos with God and the Logos in creation, whereby not only the prologue to John but *both* bring the statements of Genesis to bear on the Logos with God.[7]

There is much here that deserves comment; but I want to draw special attention to the role of the divine Logos in creation. Both Philo and John connect the Logos with the beginning of the cosmos. John says that the Logos existed in the beginning and that the cosmos came to be through him (1: 3, 10). Philo, citing Genesis 1: 1: 'In the beginning God made the heavens and the earth', also connects the Logos with the beginning of the world (*On the Creation of the World* 26–7). They both understand the Logos to be the agent of creation, through whom the world was made. The use of the preposition *dia* + genitive to express instrumental creation is not derived from Jewish Wisdom literature, but is rather an earmark of Middle Platonism; indeed, so much so that scholars of this movement like to speak of its 'prepositional metaphysics', whereby various prepositional phrases are employed to express causal categories:[8]

phrase:	*to huph' hou*	*to eks hou*	*to di' hou*	*to di' ho*
category:	*to aition* efficient cause	*hē hulē* material cause	*to ergaleion* instrumental cause	*hē aitia* final cause
entity:	God the Creator	four elements	Logos of God	God's goodness

Philo identifies Aristotle's four kinds of causes by these prepositional phrases, stating that 'through which' (*to di' hou*) represents creation

---

[7] Jutta Leonhardt-Balzer, 'Der Logos und die Schöpfung: Streiflichter bei Philo (Op 20–25) und im Johannesprolog (Joh 1, 1–18)', in Jörg Frey und Udo Schnelle (eds), *Kontexte des Johannesevangeliums* (Tübingen: Mohr Siebeck, 2004), 318. The abbreviations indicate the Latin titles of Philo's *De opificio mundi* (*On the Creation of the World*), *De somniis* (*On Dreams*), *De confusione linguarum* (*On the Confusion of Tongues*), and *De cherubim* (*On the Cherubim*).

[8] D. T. Runia, *Philo of Alexandria and the 'Timaeus' of Plato* (Amsterdam: Free University of Amsterdam, 1983), 140–3; Gregory E. Sterling, '"Day One": Platonizing Exegetical Traditions of Genesis 1: 1–5 in John and Jewish Authors', paper presented at the Philo section of the Society of Biblical Literature, San Antonio, TX, 20–3 Nov. 2004.

by the Logos (*On the Cherubim* 124–7). Philo frequently refers to the Logos as the instrumental cause of creation.[9] Although some commentators on John's Gospel have rightly insisted that John is not interested primarily in metaphysics, but in salvation, we cannot ignore his explicitly metaphysical affirmations that all things came into being through the Logos (*di' autou*) and that the world (*kosmos*) came into being through him (*di' autou*) (1: 3, 10).

The similarities between Philo and John's doctrines of the Logos are so numerous and so close that most Johannine scholars, while not willing to affirm John's direct dependence on Philo, do recognize that the author of the prologue of John's Gospel shares with Philo a common intellectual tradition of a Middle Platonic interpretation of Genesis 1.[10]

Now, interested as he is in the incarnation of the divine Logos, John does not pause to reflect on the role of the Logos 'in the beginning', causally prior to creation. But this pre-creation role does feature prominently in Philo's doctrine of the Logos. According to David Runia, a cornerstone of Middle Platonism was the division of reality into the intelligible and the sensible realms.[11] The perceived division is genuine, but it is somewhat misleading, I think, to draw the distinction in such terms.[12] The fundamental distinction here, originally to be found in Plato, is between the realm of static being and the realm of temporal becoming. The former realm is grasped by the intellect, while the latter is perceived by the senses. The realm of becoming comprised primarily physical objects, while the static realm

---

[9] Runia's list is helpful: *Allegorical Interpretation* 3.9; *On the Cherubim* 28; *On the Sacrifices of Abel and Cain* 8; *On the Unchangeableness of God* 57; *On the Confusion of Tongues* 62; *On the Migration of Abraham* 6; *On Flight and Finding* 12; 95; *On Dreams* 2.45; *The Special Laws* 1.81.

[10] So Leonhardt-Balzer, 'Der Logos und die Schöpfung', 309–10, with citations of extensive literature; cf. Craig S. Keener, *The Gospel of John: A Commentary*, 2 vols. (Peabody, MA: Hendrickson, 2003), i. 346–7.

[11] Runia, *Philo and the 'Timaeus'*, 68. The *locus classicus* of the distinction was Plato's *Timaeus* 27d5–28a4, which is in turn cited by Apuleius, *De Platone et eius dogmate* 193; Nicomachus, *Introduction to Arithmetic* 1.2.1; Numenius fr. 7; Justin Martyr, *Dialogue with Trypho* 3.5; Sextus Empiricus, *Adversus mathematicos* 7.142.

[12] The distinction at issue is not really intelligible vs sensible; rather, it is being vs becoming. The problem with the former characterization of the distinction is that it seems to leave no place for immaterial concrete objects like angels or souls. Given that the intelligible realm exists in the mind of God, such beings cannot be classed as part of the intelligible realm. They must be part of the sensible realm, which is thus more accurately described as the realm of concrete objects subject to temporal becoming.

of being comprised what we would today call abstract objects. For Middle Platonists, as for Plato, the intelligible world served as a model for the creation of the sensible world. As a Jewish monotheist, Philo does not think that this intelligible realm exists independently of God, but rather as the contents of His mind.

This view was not original to Philo, however. The interpretation of the Platonic Ideas as thoughts in the mind of God was characteristic of Middle Platonism and became widespread throughout the ancient world.[13] For example, Nicomachus of Gerasa (c.AD 60–120), who flourished in Roman Syria adjacent to Judaeae, held that, of the four subjects of the classical quadrivium,

> arithmetic... existed before all the others in the mind of the creating God like some universal and exemplary plan, relying upon which as a design and archetypal example, the Creator of the universe sets in order his material creations and makes them attain their proper ends....
>
> All that has by nature with systematic method been arranged in the universe seems both in part and as a whole to have been determined and ordered in accordance with number, by the forethought and the mind of him that created all things; for the pattern was fixed, like a preliminary sketch, by the domination of number preëxistent in the mind of the world-creating God, number conceptual only and immaterial in every way, but at the same time the true and the eternal essence, so that with reference to it, as to an artistic plan, should be created all these things, time, motion, the heavens, the stars, all sorts of revolutions.[14]

Philo concurred. The intelligible world (*kosmos noētos*), he maintains, may be thought of as either formed by the divine Logos or, more reductively, as the Logos itself as God is engaged in creating.

---

[13] See Audrey N. M. Rich, 'The Platonic Ideas as the Thoughts of God', *Mnemosyne*, 7/2 (1954): 123–33. Rich observes, 'Though Plato speaks of the transcendent Idea as existing "alone and by itself" and never "in anything else" [*Sympos[ium]* 211A], the tendency among many of his interpreters [*e.g.*, Albinus, Plutarch, Philo, Galen, Atticus, Origen, Stobaeus, Hippolytus, Theodoret] seems to have been to make the Idea dependent upon God as a thought resident in his mind' (123). R. M. Jones says that the doctrine of the Platonic Ideas as God's thoughts was so well known by Philo's time that Philo could employ it without hesitation: 'The Ideas as the Thoughts of God', *Classical Philology*, 21 (1926): 317–26.

[14] Nicomachus of Gerasa, *Introduction to Arithmetic* 1.4, 6, tr. Martin Luther D'Ooge (New York: Macmillan Co., 1926), 187, 189.

Although references to this role of the Logos are frequent in Philo,[15] the fullest exposition of his doctrine comes in his *On the Creation of the World according to Moses*:

> God, because He is God, understood in advance that a fair copy would not come into existence apart from a fair model, and that none of the objects of sense-perception would be without fault, unless it was modeled on the archetypal and intelligible idea. When he had decided to construct this visible cosmos, he first marked out the intelligible cosmos, so that he could use it as an incorporeal and most god-like paradigm and so produce the corporeal cosmos, a younger likeness of an older model, which would contain as many sense-perceptible kinds as there were intelligible kinds in that other one.
>
> To declare or suppose that the cosmos composed of the ideas exists in some place is not permissible. How it has been constituted we will understand if we pay careful attention to an image drawn from our own world. When a city is founded, in accordance with the high ambition of a king or a ruler who has laid claim to supreme power and, because he is at the same time magnificent in his conception, adds further adornment to his good fortune, it can happen that a trained architect comes forward. Having observed both the favourable climate and location of the site, he first designs in his mind a plan of virtually all the parts of the city that is to be completed—temples, gymnasia, public offices, market-places, harbours, shipyards, streets, construction of walls, the establishment of other buildings both private and public. Then, taking up the imprints of each object in his own soul like in wax, he carries around the intelligible city as an image in his head. Summoning up the images by means of his innate power of memory and engraving their features even more distinctly in his mind, he begins, like a good builder, to construct the city out of stones and timber, looking at the model and ensuring that the corporeal objects correspond to each of the incorporeal ideas.
>
> The conception we have concerning God must be similar to this, namely that when he had decided to found the great cosmic city, he first conceived its outlines. Out of these he composed the intelligible cosmos, which served him as a model when he also completed the sense-perceptible cosmos. Just as the city that was marked out beforehand in the architect had no location outside, but had been engraved in the soul of the craftsman, in the same way the cosmos composed of the

---

[15] E.g. *Allegorical Interpretation* 3.96; *On the Migration of Abraham* 6; *On Flight and Finding* 12; *On Dreams* 1.75; 2.45; *Special Laws* 1.81; *On the Confusion of Tongues* 60–3, 172.

God: The Sole Ultimate Reality

ideas would have no other place than the divine Logos who gives these (ideas) their ordered disposition. After all, what other place would there be for his powers sufficient to receive and contain, I do not speak about all of them, but just a single one of them in its unmixed state? If you would wish to use a formulation that has been stripped down to essentials, you might say that the intelligible cosmos is nothing else than the Logos of God as He is actually engaged in making the cosmos. For the intelligible city too is nothing else than the reasoning of the architect as he is actually engaged in planning the foundation of the city (*On the Creation of the World* 16–20, 24).

Especially noteworthy is Philo's insistence that the world of ideas cannot exist anywhere but in the divine Logos. Just as the ideal architectural plan of a city exists only in the mind of the architect, so the world of ideas exists solely in the mind of God.

In Philo's view, then, there is no realm of independently existing abstract objects. As Runia states, the intelligible world, while not part of the created realm, 'must be considered dependent for its existence on God'.[16]

Given the close similarity of the Logos doctrine of John's prologue to Philo's doctrine, it is not at all impossible that the author of the prologue was aware of the relation of the Logos to the realm of ideas. It is striking how verbs of being dominate vv. 1–2 of John's prologue, while verbs of becoming dominate vv. 3–5.[17] It may well be that the prologue's author thought that only concrete objects had been created by God because the intelligible realm exists only in the mind of God. The intelligible realm has no reality outside the divine Logos.

I think it not at all improbable that the prologue's author, if not the evangelist himself, held to the Middle Platonic view of God and abstract objects. But whether or not he did, it is clear that the author of John's Gospel conceives of God as the Creator of everything apart

---

[16] Runia, *Philo and the 'Timaeus'*, 138. Philo interpreted Gen. 1: 1–5 to relate the creation, not of the concrete world, but of the ideal world in the mind of God, which then served as His model for the concrete world. Philo thereby underlines the fact that ideal objects do not exist *a se*.

[17] According to Sterling, 'Platonizing Exegetical Traditions', this verbal contrast 'became a standard way for later Platonists to distinguish between the eternal world of the ideas and the sense perceptible world in which we live. I suggest that the author of the [Johannine] hymn understood the shift from ἦν to ἐγένετο in Genesis 1 as a textual warrant for a Platonic understanding.' The point is especially strong if we include the phrase *ho gegonen* in v. 3 rather than in v. 4.

from Himself through His Word. There are no uncreated, independently existing, eternal objects, for God exists uniquely *a se*.

Paul's Letters

We turn now to what Paul has to say in his various letters about God's status as the sole ultimate reality. The same Hellenistic Judaism, epitomized in Philo, that forms the background of John's prologue shapes the traditions that Paul hands on. Consider the following Pauline texts:

> there is one God, the Father, from whom are all things and for whom we exist, and one Lord, Jesus Christ, through whom are all things and through whom we exist. (1 Cor. 8: 6 NRSV)
>
> For just as woman came from man, so man comes through woman; but all things come from God. (1 Cor. 11: 12 NRSV)
>
> For from him and through him and to him are all things. (Rom. 11: 36 NRSV)
>
> He [Christ] is the image of the invisible God, the first born of all creation; for by him all things in heaven and on earth were created, things visible and invisible, whether thrones or dominions or rulers or powers—all things have been created through him and for him. (Col. 1: 15–16 NRSV)

Paul, like John, ascribes the origin of 'all things' to God. A faithful Jew, Paul held to the traditional monotheistic understanding that God is the source of everything other than Himself.

Notice Paul's use of prepositional phrases like 'from him', 'through him', and 'to him'. Douglas Moo comments on Romans 11: 36, 'The concept of God as the source (*ek*), sustainer (*dia*), and goal (*eis*) of all things is particularly strong among the Greek Stoic philosophers. Hellenistic Jews picked up this language and applied it to Yahweh; and it is probably, therefore, from the synagogue that Paul borrows this formula.'[18] Yes, but Stoic thought is the more distant progenitor; more immediately what we see here are variations on the prepositional metaphysics of Middle Platonism that shaped Hellenistic Judaism.

---

[18] Douglas J. Moo, *The Epistle to the Romans* (Grand Rapids, MI: Wm. B. Eerdmans, 1996), 743. James D. G. Dunn conveniently provides excerpts of parallel texts in his commentary *Romans 9–16* (Nashville, TN: Thomas Nelson, 1988), 702.

God: The Sole Ultimate Reality

Richard Horsley observes how unusual such prepositional formulations are for Paul and argues that the provenance of Paul's expressions is to be found in Philo. Noting that 'numerous passages in Philo's writings provide an analogy for nearly every aspect of the Corinthians' religious language and viewpoint',[19] Horsley comments,

> I Cor. 8.6 is an adaptation of the traditional Hellenistic Jewish form of predication regarding the respective creative and soteriological roles of God and Sophia/Logos, which Philo or his predecessors had adapted from a Platonic philosophical formula concerning the primal principles of the universe. What was already a fundamental tenet of the Hellenistic Jewish religion expressed in the book of Wisdom appears in more philosophical formulation in Philo; that God is the ultimate Creator and final Cause of the universe, and that Sophia/Logos is agent (and paradigm) of creation or the instrumental (and formal) cause.[20]

Notice Horsley's comment that, whereas God is regarded as the efficient and final cause of the universe of created things, Sophia/Logos (Wisdom/Word) is the instrumental cause and the formal cause (or paradigm) of creation. This latter role makes Sophia/Logos specifically the source or ground of the *kosmos noētos* or intelligible world. Paul's innovation is that he substitutes Christ for Sophia/Logos, having 'Christ take over what were the functions of Sophia, according to the *gnosis* of the Corinthians.'[21]

In the same way, Paul in his letter to the Colossians seems to have adapted traditional Hellenistic Jewish hymnic material about Sophia/Logos to make Christ the agent of creation. Peter O'Brien comments:

> while there are points of linguistic contact with Stoicism especially, and thus the language of the hymn may well have served as a bridge for those from such a background (cf. the similar function of λόγος in John 1), nevertheless Pauline thought is different from the pantheistically conceived world-soul of Stoicism.... the parallels from Hellenistic Judaism, especially the LXX, are much closer.[22]

For example, we read in Wisdom (or Sirach) 43: 26 that 'through his word all things hold together'. The parallels become even closer if the majority of commentators are correct that the original material

---

[19] Richard A. Horsley, 'Gnosis in Corinth: I Corinthians 8.1–6', *New Testament Studies*, 27/1 (1980): 46.
[20] Ibid., 46.   [21] Ibid., 51.
[22] Peter T. O'Brien, *Colossians, Philemon* (Nashville, TN: Thomas Nelson, 2000), 47.

adapted by Paul spoke of the cosmos rather than the church as the body of which Sophia/Logos is the head.[23]

It is interesting that whereas in Colossians 1: 15–16 and 1 Corinthians 8: 6, Paul names Christ as the instrumental cause of creation, in Romans 11: 36 Paul declares the Father to be the source, sustainer, and goal of all things. Romans 11: 36 is thus, in Moo's words, 'a declaration of God's ultimacy'.[24] James D. G. Dunn concurs: 'Where the focus is so exclusively on the supreme majesty and self-sufficiency of God, the Stoic type formula provides a fitting climax: he is the source, medium, and goal of *everything*, the beginning, middle, and end of all that is.'[25]

Again, the would-be Christian Platonist must maintain that the domain over which Paul quantifies in saying 'all things' is restricted in such a way that abstract objects, if they exist, escape his quantifiers. But the unrestrictedness of the domain of Paul's quantifiers is evident from the fact that the expression 'the heavens and the earth' (Col. 1: 15–16) is a typical Jewish merism or totalizing idiom comprising everything other than God.[26] Paul's characterization of the created realm as 'all things in heaven and on earth' was not, in the mind of a first-century Jew, any sort of restriction. Moreover, Paul characterizes the Son as the creator of 'all things visible and invisible' (Col. 1: 15–16), a characterization which is collectively exhaustive: Christ has created everything, whether it be *A* or not-*A*. Indeed, Paul's thinking in Colossians is expansive: he moves from speaking of all things in heaven and on earth, to all things visible and invisible, and finally to all things *simpliciter*. His intention is that the domain of his quantifiers be unrestricted.

The unrestrictedness of Paul's domain of quantification is not compromised by the fact that only concrete things in fact inhabit the domain. As we have seen, in Hellenistic Judaism, the *kosmos noētos* was *not* taken to be part of the created world, but to exist in

---

[23] O'Brien rejects the majority view because 'body' is typically used by Paul of the church, but never of the world. But this objection is not very powerful, even if O'Brien's scepticism about attempts to recover the original wording is justified. For Paul's view of the church as Christ's body might motivate Paul to adapt such material to fit his theology.

[24] Moo, *Epistle to the Romans*, 740.   [25] Dunn, *Romans 9–16*, 704.

[26] See Paul Copan and William Lane Craig, *Creation out of Nothing: A Biblical, Philosophical, and Scientific Exploration* (Grand Rapids, MI: Baker Academic, 2004), 43.

the mind of the Logos and to serve as the pattern for God's creation of the concrete world. Ideal objects are not part of creation or the world, but are rather God's ideas. They have no existence outside the divine mind. So in ascribing to Christ the role of the Logos in creating the world, Paul is affirming that everything apart from God has been created by God through Christ. The domain of Paul's quantifiers is unlimited: everything other than God has been created by God.

Perhaps biblical authors like John and Paul followed the lead of Hellenistic Judaism in locating mathematical objects and their kin in the mind of the Logos; perhaps they had never considered the subject. We do not know. But just as the discovery of extraterrestrial planets would not have led them to think that these objects somehow escaped Christ's creation, so the discovery that there are mind-independent abstract objects would not lead them to think that such objects are uncreated. Leftow is surely correct when he says, 'they meant "all things" to cover things known *and unknown*: they could not have believed that they knew *everything* "all things" ranged over. But once grant this point, and it is hard to see why we should limit its scope to the concrete.'[27] Thus, 'Biblical authors who came to believe in abstracta would want to hold God responsible for them all. Their idea surely is not that God has done *enough* to deserve praise and so on (that is, made a *big* part of reality), but that there are realms of reality for which He does not deserve praise and so on.'[28] Rather, God and Christ deserve praise for everything that exists because everything finds its source in God.

Two Theological Questions

Before we leave the biblical authors, there are two further questions about the biblical doctrine that deserve attention. I noted that the biblical writers' affirmation that all things other than God have been created by God doubtlessly looks back to the creation account in Genesis 1. The form of John 1: 1 mirrors Genesis 1: 1, and the consistent use of past-tense verbs for creation—for example, 'All things came into being through him' (John 1: 3) and 'For by him all things in heaven and on earth were created' (Col. 1: 15)—indicates that some event in the past is in view. But what about things that were

[27] Brian Leftow, *God and Necessity* (Oxford: OUP, 2012), 63 (my emphasis).
[28] Ibid., 64 (my emphasis).

not created in God's original act of creation, but have only lately arrived on the scene? In what sense can they be said to have been created by God? This is a question which the biblical authors themselves might have pondered. For they were aware that new living organisms are born every day through apparently natural processes and that human beings produce new artefacts through natural causes on a daily basis. In what sense can the Logos be said by John or Paul to have brought these things into being?

Leftow calls the creation of such things 'late creation' and offers several models of it.[29]

(i) God created out of nothing the fundamental particles ('atoms') which compose material things. If there are no fundamental particles, then at some level God created out of nothing the composite stuff of which material things consist. Composite objects therefore owe their existence to God.

(ii) God not only created the stuff out of which material things are made, but also established deterministic causal systems primed to produce certain effects at later times. God can be said to create these later effects by setting up the causal chains leading to them according to his intention. One can supplement this model by including free agents among the things God intends to be produced, as well as the artefacts He then leads them to produce or knew they would freely produce. On this model, God is the remote cause and creatures the proximate causes of things' coming into being.

(iii) God could will and cause an entire causal sequence of events terminating in the production of some creature. On this model, God causes, not merely the first member of a causal sequence, but the entire sequence. Nevertheless, each member of the sequence has causal antecedents in the sequence. Again, this model can be enhanced by making some of the creaturely causes free agents, whose choices produce effects intended by God.

(iv) Model (iii) can be extended by adding that God conserves objects in being moment by moment by willing that they persist from one time until a later time. Thus, at every moment of their existence they are being created out of nothing, in the

[29] Ibid., 15–20.

sense that God wills that they persist in being rather than be annihilated. On this model, late creation is a matter of God's conserving the world in being.

Obviously, not all of these models would be applicable to God's creation of immaterial entities like angels, souls, or abstract objects. But late creation either does not come into view for most of these things or is unproblematic. Angels may have been created once only, perhaps at the moment of creation and never again. Souls could be created immediately by God throughout history at the various appropriate times. Abstract objects come in such diverse types that no one model applies.[30] Since our concern here is with biblical, not systematic theology, let us leave aside for the moment God's creation of abstract objects, since these do not come explicitly into view in the biblical text.

While the systematic theologian will typically want to affirm a doctrine of divine conservation in line with option (iv), it is doubtful that John and Paul had such a model in mind in the passages we have examined, given their use of past-tense verbs of creation.[31] They probably looked rather to God's initial act of creation 'in the beginning'. Given that they were not natural law theorists, they probably had something like option (i) in mind rather than (ii) or (iii), though perhaps supplemented by God's providential intentions that later things should come to be. I do not mean to suggest that John and

---

[30] Many, like numbers, are plausibly timeless, if they exist at all, and so, properly speaking, can be neither created nor conserved in being by God, since these are both temporal activities. So late creation does not even come into view for them. At most, they could be said to be sustained (tenselessly) by God (see Copan and Craig, *Creation out of Nothing*, 164). On the other hand, if we are talking about temporal abstract objects, then some of them, like the Equator or the centre of mass of the solar system, could either be brought into being immediately by God when the material stuff is appropriately arranged or else be late-created along the lines of models (ii), (iii), or (iv). Similarly, the same models could account for the late creation of abstract objects which are the products of free agents, like literary and musical compositions. Unfortunately, some temporal abstract objects, like properties, would exist from eternity past and so would elude being created. At most, they are conserved in being by God. Thus, the Platonist is stuck with an infinitude of uncreated objects, both temporal and atemporal.

[31] Although present-tense verbs appear in 1 Cor. 8: 6, 11: 12, Rom. 11: 36, these seem to look back to God's initial creation via the Logos. Passages like Col. 1: 17b; Heb. 1: 3b might be more plausibly construed in terms of God's conservation of the world in being. For more on the biblical witness to God's initial act of creating everything, see Copan and Craig, *Creation out of Nothing*, chs 1-2.

Paul were atomists, but merely that they believed that, in addition to angels and souls, God created the stuff out of which physical things are made, and so He can be said to be the Creator of all things, including things which have only lately been configured. Nor am I ascribing to the biblical writers some sort of mereological nihilism, the view that there are no composite objects. For they could consistently believe and no doubt did believe that things like bricks and swords and horses do exist as bona fide things, even if they are composed of parts. Finite agents are artificers who shape stuff into things like knives and bricks or beget progeny via material stuff like semen. They are thus, as option (ii) affirms, proximate causes of what exists. God remains the ultimate Creator in that He is the source of the stuff of which every material thing is made, as well as the Creator of angels and souls.

Now to our second question. Shall we take aseity to be an essential attribute of God or merely a property that God happens to possess contingently? While the biblical writers do not address this question, Leftow rightly argues:

> the more central and prominent an attribute is in the Biblical picture of God, the stronger the case for taking it to be necessary to being God, *ceteris paribus*: this is the only reason philosophers usually treat being omniscient or omnipotent as thus necessary. . . . If creating everything is prominent and central in the Biblical account, and this is our only sort of reason for taking accepted necessary conditions of deity as necessary conditions, we have as good a reason to take creating everything as a requisite as we do in any other case.[32]

We have seen that God's being the sole ultimate reality lay at the very heart of Jewish monotheism. It is unthinkable that biblical writers might have considered aseity to be a property which God merely happened to have but might have lacked, so that God could have been dependent for His existence upon something else. Anything so dependent would not deserve to be called God. Furthermore, the fact that God alone exists *a se* would not seem to be a contingent matter. If God is the sole ultimate reality in the actual world, it is hard to imagine why He would not be so in any possible world in which He exists. To suggest that in some other possible world God finds Himself confronted with some independently existing, contingent

---

[32] Leftow, *God and Necessity*, 412–13.

being, uncreated by Him, would impugn God's power and majesty. Thus, we should take God's being the sole ultimate reality as belonging to God's nature.

At any rate, even if we must rely upon prominence and centrality as our sole guides when doing biblical theology, nevertheless, when we do systematic theology, in particular, perfect being theology, then the conception of God as the greatest conceivable being comes crucially into play, as we shall see. Thomas Morris observes that it is 'a fairly uncontroversial judgment among perfect-being theologians' that aseity is a great-making property or ingredient of perfection.[33] God must therefore exist *a se*. When we couple the attribute of divine aseity with God's attribute of metaphysical necessity, we are well on our way towards a truly great conception of God which is worthy of the biblical God.

TEACHING OF THE CHURCH FATHERS

The early Church Fathers, frequently citing John and Paul, understood God to be the sole ultimate reality. That conviction attained credal status in 325 at the Council of Nicaea. The Nicene Creed affirms:

> I believe in one God, the Father, Almighty, Maker of heaven and earth and of all things visible and invisible;
>
> And in one Lord, Jesus Christ, the only Son of God, begotten of the Father before all ages, light from light, true God from true God, begotten not made, consubstantial with the Father, through whom all things came into being.

The phrase 'Maker of heaven and earth and of all things visible and invisible' derives from Paul, and the expression 'through whom all things came into being' from the prologue to John's Gospel. The Council affirms that everything other than God was created by God through the Son, so that God alone is uncreated. Once again, the

---

[33] Thomas V. Morris, 'Metaphysical Dependence, Independence, and Perfection', in Scott MacDonald (ed.), *Being and Goodness: The Concept of the Good in Metaphysics and Philosophical Theology* (Ithaca, NY: Cornell University Press, 1991), 287.

would-be Christian Platonist, if he is to hold to Nicene orthodoxy, must regard the Fathers' domain of quantification to be tacitly restricted in such way that abstract objects escape the creed's universal quantifiers.

The Sole *Agenētos*

We have, however, convincing evidence that the Church Fathers took the domain of quantification, once God is exempted, to be unrestricted in its scope. At the heart of the theological controversy which led up to the Council of Nicaea lay a pair of terminological distinctions: *agenētos/genētos* and *agennētos/gennētos*.[34] The word pair *agenētos/genētos* derives from the Greek verb *ginomai*, which means to become or to come into being. *Agenētos* means unoriginated or uncreated, in contrast to *genētos*, that which is created or originated. The second word pair *agennētos/gennētos* derives from a different verb *gennaō*, which means to beget. That which is *agennētos* is unbegotten, while that which is *gennētos* is begotten. Most of us are familiar with the famous 'i' which marked the difference between the orthodox confession that Christ is *homoousios* (same in essence) with the Father and the Arian confession that Christ is *homoiousios* (similar in essence) with the Father, so that the difference between orthodoxy and heresy could rightly be said to hang on a single iota. But a similar world of difference lay in the single 'n', by means of which Christ could be said to be uncreated (*agenētos*) but begotten (*gennētos*), in contrast to the Father, who is both uncreated (*agenētos*) and unbegotten (*agennētos*).

Athanasius, the great champion of Nicene orthodoxy in the years following the Council, explains that Arians had borrowed the term *agenētos* from Greek philosophy and applied it exclusively to God the Father (*Defense of the Nicene Definition* 7: 'On the Arian symbol "Agenētos"'; cf. *Discourses against the Arians* 1.9.30; *On the Councils of Ariminum and Seleucia* 46–7). The relevant meaning of the term, he notes, is 'what exists but was neither originated nor had origin of being, but is everlasting and indestructible'. He complains with obvious indignation that the Arian strategy was to ask the unsuspecting

---

[34] In Greek, ἀγένητος/γενητός and ἀγέννητος/γεννητός.

God: The Sole Ultimate Reality 33

layman whether there exists one uncreated being or two. When the person replied that there is only one uncreated being, the Arians would spring the trap by exclaiming, 'Then the Son is created!' and therefore a creature. Not surprisingly, then, Athanasius says that he prefers to use the term 'Father' rather than *agenētos*, though he recognizes that the latter term has a proper and religious use (*Defense* 7.31–2; *Discourses* 1.9.33–4).

The ante-Nicene and Nicene Church Fathers, as well as the Arians themselves, all agreed that there are no *agenēta* apart from God alone. Consider these representative texts:

> there is not a plurality of uncreated beings: for if there were some difference between them, you would not discover the cause of the difference, though you searched for it; but after letting the mind ever wander to infinity, you would at length, wearied out, stop at one uncreated being, and say that this is the Cause of all things. (Justin, *Dialogue with Trypho, a Jew* 5)
>
> it is impossible for two uncreated beings to exist together (Methodius, *On Free Will* 5)
>
> in all things God has the pre-eminence, who alone is uncreated, the first of all things, and the primary cause of the existence of all, while all other things remain under God's subjection (Irenaeus, *Against Heresies* 4.38.3)
>
> For before all things God was alone, himself his own world and location and everything—alone, however, because there was nothing external beside him (Tertullian, *Against Praxeas* 5.13–15).
>
> We have never heard that there are two unbegotten beings, nor that one has been divided into two ... ; but we affirm that the unbegotten is one. (*Letter of Eusebius of Nicomedia to Paulinus of Tyre*, in Theodoret, *Ecclesiastical History* 1.5)
>
> God, subsisting alone, and having nothing contemporaneous with Himself, determined to create the world. And conceiving the world in mind, and willing and uttering the Word, He made it; and straightaway it appeared formed as it had pleased Him. For us, then, it is sufficient simply to know that there was nothing contemporaneous with God. Beside Him there was nothing. (Hippolytus, *Against Noetus* 10.1; cf. *Refutation of All Heresies* 10.28)
>
> the Father is the one uncreated being (Epiphanius, *Panarion* 33.7.6)

It would be simply flawed exegesis, I think, to suggest that the domain over which the Fathers' quantifiers range in these statements is not intended to be unrestricted.

Agenētos is thus the word which the Church Fathers used to denote the Jewish idea of what Bauckham calls God's 'transcendent uniqueness'. Prestige explains:

> Since transcendence, though a characteristically Hebrew idea, is nowhere philosophically expounded in the Bible, a term had to be adopted to express its definition. This was found in the word *agenetos*, 'uncreated'. The idea of creation was therein contrasted with that of self-grounded existence. To call God uncreated was tantamount to calling Him infinite perfection, independent reality, and the source of all finite being: He alone is absolute; all else is dependent and contingent.[35]

The Church Fathers took this property to be unique to God: 'the emphasis... on God being uncreated (ἀγένητος) implies that He is the sole originator of all things that are, the source and ground of existence; and the conception is taken as a positive criterion of deity'.[36] According to the patristics scholar Harry Austryn Wolfson,[37] the Church Fathers all accepted the following three principles:

1. God alone is uncreated.
2. Nothing is co-eternal with God.
3. Eternality implies deity.

Each of these principles implies that there are no *agenēta* apart from God alone.

Properties and Numbers

But lest it be suggested that abstract objects were somehow exempted from these principles, we should note that the ante-Nicene Church Fathers explicitly rejected the view that entities such as properties and numbers are *agenēta*. The Fathers were familiar with the metaphysical world views of Plato and Pythagoras and agreed with them that there is one *agenētos* from which all reality derives; but the Fathers identified this *agenētos*, not with an impersonal form or number, but with the Hebrew God, who has created all things (other than Himself) *ex nihilo*.

---

[35] George L. Prestige, *God in Patristic Thought* (London: SPCK, 1964), p. xx.
[36] Ibid., 5.
[37] Harry A. Wolfson, 'Plato's Pre-existent Matter in Patristic Philosophy', in Luitpold Wallach (ed.), *The Classical Tradition* (Ithaca, NY: Cornell University Press, 1966), 414.

God: The Sole Ultimate Reality

Consider first properties. Although the Fathers' primary target in their defence of *creatio ex nihilo* was the doctrine of the independence and eternality of matter, they did not countenance the idea that, although matter might be originated, properties might nonetheless be beginningless and uncreated. Athenagoras characterizes Christians as those who 'distinguish and separate the uncreated and the created' (*Plea for the Christians* 15). Although Athenagoras assumed that the created realm was the material world (including material spirits), that is not because he considered properties to be uncreated. Rather, he considered properties to lack any existence independent of concrete objects. His conviction is evident in his comment on how Satan is opposed to God's goodness:

> to the good that is in God, which belongs of necessity to Him and co-exists with Him, as colour with body, *without which it has no existence* (not as being part of it, but as an attendant property co-existing with it, united and blended, just as it is natural for fire to be yellow and the ether dark blue)—to the good that is in God, I say, the spirit which is about matter... is opposed. (*Plea* 24; my emphasis)

Athenagoras here clearly rejects the idea that properties have some sort of independent existence apart from concrete objects.

His fellow Apologist Tatian affirms that God alone is without beginning and attributes to Him the creation of both matter and form:

> Our God did not begin to be in time; He alone is without beginning, and He Himself is the beginning of all things. God is a Spirit, not pervading matter, but the Maker of material spirits and of the forms (*schematōn*) that are in matter; He is invisible, impalpable, being Himself the Father of both sensible and invisible things. (*Address to the Greeks* 4.10–14)

Tatian rejected the notion that there is besides God any eternal, uncreated thing, even pure forms. Instantiated forms he would presumably take to belong to the realm of things invisible.

Origen, who was trained in neo-Platonic philosophy, repudiated the identification of the realm of Platonic ideas with the biblical heavenly realm whence Christ came, commenting,

> It is difficult for us to explain this other world; and for this reason, that if we did so, there would be a risk of giving some men the impression that we were affirming the existence of certain imaginary forms which the

Greeks call 'ideas'. For it is certainly foreign to our mode of reasoning to speak of an incorporeal world that exists solely in the mind's fancy or the unsubstantial region of thought; and how men could affirm that the Saviour came from thence or that the saints will go thither I do not see. (*On First Principles* 2.3.6)

Like Philo, Origen believed that the forms of worldly things pre-existed as ideas in the second person of the Trinity, biblically identified as the Wisdom or Logos of God.[38] He wrote:

God the Father always existed, and . . . he always had an only-begotten Son, who at the same time . . . is called Wisdom. This is that Wisdom in whom God delighted when the world was finished. . . . In this Wisdom, therefore, who ever existed with the Father, the Creation was always present in form and outline, and there was never a time when the prefiguration of those things which hereafter were to be did not exist in Wisdom. (*On First Principles* 1.4.4[39])

The genera and species of all things have therefore always existed, being contained in God's Wisdom (*On First Principles* 1.2.2–3, 1.4.5). Origen contrasts the way in which things pre-exist in Wisdom with their later substantial existence: 'Since Wisdom has always existed, there have

---

[38] In his *Commentary on the Gospel of John*, Origen regards Christ, insofar as he is God's Wisdom, as the beginning or source of all things, including their forms:

For Christ is, in a manner, the demiurge, to whom the Father says, 'Let there be light,' and 'Let there be a firmament.' But Christ is demiurge as a beginning (*archē*), inasmuch as he is Wisdom. It is in virtue of his being Wisdom that he is called *archē*. . . . Consider, however, if we are at liberty to take this meaning of *archē* for our text: 'In the beginning was the Word,' so as to obtain the meaning that all things came into being according to Wisdom and according to the models of the system which are present in his thoughts. For I consider that as a house or a ship is built and fashioned in accordance with the sketches of the builder or designer, the house or the ship having their beginning (*archē*) in the sketches and reckonings in his mind, so all things came into being in accordance with the designs of what was to be, clearly laid down by God in Wisdom. And we should add that having created, so to speak, ensouled Wisdom, he left her to hand over, from the types which were in her, to things existing and to matter, the actual emergence of them, their moulding and their forms. But I consider, if it be permitted to say this, that the beginning (*archē*) of real existence was the Son of God, saying: 'I am the beginning and the end, the A and Ω, the first and the last' (1.22).

[39] Sections 3–5 of ch. 4, which contain this passage, are not included in the old edition of the Ante-Nicene Fathers edited by Roberts and Donaldson in 1885, but are included, on the basis of the reconstructed text by Koetschau, in Butterworth's more recent translation (Gloucester, MA: Peter Smith, 1973).

always existed in Wisdom, by a pre-figuration and pre-formation, those things which afterwards have received substantial existence' (*On First Principles* 1.4.5). We see here a pointed contrast between the substantial existence enjoyed by concrete objects and the unsubstantial and even imaginary existence that ideas are said to have, even in the Logos.

Methodius, in his dialogue *On Free Will*,[40] after declaring that there cannot be two *agenēta,* defends *creatio ex nihilo* by having Orthodoxus say to Valentinian:

> ORTHODOXUS. Do you say then, that there co-exists with God matter without qualities out of which He formed the beginning of this world?
>
> VALENTINIAN. So I think.
>
> ORTHODOXUS. If, then, matter had no qualities, and the world were produced by God, and qualities exist in the world, then God is the maker of qualities?
>
> VALENTINIAN. It is so.
>
> ORTHODOXUS. Now, as I heard you say some time ago that it is impossible for anything to come into being out of that which has no existence, answer my question: Do you think that the qualities of the world were not produced out of any existing qualities?
>
> VALENTINIAN. I do.
>
> ORTHODOXUS. And that they are something distinct from substances?
>
> VALENTINIAN. Yes.
>
> ORTHODOXUS. If, then, qualities were neither made by God out of any ready at hand, nor derive their existence from substances, because they are not substances, we must say that they were produced by God out of what had no existence. Wherefore I thought you spoke extravagantly in saying that it was impossible to suppose that anything was produced by God out of what did not exist.

Here Orthodoxus, who obviously speaks for the orthodox faith, will not allow that even properties are uncreated by God. For God alone is uncreated.

---

[40] Patristics scholar Mark Edwards informs me that *On Free Will* is not universally assigned to Methodius. Some ascribe it to Origen, some to an otherwise unknown Maximus.

Nor did the Church Fathers think that numbers exist independently of God as *agenēta*. Thus, Hippolytus traces the heresy of Valentinian Gnosticism to the systems of Plato and Pythagoras, and ultimately to the Egyptians (*Refutation* 6.16). The latter asserted that ultimate reality is an *agennētos* unit and that the other numbers are generated from it (*Refutation* 4.43). 'Pythagoras, then, declared the originating principle of the universe to be the unbegotten monad, and the generated duad, and the rest of the numbers' (*Refutation* 6.18). The material world was thought to be in turn generated from these incorporeal principles. 'There are, then, according to Pythagoras, two worlds: one intelligible, which has the monad for an originating principle; and the other sensible.... Nothing, he says, of intelligibles can be known to us from sense. For he says neither has eye seen, nor ear heard, nor whatsoever any of the senses known that (which is cognized by mind)' (*Refutation* 6.19; cf. Clement of Alexandria, *Stromata* 5.14). Hippolytus then makes the connection with Valentinus: 'And from this (system), not from the Gospels, Valentinus... has collected the (materials of) heresy—and may (therefore) justly be reckoned a Pythagorean and Platonist, not a Christian' (*Refutation* 6.24). Hippolytus charges that 'Valentinus... and the entire school of these (heretics), as disciples of Pythagoras and Plato, (and) following these guides, have laid down as the fundamental principle of their doctrine the arithmetical system. For, likewise, according to these (Valentinians), the originating cause of the universe is a Monad, *agennētos*, imperishable, incomprehensible, inconceivable, productive, and a cause of the generation of all existent things' (*Refutation* 6.24).

Logos Christology

The Church Fathers turned to the Logos doctrine of the early Greek Apologists as the means of grounding the intelligible realm in God rather than in some independent realm of self-subsisting entities like numbers or forms.[41] Combining the Gospel of John's presentation of Christ as the pre-existent Logos, who in the beginning was with

---

[41] For a discussion of texts taken from pseudo-Justin, Irenaeus, Tertullian, Clement of Alexandria, Origen, and Augustine, see Harry Austryn Wolfson, *The Philosophy of the Church Fathers*, i. *Faith, Trinity, and Incarnation*, 3rd edn rev. (Cambridge, MA: Harvard University Press, 1970), ch. 13: 'The Logos and the Platonic Ideas'. According to Wolfson, every Church Father who addressed the issue rejected the view that the ideas were self-subsisting entities, but instead located the intelligible world in the Logos and, hence, in the mind of God.

God: The Sole Ultimate Reality

God and was God and through whom all things came into being (John 1: 1-3), with Philo of Alexandria's conception of the Logos as the mind of God in which the Platonic realm of ideas subsists, Tatian offers one of the earliest Christian expositions of this doctrine:

> God was in the beginning; but the beginning, we have been taught, is the power of the Logos. For the Lord of the universe, who is Himself the necessary ground of all being, inasmuch as no creature was yet in existence, was alone; but inasmuch as He was all power, Himself the necessary ground of things visible and invisible, with Him were all things; with Him by Logos-power, the Logos himself also, who was in Him, subsists. And by His simple will, the Logos springs forth; and the Logos, not coming forth in vain, becomes the first-begotten work of the Father. Him (the Logos) we know to be the beginning of the world. (*Address to the Greeks* 5.1-9)[42]

The invisible, intelligible realm of exemplar ideas exists in the immanent Logos, who, proceeding out from God the Father (whether eternally or at the moment of creation), is begotten as God the Son. He then creates the sensible world of things that we experience.

Hippolytus, in language that would later echo at Nicaea, exults in the fact that even the opponents of orthodoxy must finally concede that there is but one *agenētos* which is the source of all reality:

> God, subsisting alone, and having nothing contemporaneous with Himself, determined to create the world. And conceiving the world in mind, and willing and uttering the Word, He made it; and straightaway it appeared, formed as it has pleased Him. For us, then, it is sufficient simply to know that there was nothing contemporaneous with God. Beside Him there was nothing; but He, while existing alone, yet existed in plurality. For He was neither without reason, nor wisdom, nor power, nor counsel. And all things were in Him, and He was the All.... He begat the Word; ... and thus there appeared another beside Himself. But when I say another, I do not mean that there are two Gods, but that it is only as light of light.... Who then adduces a multitude of gods

---

[42] Similarly, Athenagoras declares that 'our doctrine acknowledges one God, the Maker of this universe, who is Himself uncreated ... but has made all things by the Logos which is from Him' (*Plea for the Christians* 4). The patterns after which all created things are made (8) are to be found in the Logos, who is the mind of the Father: 'The Son of God is the Logos of the Father, in idea and in operation; for after the pattern of him and by him were all things made, the Father and the Son being one. And the Son being in the Father and the Father in the Son ..., the understanding and reason of the Father is the Son of God' (10; cf. Theophilus, *To Autolycus* 2.22; Eusebius, *Demonstratio evangelica* 4.13).

brought in, time after time? For all are shut up, however unwillingly, to admit this fact, that the all runs up into One. If, then, all things run up into One, even according to Valentinus, and Marcion, and Cerinthus, and all their fooleries, they are also reduced, however unwillingly, to this position, that they must acknowledge that the One is the cause of all things. Thus, then, these too, though they wish it not, fall in with the truth, and admit that one God made all things according to His good pleasure. (*Against Noetus* 10–11; cf. *Refutation* 10.28–9)

It is ironic, in view of the contemporary debate among Christian philosophers over God and abstract objects, that even the heretics against whom the Church Fathers contended did not think to postulate a plurality of *agenēta*. Whether Gnostic, Arian, or Christian, all were committed to there being a single *agenētos*.[43] The challenge facing the framers of Nicaea was how to preserve the deity and distinctness of the Son without admitting a plurality of *agenēta*.

Returning to the Nicene formula, we can see in light of its historical background that when God the Father is said to be the Maker of all things visible and invisible, the domain of quantification is intended to be unlimited. There is a state of affairs in the actual world which consists of God existing in absolute solitude. Even numbers and properties do not exist outside Him, much less independently of Him, for He is the ground of all being, and nothing is co-eternal with Him. The Logos Christology of the Greek Apologists comes to expression in the Nicene affirmation that the Son of God is begotten, not made. He is said to be the one through whom all things came to be. Since he himself is unmade and everything else is *genētos*, the Son must be *agenētos* and is therefore God, even though as the Son he is begotten (*gennētos*) of the Father.

If confronted by a modern-day Platonist defending an ontology which includes causally effete objects which are *agenēta* and so co-eternal with God, the Church Fathers would have rejected such an account as blasphemous, since such an account would deny God's being the source of all things. The Fathers could not and did not exempt such objects from God's creative power, since He is the sole and all-originating *agenētos*.

---

[43] Certain Marcionite advocates of metaphysical dualism were the exception that proved the rule.

PERFECT BEING THEOLOGY

In addition to the biblical and patristic witness to God's status as the sole ultimate reality, the requirements of sound systematic theology include the affirmation that God is the source of all things apart from Himself. For divine aseity is a fundamental requirement of perfect being theology. As a perfect being, the greatest conceivable being, God must be the self-existent source of all reality apart from Himself. For being the cause of existence of other things is plausibly a great-making property, and the maximal degree of this property is to be the cause of everything else that exists.[44] God would be diminished in His greatness if He were the cause of only some of the other things that exist. If abstract entities such as mathematical objects were real existents independent of God, then God would be the source of merely an infinitesimal part of what exists. For Platonism posits infinite realms of being which are metaphysically necessary and uncreated by God. The physical universe which has been created by God would be an infinitesimal triviality utterly dwarfed by the unspeakable quantity of uncreated beings. To appreciate in some measure the vastness of the realms of uncreated being postulated by Platonism, consider the set theoretical hierarchy alone, as displayed in Figure 2.

Of course, the existence of any entities whatsoever independent of God is incompatible with God's being the Creator of all things, but the profligacy of Platonism in this respect truly takes away one's breath. God's status as the greatest conceivable being requires that He be the source of existence of all things apart from Himself. Not only so, but God's greatness would be even further augmented if it were impossible that anything exist independent of His creative power. Thus, in any possible world, God, as the greatest conceivable being, is the source of all things, if any, apart from Himself.

Seen in this light, divine aseity is a corollary of God's omnipotence, which belongs indisputably to maximal greatness.[45] For if any being exists independently of God, then God lacks the power either to annihilate it or to create it. An omnipotent being can give and take existence as He sees fit with respect to other beings. God's power would thus be attenuated by the existence of independently existing abstract objects.

---

[44] A point made by Leftow, *God and Necessity*, 22. [45] Ibid., 22.

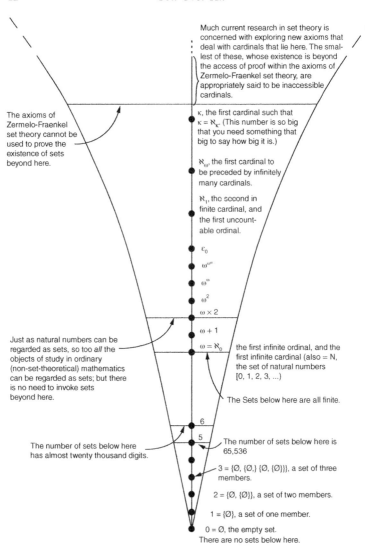

Figure 2. The set theoretical hierarchy, starting at zero and proceeding up through the natural numbers to transfinite numbers. (Adapted from A. W. Moore, *The Infinite* [London: Routledge, 1990], 157.)

Moreover, there is a powerful philosophico-theological argument against the existence of uncreated, Platonic properties.[46] Consider the cluster of divine attributes which go to make up God's nature. Call that nature *deity*. On Platonism, *deity* is an abstract object existing independently of God, to which God stands in the relation of exemplification or instantiation. Moreover, it is in virtue of standing in relation to this object that God is divine. He is God because He exemplifies *deity*. Thus, on Platonism, God does not really exist *a se* at all. For God depends upon this abstract object for His existence. Platonism does not simply postulate some object existing independently of God—a serious enough compromise of God's sole ultimacy—but makes God dependent upon this object, thus denying divine aseity. The implication? 'So deity/the Platonic realm, not God, is the ultimate reality.'[47]

Worse, if possible: since aseity, like omnipotence, is one of the essential attributes of God included in *deity*, it turns out that God does not exemplify *deity* after all. Since aseity is essential to *deity* and God, on Platonism, does not exist *a se*, it turns out that God does not exist! On Platonism, there may a demiurge, such as is featured in Plato's *Timaeus*, but the God of classical theism does not exist. Theism is thus undone by Platonism.

CONCLUSION

It seems to me, therefore, that we have very strong reasons both biblically and theologically for standing with the historic Christian tradition in affirming that God is the sole ultimate reality, that He exists *a se* and is the source of all things apart from Himself. This conclusion entails that the orthodox Christian cannot be a (metaphysically heavyweight) Platonist, for Platonism affirms that there are abstract objects which exist necessarily, eternally, and *a se*, in contradiction to the Christian affirmation that God is the sole ultimate reality. The challenge posed by Platonism to orthodox theology is therefore serious and must be squarely confronted.

---

[46] Ibid., 234.
[47] Ibid., 235. Leftow offers a second argument as well for this conclusion. See also Leftow, 'Is God an Abstract Object?', *Noûs*, 24/4 (1990): 581–98, where he presents a bootstrapping objection against God's creating His own nature, which, barring divine simplicity, leaves God dependent upon His nature for His existence.

3

The Challenge of Platonism

INTRODUCTION

The heart of the contemporary debate over Platonism is to be found in the philosophy of mathematics, and so this field shall be the focus of our investigation. The ancient problem of universals, though still discussed by contemporary metaphysicians, does not lie at the centre of today's debate—and with good reason, I think. The principal motivation for belief in universals is that it provides a solution to the ancient problem of the One over the Many. That problem concerns how to give an explanatory account of the resemblance between two things. The basic idea is that when two objects resemble each other in some respect—for example, they are the same colour—then there must be something which they have in common. This is said to be a universal or property, say *redness*, which the particular objects share. For the Platonist, talk of universals is not just a *façon de parler*. There really exist these abstract objects which particular things somehow have in common.

On the face of it, this account of resemblance sounds bizarre. Certainly, brown dogs and big elephants exist, but are we really to think that *brownness* and *bigness* are existing things, abstract entities existing in addition to elephants and dogs? Few contemporary philosophers think that the problem of the One over the Many provides an adequate reason for postulating the existence of such entities. Explaining the resemblance between two things is not really the issue, for if the anti-realist can explain, for example, why the dog is brown, then he can account for the dog's resemblance in colour to the chair simply by saying of the chair what he said about the dog.[1]

---

[1] Michael Devitt, '"Ostrich Nominalism" or "Mirage Realism"?', *Pacific Philosophical Quarterly*, 61/4 (1980): 435.

For the anti-realist, talk of properties may be regarded as just a convenient, and perhaps indispensable, *façon de parler* not to be taken ontologically seriously. If asked to explain why the dog is brown, the anti-realist can offer a perfectly plausible and, I think, adequate scientific explanation in terms of the dog's absorbing and reflecting various wavelengths of light, and so forth. By contrast, it does nothing at all to explain why the dog is brown to say that the dog has the property of *brownness*. Indeed, how does standing in a mysterious relation to a non-spatial, causally unconnected, abstract object make an otherwise colourless dog brown? It seems that Platonism has no explanatory advantage over anti-realism. It is therefore little wonder that, in the words of the philosopher of mathematics Mark Balaguer, 'The One Over Many argument is now widely considered to be a bad argument.'[2]

THE INDISPENSABILITY ARGUMENT

Rather, in the contemporary debate over Platonism, there is one argument that is predominant: the so-called Indispensability Argument. The argument's claim is that we are committed to the reality of abstract objects by many of the statements we take to be true, such as mathematical statements like '$1 + 1 = 2$'. Although the Indispensability Argument for Platonism originated with W. V. O. Quine, a giant of twentieth-century philosophy, subsequent discussion has largely overtaken Quine's version of the argument, which was predicated upon a number of idiosyncratic and now widely rejected theses.[3] Today there is a variety of versions of Indispensability Arguments on tap, free of Quine's more controversial theses. Balaguer nicely epitomizes such arguments as follows:

> I. If a simple sentence (*i.e.*, a sentence of the form '*a* is *F*', or '*a* is *R*-related to *b*', or ...) is literally true, then the objects that its singular terms denote exist. Likewise, if an existential sentence is literally true,

---

[2] 'Platonism in Metaphysics', *The Stanford Encyclopedia of Philosophy*, 7 Apr. 2009, §3, <http://plato.stanford.edu/entries/platonism>.
[3] See my account of Quine's Indispensability Argument in *God and Abstract Objects* (Berlin: Springer Verlag, 2018), ch. 3.

then there exist objects of the relevant kinds; *e.g.,* if 'There is an *F*' is true, then there exist some *F*s.

II. There are literally true simple sentences containing singular terms that refer to things that could only be abstract objects. Likewise, there are literally true existential statements whose existential quantifiers range over things that could only be abstract objects.

III. Therefore, abstract objects exist.[4]

Let us unpack these premisses for the sake of those unfamiliar with the terminology.

PREMISS (I): A CRITERION OF ONTOLOGICAL COMMITMENT

Premiss (I) states a *criterion of ontological commitment*. It does not tell us what exists, but it does claim to tell us what must exist if a sentence we assert is to be true. It is intended to reveal to us what our discourse commits us to ontologically. According to premiss (I), we make ontological commitments in two ways.

Singular Terms

According to the first part of premiss (I), we make ontological commitments by means of *singular terms*. What are they? Singular terms are words or phrases which are used to single out something. They include *proper names* like 'John', 'HMS Bounty', 'Blue Velvet', and so on; *definite descriptions* like 'the man in the grey suit,' 'your sister-in-law', 'my worst nightmare', and so on; and *demonstrative terms* like 'this pancake', 'that boy', and so on.

In premiss (I), Balaguer uses '*a*' as a logical constant for which we may substitute a singular term to form a simple sentence. '*F*' stands for any property which we might predicate of the individual picked out by the singular term, and '*R*' any relation in which that individual may be said to stand. For example, the simple sentence 'The *Queen Mary II* is a huge oceanliner' has the form *a* is *F*, '*a*' standing for the

---

[4] Balaguer, 'Platonism in Metaphysics'.

Queen Mary II and 'F' standing for *a huge oceanliner*. The simple sentence 'The Queen Mary II docks in Southampton' has the form *a is R-related to b*, '*a*' standing for the Queen Mary II, '*b*' for Southampton, and '*R*' standing for the relation *docks in*. In the following, we may ignore without detriment simple sentences involving relations and focus on those which are predications of a property to an individual.

The claim of premiss (I) is that, if a simple sentence of the form *a is F* is literally true, then the object denoted by its singular term exists. In our example, the term '*Queen Mary II*' denotes the Queen Mary II (or, in other words, the Queen Mary II is the denotation of the singular term '*Queen Mary II*').[5] Accordingly, since the sentence 'The Queen Mary II is a huge oceanliner' is literally true, the Queen Mary II exists.

Notice Balaguer's qualification that the sentence must be *literally* true. Sentences employing metaphors and other figures of speech may be true, but they are not literally true. It may be true, for example, that 'It's raining cats and dogs!', but it would be obtuse to think that someone asserting such a sentence believes that there are animals falling from the sky. He simply means that it is raining hard. Singular terms employed in non-literal speech are not ontologically committing for their user. But premiss (I) states that, if a simple sentence with a singular term is literally true, there must exist an object corresponding to the singular term used in the sentence.

Why *simple* sentences? What Balaguer is trying to avoid is not complexity, but sentences involving what are called intensional contexts. Intensional contexts are non-extensional contexts. Extensional contexts are sentence phrases which have two characteristics. (i) Singular terms referring to the same entity can be switched without affecting the sentence's truth value. For example, 'The morning star is Venus' is an extensional context because one could substitute the co-referring term 'the evening star' for 'the morning star' without affecting the sentence's truth value. By contrast, 'Ancient Babylonian astronomers believed that the morning star rises in the morning' is

---

[5] Sometimes philosophers will speak of designation instead of denotation; most often they use the word 'reference' with respect to singular terms. In premiss (II), Balaguer says that a singular term *refers* to a particular object. There is no uniform usage or understanding of these notions, but the basic idea is that if we use a singular term in a literally true sentence, then there exists some object corresponding to that term.

an intensional context because substitution of 'the evening star' for the co-referring term 'the morning star' would yield a false sentence. (ii) One can quantify into such contexts from outside the context. For example, 'Mars has two moons' permits us to infer, 'There is something which is a moon of Mars'. By contrast, 'Le Verrier sought to discover Vulcan between Mercury and the Sun' involves an intensional context because we cannot infer that 'There is something that Le Verrier sought to discover'.

The criterion of ontological commitment proposed by (I) does not apply when it comes to intensional contexts. For example, use of the singular term 'the bogeyman' in the true statement 'Johnny fears the bogeyman' does not commit us to the reality of the bogeyman. The inapplicability of (I)'s criterion of ontological commitment to intensional contexts implies that it will be useless for vast stretches of human discourse, for intentional attitudes (like fearing, hoping, believing), modal operators (like 'necessarily, . . .' or 'possibly, . . .'), and temporal operators (like 'it was the case that . . .' or 'it will be the case that . . .') all establish intensional contexts.[6] The criterion applies only to sentences which are extensional.

Existential Quantification

Singular terms are not the only devices of ontological commitment, according to (I). The second part of (I) claims that we also make ontological commitments by means of existential sentences. What are they? As Balaguer makes clear in the second part of premiss (II), he is talking about sentences which involve so-called existential (or particular) quantifiers. In contrast to universally quantified statements, which are true with respect to *all* the members of the domain of quantification[7], existentially quantified statements are true with respect to *some* of the members of the domain of quantification. For example, if our domain of quantification is bears, then the statement 'Some bears live near the North Pole' is true just in case at least one member of the domain lives near the North Pole.

---

[6] E.g. 'Possibly, there are pink unicorns' does not permit us to infer that there are possible pink unicorns, and 'There were carnivorous dinosaurs' does not permit the inference that there are dinosaurs which were carnivorous.

[7] Recall our discussion in Ch. 2, under 'John's Prologue'.

In ordinary English, there is a variety of informal existential quantifiers, such as 'some', 'at least one', 'there is/are', and 'there exists'. All of these informal expressions are captured in formal logic by the formal quantifier '∃'. A sentence like 'Some bears live near the North Pole' has the form (∃x) (x is a bear & x lives near the North Pole), which is to be read 'There is some x such that x is a bear and x lives near the North Pole'. In order for the sentence to be true, there must be at least one thing in the domain that can be the value of the variable 'x'. Balaguer is evidently talking about first-order logic, where the variables x, y, z, take individual things as their values.

Now the claim of premiss (I) is that the literal truth of simple sentences involving existential quantification of the form 'There is an F' commits us to the reality of the object which is an F. Here 'F' stands for a general term like 'a man', 'buffalo', 'facts which science has yet to discover', and so on. Such sentences can be symbolized as (∃x) (x is an F). The existential quantifier '∃' is claimed to express existence, not in a metaphysically lightweight sense, but rather in a metaphysically heavyweight sense. It is a device for making ontological commitments. Thus, the person who makes assertions involving informal quantifiers like 'some' and 'there is/are' thereby commits himself to the reality of the things in the domain of quantification which, as Balaguer puts it in premiss (II), his quantifiers 'range over', that is to say, the things which are the values of the variables in sentences he regards as true.

So, in sum, what premiss (I) expresses is not an ontological claim about what exists, but a meta-ontological claim about how a person commits himself ontologically. The claim is that singular terms and existential quantification are devices of ontological commitment. The idea is very simple, really, and I hope that I have not made it unduly complicated. My explication is necessary to prepare us for discussion of the premiss in what follows.

PREMISS (II): ABSTRACT OBJECTS

Turn now to premiss (II). It claims that the denotations or referents of certain singular terms in literally true, simple sentences, for example, '2 + 2 = 4', cannot plausibly be taken to be concrete objects of any kind. For example, the referents of such mathematical terms as '2 + 2' and '4' are clearly abstract objects. Premiss (II) also excludes taking such mathematical discourse to be some sort of figurative language, not to be taken literally. It claims that at least some abstract discourse is literally true and therefore commits its user to the reality of abstract objects.

In the second part of premiss (II), it is likewise claimed that there are literally true existentially quantified statements involving quantification over abstract objects. For example, 'There is a prime number between 2 and 4' or 'There are prime numbers greater than 100'. Again, such statements are not to be construed metaphorically, along the lines of 'There's a bee in her bonnet'. So existentially quantified abstract discourse also commits its user to the reality of abstract objects.

From (I) and (II) the conclusion (III) follows, that abstract objects exist. If such objects exist *a se*, as Platonists claim, then the classical theist must reject either (I) or (II).

RESPONSES TO THE INDISPENSABILITY ARGUMENT

Most Christian philosophers, not to speak of theologians, are largely unaware of the wide range of responses to the Indispensability Argument which are on offer today. If we take mathematical objects as a case in point, then we can portray some of the many options as in Figure 1 (p. xii).

The various options can be classed as *realist* (mathematical objects exist); *anti-realist* (mathematical objects do not exist); or *arealist* (there is no fact of the matter concerning the existence of mathematical objects). As Figure 1 illustrates, there are two brands of realism about mathematical objects: views which take them to be *abstract* objects and views which take them to be *concrete* objects. Of realist views which consider mathematical objects to be abstract, absolute creationism is a sort of modified Platonism, holding that mathematical objects have, like concrete objects, been created by God, thus safeguarding divine aseity. Concretist versions of realism can take mathematical objects to be either *physical* objects or *mental* objects, the latter either in *human* minds or in *God's* mind. The most promising concretist view is some sort of divine conceptualism, the heir to the view of Philo and the Church Fathers.

When we turn to anti-realist responses to the Indispensability Argument, we find a cornucopia of different views. Neutralism rejects the criterion of ontological commitment expressed in premiss (I), taking the use of singular terms and existential quantification to be neutral with respect to ontological commitments. Neo-Meinongianism similarly denies that existential (or particular) quantification is ontologically committing, though it agrees that there are objects referred to by abstract singular terms—with the caveat that these objects are nonexistent. Free logic, on the other hand, takes existential quantification to be ontologically committing but denies that the use of singular terms is a device of ontological commitment. Fictionalism accepts entirely the Platonist's criterion of ontological commitment but denies that mathematical statements are true. Figuralism, by contrast, holds that mathematical discourse is true but denies that it must be taken literally. Pretence theory considers mathematical discourse to be a species of make-believe, so that mathematical objects are akin to fictional characters. There are also paraphrastic strategies, which hold that we can offer paraphrases of mathematical statements which will preserve their truth value but without ontological commitment to abstract objects.[8] And so on!

In between realism and anti-realism about mathematical objects is arealism, the view that there just is no fact of the matter about the reality of mathematical objects. Is this an option that might be available to theists eager to preserve divine aseity? The classic version of arealism was the conventionalism of Rudolf Carnap.[9] He drew a fundamental distinction between what he called 'internal questions' and 'external questions', that is to say, questions which are posed *within* an adopted linguistic framework and questions posed by someone *outside* that framework. Carnap gives the illustration of what he calls the 'thing' framework or language. Once we have adopted the linguistic framework in which we speak of observable things in a spatiotemporal system, we can meaningfully pose internal questions like 'Is the moon a thing?' or 'Is a school of fish a thing?'

---

[8] These are discussed in my *God and Abstract Objects*, ch. 8.
[9] Rudolf Carnap, *'Meaning and Necessity': A Study in Semantics and Modal Logic* (Chicago: University of Chicago Press, 1956), 206–17.

Someone who rejects the language of things may choose to speak instead of mere appearances such as sense data.

Similarly, once we have adopted a linguistic framework involving terminology for abstract objects like numbers, internal questions like 'Is there a prime number greater than 100?' are meaningful. No one who has adopted the framework would seriously raise the question 'Are there numbers?', for their existence is necessary once one has adopted the number framework. For someone who is outside the framework, Carnap insisted, the question is meaningless. As a logical positivist and verificationist, Carnap was convinced that such metaphysical questions have no cognitive content. Whether one adopts the linguistic framework in which it makes sense to speak of numbers is just a matter of convenience, or convention; hence, the name conventionalism.

No philosopher today would defend Carnap's verificationism; but his conventionalism does find an echo today in what is sometimes called ontological pluralism.[10] According to these thinkers, certain ontological questions, though meaningful, do not have objective answers. The philosophers of mathematics Mark Balaguer and Penelope Maddy, for example, would deny that the question 'Do mathematical objects exist?' has an answer that is objectively true or false.[11] On arealism, there just is no fact of the matter whether or not mathematical objects exist.

Now at first blush arealism might seem a quick and easy solution to the challenge posed by Platonism to divine aseity. If there is no objective truth about whether or not mathematical objects exist, then the use of mathematical terminology is devoid of ontological significance. Internal questions about the existence of certain sets or numbers or solutions to equations may be answered affirmatively; but there just is no answer to the external question of the existence of

---

[10] See David J. Chalmers, 'Ontological Anti-Realism', in David Chalmers et al., *Metametaphysics: New Essays on the Foundations of Ontology* (Oxford: Clarendon, 2009), 77–129. Chalmers's terminology is misleading, since anti-realism on the level of ontology involves the denial of the existence of mathematical objects. It is only on the meta-ontological level that anti-realism is the denial that the ontological question has an objective answer. So it would be less misleading to call ontological pluralism 'meta-ontological anti-realism' rather than 'ontological anti-realism'.

[11] See Mark Balaguer, *Platonism and Anti-Platonism in Mathematics* (New York: OUP, 1998), 151–79; Penelope Maddy, *Defending the Axioms: On the Philosophical Foundations of Set Theory* (Oxford: OUP, 2011), 98. Maddy offers various characterizations of arealism.

such entities. In that case, one cannot truthfully assert that there are objects which God did not create.

Alas, however, there is no succour for the theist here. For given God's metaphysical necessity and essential aseity, there just is no possible world in which uncreated mathematical objects exist. Hence, there most certainly is a fact of the matter whether uncreated, abstract objects exist: they do not and cannot exist. Therefore, arealism is necessarily false, as is conventionalism about existence statements concerning mathematical and other abstract objects.

Still, Carnap's discussion is not without merit, and many contemporary philosophers find his distinction between internal and external questions to be intuitive and helpful. We shall have occasion to return to it.

Putting aside arealism, then, we are left with a number of both realist and anti-realist solutions to the challenge posed by Platonism to divine aseity. We shall want to explore which solutions offer the most promise for an answer to the Indispensability Argument and to the challenge of Platonism. We shall begin with the realist alternatives.

4

Absolute Creation

INTRODUCTION

Whatever one's reason for adopting Platonism, the most obvious response to the challenge it poses to divine aseity is to advocate a sort of modified Platonism, according to which mathematical objects and other abstract entities are not uncreated, but rather are created by God. Such a view has been called 'absolute creation' by Thomas Morris and Christopher Menzel, whose seminal article 'Absolute Creation' in 1986 sparked the contemporary debate among Christian philosophers over God and abstract objects.[1]

Actually, there are two contemporary debates going on concerning God and abstract objects, one over the challenge of Platonism to *divine aseity*, stemming from Morris and Menzel's article, and the other over the challenge of Platonism to *divine sovereignty*, sparked by Alvin Plantinga's 1980 Aquinas Lecture 'Does God Have a Nature?' at Marquette University.[2] Mathematical truths like '2+2=4' are necessarily true and so beyond the control of God, thereby presenting an ostensible challenge to God's sovereignty. Because Plantinga was concerned with the challenge posed by Platonism to divine sovereignty, not divine aseity, he dismissed nominalism, or anti-realism, as irrelevant to the discussion. For even if there are no such things as the

---

[1] Thomas V. Morris and Christopher Menzel, 'Absolute Creation', *American Philosophical Quarterly*, 23/4 (1986): 353–62.

[2] Alvin Plantinga, *Does God Have a Nature?* (Milwaukee, WI: Marquette University Press, 1980). The aseity challenge and the sovereignty challenge are often conflated in the philosophical literature. E.g. the title of the recent symposium edited by Paul Gould, *Beyond the Control of God? Six Views on the Problem of God and Abstract Objects* (London: Bloomsbury, 2014), evokes the divine sovereignty debate, when, in fact, the symposiasts are almost wholly occupied with the debate over divine aseity.

properties of *being red* and *being coloured*, for example, nevertheless, it remains necessarily true that whatever is red is coloured, and God can do nothing to make it otherwise.

Obviously, anti-realism, however irrelevant it may be to the sovereignty debate, is nonetheless central to the aseity debate, since if there are no abstract objects, the challenge their existence would pose to divine aseity simply evaporates. In the end, Plantinga opts for a conception of divine sovereignty that does not require the modal status of propositions (i.e. whether they are necessary or contingent) to be within God's control. He does not address the question whether the existence of abstract objects somehow depends on God's nature or activity.

Morris and Menzel addressed both challenges in their article. They espouse absolute creation to safeguard God's aseity and what they call 'theistic activism' to safeguard divine sovereignty. The theistic activist, unlike Plantinga, attributes even the modal status of propositions to God. Thus, Morris and Menzel refer to theistic activism as the 'modal component' of absolute creation.[3] The most sophisticated defence of theistic activism to date is Brian Leftow's massive *God and Necessity* (2012).[4] As Leftow recognizes, ascribing the existence of abstract objects like propositions to God's creative activity does not entail grounding propositions' modal status in God. In other words, absolute creation does not require theistic activism. Since our concern is divine aseity, not divine sovereignty, I shall leave largely to the side the question of theistic activism.

ABSOLUTE CREATION

When Tom Morris, in consultation with Menzel, wrote 'Absolute Creation', he had, unfortunately, not yet clearly differentiated in his thinking absolute creationism from divine conceptualism (see Figure 1).[5] As a result, the paper tends to conflate a modified Platonism, according to which abstract objects exist but are caused by God's intellective activity, and a sort of divine conceptualism, according to

---

[3] Morris and Menzel, 'Absolute Creation', 360.
[4] Brian Leftow, *God and Necessity* (Oxford: OUP, 2012).
[5] Personal communication, 1 Nov. 2013.

which objects usually taken to be abstract are really thoughts in God's mind. Since the expressed goal of Morris and Menzel's paper is to reconcile Platonism with classical theism, I shall take them as defending the view that abstract objects do exist, just as the Platonist says, but have been created by God, and I shall reserve our discussion of divine conceptualism for the next chapter.

It is worth noting in passing that the absolute creationist is not necessarily committed to the reality of a transcendent realm of abstract objects existing independently of concrete objects. That was indeed Plato's view, but his student Aristotle took a different view. Aristotle thought that universals or properties exist in the concrete things which have those properties and do not exist in the absence of such concrete things. Chris Menzel's colleague at Texas A&M, Hugh McCann, defends a view like Aristotle's. McCann thinks that abstract objects exist in the concrete world and are created by God in His creating concrete objects.[6] So, for example, in creating cats, God also creates the property *felinity*. Although McCann struggles to explain how unexemplified properties, like *unicornality*—or even *felinity* during the Jurassic age when no cats were about—exist, we may leave that to the Aristotelians to sort out. The overriding point is that absolute creationism takes abstract objects, wherever or whenever they exist, to be created by God.

PROBLEMS WITH ABSOLUTE CREATION

Two main problems arise for absolute creationism, the first troublesome and the second truly serious.

Scope and Freedom of God's Creating

The first problem is that absolute creationism's modified Platonism is theologically objectionable because it misconstrues either the scope or the nature of creation. This problem arises because of two features of

---

[6] Hugh J. McCann, *Creation and the Sovereignty of God* (Bloomington, IN: Indiana University Press, 2012), 201–2. Note that McCann's motivating concern is that of the theistic activist: divine sovereignty.

many abstract objects: their eternality and their necessity. Things like numbers, propositions, and properties do not seem to be the sort of thing that could begin to exist. If '1 + 1 = 2' is true at some moment of time, then it was obviously true at any earlier moment of time. Even if time began to exist, there is no reason to think that numbers began to exist along with time. Even if God should exist timelessly in the absence of a created world of concrete objects, it would nonetheless be the case that the number of concrete objects is 1 (namely, God). So the number 1 would exist. But if the number 1 exists, all the rest of the natural numbers generated by the successor relation also exist. God's creation of abstract objects must therefore be either timeless or from eternity past. From the perspective of the absolute creationist, such objects exist co-eternally with God in a relation of ontological dependence upon Him.

Moreover, although not all kinds of abstract objects exist necessarily, many kinds, such as numbers, propositions, and possible worlds, do seem to exist necessarily, if they exist at all. Not only do such objects exist in every possible world, but, as even most theistic activists acknowledge, they exist independently of God's will, being grounded in His nature, not in His will.[7] According to the absolute creationist, the realm of necessarily existing abstract objects flows non-voluntaristically from the very nature or being of God.

Trade-off between the Scope and Freedom of Creation

The eternality and necessity of abstract objects will force significant revisions in the traditional doctrine of creation. A biblical doctrine of creation assigns all created things to the realm of temporal becoming and implies a temporal beginning to the existence of created things.[8] If, then, we think of abstract objects as *ontologically dependent* on God but not, properly speaking, as *created* by God, then the scope of

---

[7] Even on a semi-voluntaristic version of theistic activism like Leftow's, the modal status of logical and mathematical truths is not up to God, but is a function of His nature, so that such a theory, when conjoined with absolute creationism, would subvert God's freedom in creating.

[8] See Ch. 2, 'Biblical Basis of Divine Aseity'. For an extended defence of the claim that the biblical doctrine of *creatio ex nihilo* involves not merely ontological dependence, but a temporal beginning of the created realm, see the first three chapters of Paul Copan and William Lane Craig, *Creation out of Nothing: A Biblical, Philosophical, and Scientific Exploration* (Grand Rapids, MI: Baker Academic, 2004).

divine creation becomes infinitesimal. The abstract realm dwarfs the concrete realm in its incomprehensible plenitude. Hence, scarcely anything, relatively speaking, is created by God. Most of reality is merely sustained in being by God but not, properly speaking, created by God. But, as we have seen, biblical writers bear witness to the truth that God through Christ has created all things other than Himself.

If, on the other hand, we expand the meaning of 'creation' so as to comprise eternal, ontological dependence as well as temporal origin of existence, then we subvert God's freedom with respect to creation. For in orthodox Christian thought, creation is understood to be a freely willed act of God. He does not create from a necessity of His own nature, and there are possible worlds in which God refrains from creation and so exists alone. Absolute creationism, however, robs God of His freedom with respect to creating. God is free with respect to the creation of the realm of concrete objects alone. The vast majority of beings flow from Him with an inexorable necessity independent of His will. If the existence of abstract objects is a function of God's nature, not of His will, then it is not up to God whether (or which) abstract objects exist. Thus, conceptualist Greg Welty seems to be justified in charging that Morris and Menzel have traded in a biblical doctrine of creation for neo-Platonic emanationism with respect to the realm of abstract objects, which is, as I say, nearly all of the created order.[9]

Radical Voluntarism

It seems that the only way the absolute creationist could safeguard God's freedom with respect to creating would be to ground the existence of abstract objects, not in God's nature, but in His free will. Although very few have been willing to take this line, the radical Dooyeweerdian philosopher Roy Clouser boldly affirms not only that abstract objects are created by God, but also that they are 'the created products of God's will', the result of His free choice.[10] Clouser

---

[9] Greg Welty, 'Theistic Conceptual Realism: The Case for Interpreting Abstract Objects as Divine Ideas' (D.Phil. thesis, Oxford University, 2006), 195; similarly, Keith Yandell, 'God and Propositions', in *Beyond the Control of God?*, 26. Theistic activists Gould and Davis are remarkably blasé about activism's implication of emanationism (Paul Gould and Richard Davis, 'Response to Yandell', in *Beyond the Control of God?*, 36–7).

[10] Roy A. Clouser, *The Myth of Religious Neutrality: An Essay on the Hidden Role of Religious Belief in Theories,* rev. edn (Notre Dame, IN: University of Notre Dame

maintains that even the laws of logic, including the law of contradiction, are within God's sovereign control. Clouser does not shrink from affirming that God's own properties and therefore His own nature are the result of His free choice and so are created by Him. Even monotheism, as well as trinitarianism, is the result of God's choice, not His nature. Clouser sums up his voluntaristic absolute creationism as the position that 'God chooses what he is and is what he chooses. Only God's unconditional being is divine *per se*.'[11]

What might be said in response to Clouser's radical voluntarism? First, I think it must be esteemed theologically perverse. Clouser privileges divine sovereignty even above God's essential goodness, wisdom, trinitarian nature, and so on. There is simply no theological or scriptural reason for such a weighting of theological priorities. This is Reformed theology run amok, carried to such an extreme that God is said to decide whether He exists, whether He is one being, whether He is a Trinity, and what essential properties He will have. Such a theology is so strange as to be not recognizably Christian.

Second, Clouser's voluntaristic theistic activism is self-refuting. For example, in claiming that 'The transcendent being of God is beyond the domain of the law of non-contradiction as well as all other laws',[12] Clouser assumes the validity of the law of contradiction for statements about God's transcendent being. Similarly, in saying that God's unconditional, transcendent being is propertyless and that properties are the products of God's free creation, Clouser implies that God's unconditional, transcendent being must have at least the properties of being unconditional and transcendent. Moreover, on Clouser's view, God, having created the world, now really does have, as a result of His free choice, various properties like oneness, omnipotence, omniscience, goodness, being a Trinity, and so on, and really is related to the world as its sustaining ground. But if, as Clouser affirms, 'Only God's unconditional being is divine *per se*', then it follows that God literally does not exist, nor ever has existed. For only God's conditioned,

---

Press, 2005), 212; cf. 207. Incredibly, McCann espouses the same radical voluntarism as Clouser, and out of the same motivation, to preserve God's sovereignty. McCann holds that God even freely chooses His own nature (McCann, *Creation and Sovereignty*, 231–2).

[11] Clouser, *Myth of Religious Neutrality*, 361.
[12] Ibid., 229. Cf. his claim, assumed to be true and not false, that 'His unconditional being neither conforms to nor breaks the law of non-contradiction.'

relational being actually exists, and that is not divine. Clouser's view is, in truth, atheistic.

In sum, if we take abstract objects to be ontologically dependent upon God, but not, properly speaking, created by God, then the scope of divine creation becomes unacceptably minuscule; but if we expand the meaning of 'creation' so as to comprise all dependent beings, including abstract objects, then, on pain of incoherence, we subvert God's freedom with respect to creating. Thus, the ontology of theistic Platonism is incompatible with the doctrine of creation, attenuating either God's freedom or the scope of creation.

Bootstrapping Objection

Vicious Circularity of Absolute Creation

The second, more serious difficulty with absolute creation is that absolute creationism seems to be viciously circular. In the literature, this is known as the bootstrapping objection, after the famous Baron von Münchhausen, who tried to pull himself up by his own bootstraps. The problem can be most clearly seen with respect to the creation of properties. According to absolute creationism, God has created all properties. But in order to create properties, God would already have to possess certain properties.[13] For example, in order to create the property *being powerful*, God would already have to be powerful. An impotent God obviously could not create anything. Thus, God would have to already possess a property in order to create it, which is viciously circular.

Now Morris and Menzel are acutely aware that absolute creation appears to involve what they call 'the ultimate act of bootstrapping', namely, God must be the creator of His own properties, like omniscience, omnipotence, and eternity, and, hence, of His own nature.[14] They admit that it sounds 'at least exceedingly odd', and many would say 'incoherent or absurd', to say that God creates the very properties which are logically necessary for His creative activity, or to say that

---

[13] The force of the word 'already' is obviously not temporal priority, since God's creation of properties is either timeless or from eternity. Rather, one is talking about a sort of explanatory priority. Properties exist because God creates them.

[14] Morris and Menzel, 'Absolute Creation', 358.

God creates His own nature.[15] Morris and Menzel reject any attempt to escape the problem by exempting God's essential properties from absolute creation because 'no such selective exclusion would work in the first place' and such a move would amount to abandoning absolute creation, since God would not then be the only uncreated being—there would also be all God's essential properties, which exist as independent, abstract objects.[16] They reject any appeal to purely negative theology or to divine simplicity—which they take to be 'the denial that God has discrete, distinguishable properties which exist as abstract entities distinct from each other and from him'—because such doctrines encounter insuperable obstacles, which Morris addresses elsewhere.[17] Instead, they boldly claim that it is unproblematic that God create His own essential properties.

Although they offer an analogy to God's creation of His own nature (a materialization machine which produces its own parts), Morris and Menzel insist that its value is mainly illustrative or pedagogical. Rather, the essential point is that there is no objectionable circularity in maintaining that, while God stands in a relation of *logical* dependence to His essential properties, they stand to Him in a relation of *causal, ontological* dependence.[18] Earlier in their article, they had exploited the same distinction to differentiate between the statements

1. If there were no God, there would be no abstract objects.

and

2. If there were no abstract objects, there would be no God.

(2) expresses a harmless, symmetrical, logical dependence of God on abstract objects. Since God necessarily creates abstract objects, it is impossible for Him to exist without them. So if there were no God, there would be no abstract objects, and if there were no abstract objects, there would be no God. Such a symmetrical, logical relation

---

[15] Ibid. Notice that Morris and Menzel do not distinguish between God's creating His own nature and God's creating the properties logically necessary for His creative activity. This distinction becomes crucial in discussion of the bootstrapping objection.
[16] Ibid.
[17] Ibid., 358–9. The reference is to Thomas V. Morris, 'On God and Mann: A View of Divine Simplicity', *Religious Studies*, 21/3 (1985): 299–318; repr. in Morris's *Anselmian Explorations: Essays in Philosophical Theology* (Notre Dame, IN: University of Notre Dame Press, 1987), ch. 6.
[18] Morris and Menzel, 'Absolute Creation', 359.

hardly deserves to be called dependence. By contrast, (1) expresses a more revealing, asymmetrical, causal, or ontological dependence of abstract objects on God.[19] God is responsible for the existence of abstract objects, whereas abstract objects are in no way responsible for God's existence.

Similarly, in the case of God's relation to His own nature, Morris and Menzel maintain that God is ontologically or causally prior to His nature, even though it is true that were His nature not to exist, God would not exist. There is no vicious circularity because the dependence relations are different. It does not follow that, because God's nature depends causally on God and God depends logically on His nature, therefore God depends causally on Himself. 'Relations of logical dependence are always transitive. Relations of continuous causal dependence are always transitive. But we have no good reason to think that transitivity always holds across these two relations.'[20] Since Morris and Menzel have rejected divine simplicity, or the view that God is identical to His nature, they claim that God cannot be said, on their view, to create Himself.

Unfortunately, the vicious circularity which Morris and Menzel seek to elude is not, I think, the circularity alleged by most proponents of the bootstrapping objection. Morris and Menzel want to show, in effect, that while God causes His properties, His properties do not cause God; therefore, God does not cause Himself. By contrast, the vicious circularity alleged by the detractor of absolute creationism is, I think, quite different. The vicious circle alleged by bootstrapping objectors is not that God creates Himself, but that properties, for example, must already exist prior to God's creation of them, which is incoherent. Prior to God's creating properties, there should be no properties, in which case, it is alleged, some of the causal conditions for the creation of properties are missing. This is the vicious circularity that absolute creationism seems to involve. Morris and Menzel say nothing to defeat the charge that, explanatorily prior to creating certain properties, God must already have those very properties in order to create them, which is incoherent.

---

[19] Ibid., 355.
[20] Ibid., 360. Menzel takes exactly the same line with far greater analysis and sophistication in 'Problems with the Bootstrapping Objection: A Response to Craig's "God and Abstract Objects"', paper presented at the Central Division meeting of the American Philosophical Association, Chicago, IL, 27 Feb. 2014.

The priority at issue in the bootstrapping objection is throughout a sort of causal priority—which Menzel recognizes to be asymmetric.[21] According to Menzel, '*a* is *causally dependent* on *b* iff (crudely) *b* has caused it to be the case that *a* exists'.[22] This admittedly crude characterization might be plausibly nuanced in such a way that the causal prerequisites of *a* are also causally prior to *a*. In absolute creation, God's creation of properties is causally prior to the existence of properties; but among the causal prerequisites of God's creating properties is God's having certain properties and, hence, the existence of properties. Thus, the problem with absolute creationism is that causally prior to God's creating properties, the causal prerequisites for His creating properties are missing, so that He cannot create properties. One could put the difficulty by saying that the existence of properties would have to be causally prior to the existence of properties, which is viciously circular. So the bootstrapping worry arises, not from confusion about logical priority, but from a pretty intuitive notion of the causal prerequisites for some action.

What is at stake in the bootstrapping objection is what my colleague J. P. Moreland calls one's 'ontological assay' of things.[23] Standard Platonism offers an ontological assay of things in terms of substances and properties which are exemplified by those substances. Logically prior to their exemplification of properties, substances either are mere bare particulars or simply do not exist. Since absolute creationists accept the ontological assay offered by Platonism, they are immediately confronted with a severe bootstrapping problem, since logically prior to His creation of properties, God is either a featureless particular or non-existent, in which case He is impotent to create properties. In order to create any properties, God must already have properties, which is incoherent.

Divine Simplicity

So what is the absolute creationist to do? Unlike Morris and Menzel, he might try to escape the bootstrapping problem by appealing to the doctrine of divine simplicity. According to that doctrine, God is not

---

[21] Menzel, 'Problems with Bootstrapping Objection', 14. Menzel says that the priority of an act of creation to the thing created involves the asymmetry of causation.
[22] Ibid., 3.
[23] J. P. Moreland, *Universals* (Chesham, Bucks.: Acumen, 2001), 15.

in any way composed. In particular, He transcends the distinction between a thing and its properties. Rather, God is identical to His properties, and all His properties are identical with one another. Thus, we should affirm with respect to God that omniscience = omnipotence = holiness = omnipresence = eternity = God. The doctrine of divine simplicity avoids the vicious circularity threatening absolute creationism because God does not have any properties; rather, God is a simple being identical with His own nature.

Morris and Menzel's scepticism about the plausibility of the traditional doctrine of divine simplicity seems to me, however, well justified. I shall not rehearse its problems here.[24] Suffice it to say that since, according to Platonism, properties are abstract objects, if God is identical to His properties, then God is an abstract object, which is absurd.

McCann acknowledges the problems with the traditional doctrine of divine simplicity, which in his mind render that doctrine implausible, if not wholly untenable. But he proposes an amended doctrine of divine simplicity by means of which he hopes to solve the bootstrapping problem, while avoiding the pitfalls of the traditional doctrine. McCann suggests that God be identified, not with His properties, but with a concrete state of affairs—not, indeed, a static state of affairs, but a dynamic state of affairs. God is, then, an event. McCann holds that God creates His own properties just by being God. Just as *felinity* exists because cats exist, so God's nature exists because God exists; and just as *felinity* exists only in cats, so God's nature exists only in God. God, then, does have properties, but they are created by God. On McCann's view, there just is nothing prior to the actual state of affairs that is God; therefore, God cannot be dependent on His nature, and the bootstrapping problem is avoided.

Very little reflection is needed, I think, to see that McCann has abandoned any claim to divine simplicity. For on his view, God does have a nature which exists immanently in Him, just as *felinity* exists in cats. Moreover, even on McCann's novel view that God is an event, that dynamic state of affairs, like any concrete state of affairs, is, on McCann's view, also ineliminably composed of a subject and a property.[25] So God is not simple.

---

[24] For a discussion, see my *God and Abstract Objects* (Berlin: Springer Verlag, 2018), ch. 4.
[25] McCann, *Creation and Sovereignty*, 227.

But then it is evident that McCann has done nothing to solve the bootstrapping problem. McCann thinks that he has solved it because he would make God's nature asymmetrically dependent upon God, thereby avoiding God's depending on His nature. But that, as we have seen, is not the problem. The problem is that, in order to create properties, God must already have properties, which is viciously circular. McCann would solve the problem by having God's properties depend upon God for their being. But unless God is already omnipotent explanatorily prior to having properties, there is no explanation why He will have the property of *omnipotence* in the explanatorily posterior moment. The only apparent way to avoid the vicious circularity is to maintain with the anti-realist that in that explanatorily prior moment, God can be omnipotent without exemplifying the property of *omnipotence*, which just is to abandon the Platonistic assay of things. In fact, McCann's view threatens to make universals metaphysically superfluous; they seem to just float along as concomitants of God's creation of concrete things and do not do any metaphysical work.

Worse, McCann's view seems to be incoherent. For the complex state of affairs which McCann identifies as God is itself a composition of (God + a property). But then what entity is the subject of that dynamic state of affairs? If it is not God, then the view is self-contradictory, since the subject of that state is said to be God. If it is, indeed, God, then we are launched on an infinite regress in which every concrete state of affairs that is God is itself partly composed of a subject which just is that same concrete state of affairs: God = (God + a property) = ((God + a property) + a property) = (((God + a property) + a property) + a property) = ((((God + a property) + a property) + a property) + a property)... This regress is explanatorily vicious, since at every prior level, the existence of the property is already posited, so that no explanation is given of God's nature.[26] Far from avoiding bootstrapping, this view affirms it: in order to create the property, God must already have it.

---

[26] Cf. Stewart Shapiro's observation that impredicative notions cannot be constructed because the object is already contained in the class used to construct it: 'Philosophy of Mathematics and its Logic: Introduction', in Shapiro (ed.), *The Oxford Handbook of Philosophy of Mathematics and Logic* (Oxford: OUP, 2005), 7; see also Carl Posy, 'Intuitionism and Philosophy', in *Oxford Handbook of Philosophy of Mathematics and Logic*, 321–34. But absolute creationism is a form of constructionism, since God constructs sets via His collecting activity.

Thus, McCann, far from exploiting the doctrine of divine simplicity to avoid vicious circularity, not only abandons divine simplicity, but also, it seems to me, plunges headlong into the maelstrom of the bootstrapping problem.

Created and Uncreated Properties

With their backs apparently to the wall, some absolute creationists have conceded that God does not create His own properties; but they insist that God has created all other properties. This recourse, however, will either sacrifice divine aseity on the altar of Platonism or else seems to yield the palm of victory to the anti-Platonist. Consider the options.

On the one hand, the absolute creationist might affirm that God's properties, or at least His essential properties, are exemplified by Him logically prior to His creation of all remaining properties and so are not created by Him.[27] Thus, there are two sorts of properties: uncreated properties and created properties. Unfortunately, this recourse constitutes an abandonment of the doctrine of divine aseity in favour of Platonism; it just is the theologically unacceptable position that in addition to God there exist other uncreated entities.

The absolute creationist might insist that objects which are parts, aspects, or attributes of God should not be taken to detract from God's being the sole ultimate reality.[28] While this claim is not in general unreasonable, in the case of a Platonistic ontological assay of things, the exceptions do seem objectionable. For on a Platonistic ontological assay, the standard view is that properties are constituents

---

[27] Thus, Paul Gould and Richard Davis affirm that 'God's essential platonic properties exist *a se* (i.e. they are neither created nor sustained by God, yet they *are exemplified by* the divine substance)': 'Response to Critics', in *Beyond the Control of God?*, 76. But they insist that divine aseity is not sacrificed by God's exemplifying Platonic abstract properties, whether on a relational or a constituent ontology. That claim seems clearly false on a relational ontology, since on such a view, God stands in relation to uncreated objects which are in no sense a part of Him but are utterly separate beings. And even on a constituent ontology, where properties are taken to be parts of God, the notion of parthood involved is still cashed out in terms of God's exemplifying abstract objects which are distinct from Him. Gould and Davis's exposition of their view is considerably muddied, moreover, by their bizarre affirmation that God's thoughts are abstract objects.

[28] So Leftow, *God and Necessity*, 20.

of things or in things only by way of exemplification.[29] Things have properties, only in the sense that they stand in a primitive relation of exemplification to separately existing abstract objects. Thus, properties remain objects apart from God. On this view, there exist uncreated, necessary, eternal abstract objects to which God stands in a relation of exemplification. God is not, therefore, the sole ultimate reality.

It gets arguably even worse. For as we saw in our discussion of philosophico-theological objections to Platonism, on Platonism, God's essential properties or nature, what Brian Leftow calls *deity*, serve to explain why God is God.[30] Leftow's objection to a realist view of *deity* is all the more powerful if the absolute creationist resorts to the position that God's properties are uncreated. For then God's nature is causally independent of Him, and He depends for His Godhood on His exemplifying the relevant properties. This makes God actually dependent upon His independently existing nature for His existence as God. The problem, then, is not merely that things other than God exist *a se*; the problem is that on Platonism, God does not exist *a se*, a flat denial of divine aseity.

In fact, if *deity* includes, as it must, the property of *aseity*, then absolute creationism of this variety becomes incoherent. For in order to exemplify *deity,* God must exemplify *aseity* and so exist *a se*. But if His aseity derives from His exemplifying *aseity*, then He does not exist *a se*. For He depends upon *aseity* for His aseity, which is incoherent. Thus, absolute creationism becomes necessarily false.

On the other hand, if the absolute creationist affirms that, explanatorily prior to His creation of properties, God has no properties but is as He is without exemplifying properties (since they have not yet been created), then we have abandoned the Platonistic ontological assay of things with respect, at least, to God and conceded to the anti-Platonist

---

[29] This is the case even on the Aristotelian view that properties are in things. Thus, Moreland writes, 'it is entirely unclear how a property can be a constituent of a particular (e.g. a concrete particular, a moment, or an event) without doing so by way of exemplification. Throughout history, the overwhelming majority of realists have agreed that *qua* universals, properties are the sorts of things that enter other things by way of the nexus of exemplification....': *Universals*, 126. Cf. Devitt's complaint that, on D. M. Armstrong's immanent realism, we have not the 'remotest idea' what 'in' or 'have' mean: Devitt, '"Ostrich Nominalism" or "Mirage Realism"?', *Pacific Philosophical Quarterly*, 61/4 (1980): 438. This situation has led Peter van Inwagen to confess, 'I do not understand this idea': 'God and Other Uncreated Things', in Kevin Timpe (ed.), *Metaphysics and God* (London: Routledge, 2009), 9.

[30] See Ch. 2, under 'Perfect Being Theology'.

that in order to be, for example, powerful, God need not exemplify the property of *being powerful*. Then it becomes unexplained why creatures also cannot be as they are without exemplifying properties. The problem is especially pressing in the cases of resemblance between God and creatures. Indeed, Platonists who appeal to the problem of the One over Many to explain similarity relations will be hard-pressed to explain how creatures resemble God in being powerful, since God and creatures do not share the relevant property.

Perhaps the absolute creationist will say that only logically posterior to His creation of properties does God come to acquire properties; prior to His creation of properties, God is, for example, powerful, even though the property of *being powerful* has not yet been created. But then properties are not doing any metaphysical work, since God is already powerful before coming to exemplify *being powerful*.[31] This is to deny the standard Platonist ontological assay of things. By rejecting the Platonist's ontological assay of things, the conceptualist, for example, can hold coherently that logically prior to His abstraction of any property, God is as He is without standing in an exemplification relation to properties. Similarly, an absolute creationist who denies that properties are fundamental ontological constituents of things could maintain that logically prior to His creation of properties, God is as He is without having properties. Deny the Platonist's ontological assay of things, and the bootstrapping problem will not arise.

Metaphysically Heavy Absolute Creationism

Thus, it seems to me that an absolute creationism which rejects the Platonistic ontological assay of things is a defensible option for the classical theist. But in adopting such a view of *abstracta*, the absolute creationist seems to have lost any rationale for positing the existence—in a metaphysically heavy sense—of such objects. They are not doing any metaphysical work, as they do in the usual Platonist scheme of things. As Moltmann says, they simply enable reference for reifying expressions like 'the number 7' or 'the property wisdom'.

---

[31] Just such a view is suggested by Friederike Moltmann's recent analysis of how we make ontological commitments in ordinary language: *Abstract Objects and the Semantics of Natural Language* (Oxford: OUP, 2013). This is similar to McCann's view that in creating cats, God also creates *felinity*.

This smacks of lightweight Platonism, which does not involve serious ontological commitment to abstract objects.

It might be said that we are involved in metaphysically heavy commitments to the reality of such entities by the customary neo-Quinean criterion of ontological commitment, which comes to expression in premiss (I) of the Indispensability Argument. This is, in fact, Peter van Inwagen's view. Van Inwagen classifies ontologies as either constituent ontologies or relational ontologies. He rejects constituent ontologies, which ascribe to particular things an ontological structure.[32] He therefore repudiates the Platonist's ontological assay of things, denying that properties are ontological constituents of things.[33]

The reason for van Inwagen's scepticism is that he cannot make sense of constituent ontologies. 'I do not understand the words and phrases that are the typical items of the core vocabulary of any given constituent ontology. "Immanent universal", "trope", "exist wholly in", "wholly present wherever it is instantiated," "constituent of" (said of a universal and a particular in that order): these are all mysteries to me.'[34] With respect to properties, he is mystified by exemplification. He asks, 'How does a concrete object (like a green ball) reach out and take hold of a property (like the color green), an abstract object, and make it *had* or *exemplified* or *instantiated*?'[35] On van Inwagen's view, properties are metaphysically idle, serving to explain neither why objects are the way they are nor their resemblance to one another. He insists, 'I do believe that there is an object I call "the color green." . . . But I should never want to say that the fact that greenness was a property of both the apple and the book explained the fact that they were both green or the fact that they were both of the same color.'[36]

So why include abstract objects at all in one's ontology? Van Inwagen confesses, 'I'd really *like* to be an austere nominalist', but he finds himself reluctantly committed to the reality of properties by ineliminable quantification over abstract objects in our discourse.[37]

---

[32] Peter van Inwagen, 'Dispensing with Ontological Levels: An Illustration', LanCog Lectures in Metaphysics 2013, *Disputatio*, 6/38 (2014): 41–2.
[33] Ibid., 33.
[34] Peter van Inwagen, 'Relational *vs.* Constituent Ontologies', *Philosophical Perspectives*, 25/1 (2011): 393.
[35] Ibid., 396.   [36] Ibid., 398.
[37] Ibid., 400; cf. Peter van Inwagen, 'God and Other Uncreated Things', in *Metaphysics and God*, 19. NB that van Inwagen's repudiation of the Quine-Putnam

An absolute creationist of van Inwagen's stripe, who similarly holds to the neo-Quinean criterion of ontological commitment, could hold to the reality of abstract objects without falling prey to the bootstrapping objection because his favoured ontology denies the typical Platonist ontological assay of things.

Van Inwagen himself rejects absolute creationism, taking properties and other abstract objects to be uncreated beings alongside God. But his cursory dismissal of absolute creationism does not do justice to this viewpoint. In his fullest treatment of the viewpoint that I am aware of, van Inwagen criticizes absolute creationism on the grounds that (1) it is hard to make sense of God's deciding to create an abstract mathematical object, and (2) creation is a causal relation, and abstract objects cannot enter into causal relations.[38] With respect to (1), absolute creationists (unless they are radical theistic activists) do not typically root mathematical necessities in God's *will*, but in God's *nature*.[39] Hence, though mathematical objects depend ontologically on God, they are not the result of His deciding. As for (2), while abstract objects have no causal powers and so cannot be causes, why can they not be effects? Most philosophers of aesthetics who are, like van Inwagen, realists about fictional characters take them to be abstract objects created by their authors.[40] So why could God not be the author of mathematical objects?

Thus, a Christian Platonist like van Inwagen ought to find absolute creationism to be an attractive option. Nevertheless, to my knowledge,

---

Indispensability Argument is based on his rejection of the claim that the success of science 'is *best explained* by postulating the existence of the real numbers' (19). That claim is not at all essential to the Indispensability Argument. Van Inwagen's argument for properties is, in fact, a sort of indispensability argument. See Peter van Inwagen, 'A Theory of Properties', in Dean Zimmerman (ed.), *Oxford Studies in Metaphysics*, i (Oxford: Clarendon Press, 2004), 113–15.

[38] Peter van Inwagen, 'Did God Create Shapes?' *Philosophia Christi*, 17/2 (2015): 285–90.

[39] See Morris and Menzel, 'Absolute Creation', 355–6, 360. Cf. Brian Leftow's development in *God and Necessity*. Among theistic modal theories, Leftow distinguishes between theories which ground modality in God's nature and theories which ground modality in God's activity. Leftow endorses a partial activist view, but even so grounds necessary truths of logic and mathematics in God's nature, not His activity. If the absolute creationist elects to ground abstract objects in God's nature rather than His will, that does leave us with the aforementioned problem of the attenuation of God's freedom with respect to creation, and perhaps that is van Inwagen's concern.

[40] Christy Mag Uidhir, 'Introduction: Art, Metaphysics, and the Paradox of Standards', in Christy Mag Uidhir (ed.), *Art and Abstract Objects* (Oxford: OUP, 2012), 7.

no one has adopted this viewpoint. Van Inwagen reports, 'I am the only proponent of the Favored Ontology I am aware of',[41] and he is not an absolute creationist! Nor do I personally find his favoured ontology attractive. To my mind, having to include such metaphysically idle entities as are countenanced by van Inwagen's favoured ontology ought to prompt us to call into question the criterion of ontological commitment that foists such unwanted freeloaders upon us.

CONCLUDING REMARKS

I conclude, therefore, that absolute creationism may be, after all, a tenable option for theists who want to preserve God's status as the sole ultimate reality in the face of Platonism's challenge to that doctrine. In particular, by denying a constituent ontology, the absolute creationist can avoid the bootstrapping objection, since explanatorily prior to His creation of properties, God can be just as He is without exemplifying properties. So there is no vicious circularity in His creation of properties and other abstract objects. Still, in light of the metaphysical idleness of such entities—not to mention the theological dislocations forced in the doctrine of creation—it seems to me that theists would be well-advised to look elsewhere for a solution to the challenge posed by Platonism to the doctrine of divine aseity.

---

[41] Van Inwagen, 'Relational *vs.* Constituent Ontologies', 398.

5

Divine Conceptualism

Absolute creationism proffers the easiest solution to the challenge posed by Platonism to divine aseity, but it is not the historic Christian position. Rather, as we have seen, the Church Fathers, if not the biblical writers themselves, embraced a different solution: divine conceptualism. This view also dominated medieval thought and receded only with the advent of modernity. Like absolute creationism, divine conceptualism is a realist view of mathematical objects, but it is a non-Platonic realism. That is to say, it takes mathematical objects and other allegedly abstract entities to be, in fact, concrete objects, namely, thoughts in God's mind.

As Figure 1 displays, there are other versions of non-Platonic realism on offer, but these were subjected to such withering criticism by the nineteenth-century mathematician and philosopher Gottlob Frege that such views are scarcely taken seriously today. Frege's objections to psychologism, which takes mathematical objects to be thoughts in human minds, do not, however, touch divine conceptualism. The necessity, plenitude, and intersubjectivity of mathematical objects may be impossible to square with psychologism, but they constitute no obstacle to identifying such objects with thoughts of God. That Frege could simply overlook what had historically been the mainstream theistic position with respect to putative abstract objects is testimony to how utterly detached nineteenth-century philosophical thinking had become from the historic Christian tradition.[1]

---

[1] For a brief survey of the pre-modern tradition, see Reuben Hersh, *What is Mathematics Really?* (New York: OUP, 1997), ch. 6: 'Mainstream before the Crisis'. In Hersh's view, divine conceptualism was a complete and simple solution to the ontology of mathematics. 'Recent troubles in the philosophy of mathematics are ultimately the consequence of the banishing of religion from science.... The present trouble with the ontology of mathematics is an after-effect of the spread of atheism' (122, 126).

CONCEPTUALISM

With the late twentieth-century renaissance of Christian philosophy, divine conceptualism is once again finding articulate defenders. For example, Al Plantinga, the most influential theist philosopher writing today, has lately endorsed divine conceptualism. He locates himself in the Augustinian tradition 'in thinking of numbers, properties, propositions and the rest of the Platonic host as *divine ideas*'.[2] Plantinga does not always clearly differentiate divine conceptualism from absolute creationism. But he says that 'perhaps the most natural way to think about abstract objects... is as divine thoughts'.[3] Specifically, he advocates construing propositions as God's thoughts, properties as God's concepts, and sets as God's collections.[4] By so construing propositions, properties, sets, and the like, Plantinga means to safeguard divine aseity, since God's thoughts depend causally upon God. 'According to classical versions of theism, sets, numbers and the like... are best conceived as divine thoughts. But then they stand to God in the relation in which a thought stands to a thinker. This is presumably a *productive* relation: the thinker produces his thoughts. It is therefore also a causal relation.'[5] In that case, such objects do not exist independently of God, but depend causally upon Him, so that God exists uniquely *a se*.

Unfortunately, Plantinga's endorsement of divine conceptualism amounts to little more than a nod in its direction. But a fuller development of a conceptualist viewpoint is to be found in Greg Welty's defence of what he calls 'theistic conceptual realism' concerning propositions and possible worlds.[6] As a realist, Welty is entirely

---

[2] Alvin Plantinga, 'Response to William Lane Craig's Review of *Where the Conflict Really Lies*', *Philosophia Christi*, 15/1 (2013): 178.

[3] Alvin Plantinga, *Where the Conflict Really Lies: Science, Religion, and Naturalism* (Oxford: OUP, 2011), 288.

[4] Plantinga writes: 'Theists... may find attractive a view popular among medieval philosophers from Augustine on: the view that abstract objects are really divine thoughts. More exactly, propositions are divine thoughts, properties divine concepts, and sets divine collections', *Warrant and Proper Function* (Oxford: OUP, 1993), 121. I take it, then, that Plantinga does not think of concepts and collections as abstract objects produced by divine thinking, but as divine thoughts.

[5] Plantinga, *Where the Conflict Really Lies*, 291.

[6] Welty's principal work is his unpublished 'Theistic Conceptual Realism: The Case for Interpreting Abstract Objects as Divine Ideas' (D.Phil. thesis, University of Oxford, 2006). Fortunately, a precis of Welty's thesis is available in Greg Welty,

sympathetic to Indispensability Arguments for the existence of propositions and possible worlds. In fact, upon inspection, almost all of Welty's arguments for the reality of propositions and possible worlds are various incarnations of the Indispensability Argument.[7] If we reject, as I think we should, the soundness of the Indispensability Argument, then the nerve of Welty's case for divine conceptualism will be cut. Divine conceptualism might remain a coherent option for the classical theist for meeting Platonism's challenge, but it will not be philosophically incumbent upon him.

The key to Welty's case for conceptualist realism over against Platonic realism (as well as other non-Platonic realisms) is the intentionality of propositions and possible worlds. Intentionality is the property of being *about* something or *of* something. It signifies the *object-directedness* of something. Our thoughts, for example, have intentionality. Welty draws our attention to two characteristics of thoughts' intentionality:

> Thoughts have intentionality, which is to say they exhibit the two characteristics of 'directedness' and 'aspectual shape.'...
>
> Directedness is the 'apparently relational structure' of intentionality, due to the fact that every intentional state is 'about' something else. A thought is always a thought 'of' something....
>
> Aspectual shape denotes 'the perspectival or fine-grained nature of intentionality.' Objects of intentional states are 'always apprehended in a certain way.' So, for instance, my thought that Lewis Carroll authored *Alice in Wonderland* is not only about Lewis Carroll, but also picks him out in a certain way, namely, as 'Lewis Carroll' (the bearer of that name). Thus, it would not be correct to report my thought as being that Charles Dodgson authored *Alice in Wonderland*.[8]

'Theistic Conceptual Realism', in Paul M. Gould (ed.), *Beyond the Control of God? Six Views on the Problem of God and Abstract Objects* (London: Bloomsbury, 2014), ch. 3.

[7] See Welty, 'Theistic Conceptual Realism' (doctoral thesis), ch. 2; cf. his 'Theistic Conceptual Realism' (essay), 82–4, along with my 'Response to Greg Welty', in *Beyond the Control of God?*, 101–2.

[8] Welty, 'Theistic Conceptual Realism' (doctoral thesis), 112–13. Welty draws upon the work of Tim Crane, 'Intentionality as the Mark of the Mental', in A. O'Hear (ed.), *Current Issues in Philosophy of Mind* (Cambridge: CUP, 1998), 243; Tim Crane, 'Intentionality', in Edward Craig (ed.), *The Routledge Encyclopaedia of Philosophy*, 2nd edn (London: Routledge, 1998), §2; Tim Crane, *Elements of Mind* (Oxford: OUP, 2001), 13–21. With respect to the illustration of aspectual shape, the point is that even though 'Lewis Carroll' is the name of Charles Dodgson, my thought that Lewis Carroll wrote *Alice in Wonderland* is not the same thought as the thought that Charles Dodgson wrote *Alice in Wonderland*, for I may not be aware that Lewis

Divine Conceptualism 75

Welty argues that propositions also exhibit intentionality. For only if propositions are about the world can they be true/false and believed/disbelieved. Welty calls a proposition's having a truth value its alethicity (from the Greek *aletheia*, or truth), and he calls a proposition's being the potential object of a person's attitudes like belief and disbelief its doxasticity (from the Greek *doxa* or opinion). As this is a very important point for our study of abstract objects, I quote Welty at length:

> Once we recognize the intentionality of propositions, we can see that alethicity is a corollary of it. That is, the fact that proposition *p* has a truth-value (and indeed can have a truth-value) presupposes the intentionality of *p*. For it is only because *p* is *about* something—represents it as being a certain way—that *p* is susceptible to either *correctly* or *incorrectly* representing something to be the case, that is, being true or false. Thus, *p*'s capacity to be truth-valued presupposes *p*'s intentionality. The 'aboutness' of *p* is what enables it to make a claim, and it is the fact that it makes a claim that entails that it can be true or false....
>
> ... what has been said here of alethicity can also be said on behalf of doxasticity. It too presupposes intentionality. It is only because propositions make claims, and represent something to be the case, that we can either *agree or disagree* that it correctly represents what it claims to represent. This agreement or disagreement is constituted by our believing or disbelieving the proposition in question.[9]

But Welty observes the following difference between our thoughts' intentionality and the intentionality exhibited by abstract propositions. Our thoughts are intrinsically intentional—we think about things or of things. By contrast, abstract objects are not intrinsically intentional. They have at best an extrinsic or derivative intentionality by being the objects of doxastic attitudes.

In virtue of our acquaintance with our own thoughts, we are already committed to the reality of thoughts. So if propositions can be taken just to be thoughts rather than abstract objects, we shall have

---

Carroll is Charles Dodgson. Recalling our distinction between extensional and intensional contexts in our discussion of premiss 1 of the Indispensability Argument (Ch. 3, under 'Singular Terms'), we see that thoughts supply intensional contexts: we cannot switch the co-referring singular terms 'Lewis Carroll' and 'Charles Dodgson' in 'Bill thinks that Lewis Carroll wrote *Alice in Wonderland*' and guarantee that the truth value of the sentence will remain the same. Thus, states of intentionality (with a 't') set up contexts which are intensional (with an 's').

[9] Welty, 'Theistic Conceptual Realism' (doctoral thesis), 114–16.

a more economical or parsimonious ontology as a result, and therefore, Welty thinks, a theory which is more likely to be true.

Welty similarly argues that possible worlds—whatever they are, metaphysically speaking—must have intentionality because they are about how the world could be. Moreover, possible worlds discourse represents not only the world as a whole, but also particular objects in the world. For they represent ways in which, for example, Hubert Humphrey might be. The representative function of possible worlds requires that they have intentionality. As Welty says, 'If they are ... ways *the World* (or universe) could be, then they are *about* the World, representing it as such-and-such', and so have intentionality.[10]

Again, Welty argues that the intentionality of possible worlds is better explained by conceptualism than by other forms of realism. He explains,

> If spatiotemporal particulars derive their intentionality from the intentionality of thinkers, why should it be any different for the intentionality of abstract simples?
> ... Perhaps the reason why *neither* of these theories is particularly illuminating on this matter of representation is because something fundamental has been left out: the intrinsic intentionality of thoughts, from which all other intentionality is derived.[11]

Since the intentionality of possible worlds is ultimately derivative from persons, a kind of thing to which we are already ontologically committed, conceptualism, by identifying possible worlds with thoughts of a certain kind, enjoys the advantage of being simpler than both Platonist and other anti-Platonist realisms. Welty says:

> If indeed the entities posited by set-theoretic nominalism, linguistic nominalism, and realism ultimately receive their status as representations in virtue of the intrinsic intentionality of thoughts, then the fortunes of these three positions are tied to those of conceptualism itself. In short, advocates of these three positions—initially advertised as distinct alternatives to conceptualism—are implicitly committed to some version of conceptualism anyway, because in each case the status of possible worlds as representations requires the conceptual activity of thinkers. In that case conceptualism would truly be the only game in

---

[10] Welty, 'Theistic Conceptual Realism' (essay), 86.
[11] Welty, 'Theistic Conceptual Realism' (doctoral thesis), 152–3.

town, and its chief alternatives would be parasitic upon its adequacy, and therefore superfluous.[12]

Such parasitic alternatives will not survive the application of Ockham's Razor. Thus, Welty sees conceptualism as the best realist theory of possible worlds.

Having argued that conceptualism is the best form of realism about propositions and possible worlds, Welty proceeds to argue that propositions and possible worlds are, respectively, to be identified with divine thoughts of various sorts. With respect to propositions, Welty observes that, although some thoughts have alethicity and doxasticity, not all do. For example, my mere thought of the letter B is not true or false or capable of being believed; but my thought that *B is a letter of the alphabet* is. God's thoughts, which stand in for the Platonist's propositions, will be thoughts that exhibit alethicity and doxasticity. By contrast, possible worlds have neither alethicity nor doxasticity and therefore are not propositions. Rather, they are divine thoughts of a different sort. Welty distinguishes narrow intentionality (which entails alethicity and doxasticity) from broad intentionality (which entails a capacity to represent). 'Possible worlds are broadly intentional entities even if they are not narrowly intentional entities. They exhibit directedness (they are about the universe) and aspectual shape (they are fine-grained in their aboutness), but they fall short of alethicity and doxasticity.'[13] They are God's thoughts of how the world might have been.

Because of God's omniscience, omnipotence, and metaphysical necessity, divine conceptualism, in contrast to human psychologism, can satisfy the conditions of plenitude and necessity with respect to propositions and possible worlds. Once we have God's thoughts, abstract objects like propositions and possible worlds become superfluous. So on Welty's view, propositions and possible worlds are not abstract objects, but rather are concrete entities, namely, divine thoughts of different sorts.[14] By denying the existence of uncreated, abstract objects, Welty would preserve divine aseity.

---

[12] Ibid., 153. Notice that the nominalisms of which Welty speaks are, in fact, realist views. Welty uses the Indispensability Argument to dispatch anti-realist views.
[13] Ibid., 150.
[14] Thus, Welty's affirmations that abstract objects exist as ideas in God's mind are misleading. When he says such a thing, he is, as he puts it, speaking merely functionally. That is to say, God's thoughts play the roles normally assigned to various abstract objects.

CONCEPTUALISM AND DIVINE ASEITY

Conceptualism will be an attractive view for theists who feel the force of realist arguments for abstract objects and yet who want to preserve classical theism's commitment to God as the sole ultimate reality. Indeed, conceptualism is historically the mainstream position among Christians, Jews, and Muslims. It is the position that I assumed I would eventually adopt when I began this study. But does conceptualism succeed in safeguarding divine aseity? The answer is unclear.

Are God's Thoughts Uncaused?

One of the peculiar features of Welty's conceptualism is that he takes God's thoughts to be uncreated.[15] In order to avoid the bootstrapping problem that threatens absolute creationism, Welty denies that the relation between God and His thoughts is causal. He believes that absolute creationism 'succumbs in the end to a series of successful objections, primarily because it construes the dependence relation between God and abstract objects in terms of *causation* (more specifically, creation).'[16] But Welty's version of theistic conceptual realism rejects absolute creationism's causal, creative dependence relation and merely posits an identity relation between God's thoughts and propositions and possible worlds.[17] Welty admits that a causal account is 'a very plausible account of the *thinker/thought relation* in human beings'.[18] But he refuses to extend such a model to God's case.

Such a refusal strikes me as both implausible and ad hoc. As Paul Gould and Richard Davis point out in response to Welty, 'the relation between a thought and a thinker is most naturally understood as a *productive* relation: the thinker produces his thoughts'.[19] So God's thoughts are plausibly taken to be produced by God. Thinking, after all, is something that God does; it is an activity, even if timeless, in

---

[15] 'On my model, God in no way *creates* abstract objects. Rather, a particular range of the *uncreated* divine thoughts function as abstract objects' (ibid., 213; cf. 222).
[16] Ibid., 192. [17] Ibid., 210. [18] Ibid., 193.
[19] Paul M. Gould and Richard Brian Davis, 'Response to Greg Welty', in *Beyond the Control of God?*, 99–100; cf. Welty's own development of this point in Welty, 'Theistic Conceptual Realism' (doctoral thesis), 192–4. Gould and Davis are clearly echoing Plantinga, *Warrant and Proper Function*, 121.

Divine Conceptualism 79

which God is engaged. The result of such activity is God's thoughts. That plausibly suffices for a causal relation. So far as I can see, Welty offers no reason why the relationship between God and His thoughts should not be characterized as a causal relationship—apart from the fact that conceptualism would then become susceptible to the same bootstrapping problem that attends absolute creationism:

> there is a serious question as to whether the thinker/thought model ought to be extended from the human context with which we are most familiar, to the divine context. Ought we to hold that God literally *creates* or *causes* his thoughts? Does this not imply that God creates his own attribute of omniscience (since divine omniscience is constituted by the thoughts in question)? If so, then we are in for a real shocker: the problems about God creating himself or creating his nature would not just be an unfortunate quirk of theistic activism, but would attach to traditional theism itself. This is probably as good a reason as any to resist extending the thinker/thought model—construed in any *causal* sense—to the divine context.[20]

I think that it is worth observing that the bootstrapping problem will attach to theism, given a causal account of the thinker/thought relation, only if one is a realist about properties (and other abstract objects). Since on anti-realism there is no such object as omniscience, God's causing His thoughts, as we do ours, does not bring His properties into being. If there is a problem here, it is a problem only for realists.

But would, as Welty fears, the affirmation of the causal dependence of God's thoughts upon God, in fact, render conceptualism susceptible to the bootstrapping problem? I think not. For that problem arises, not, as Welty thinks, from the causal dependence thesis, but rather, as we saw in our discussion of absolute creationism, from the Platonist's ontological assay of things.[21] Consider Bergmann and Brower's intuitive statement of the bootstrapping objection:

> If a view such as theistic activism is true, then every property (or exemplifiable) will be a product of God's creative activity. But this implies the general principle that, for any property *F,* God's creating *F* is a prerequisite for, and hence logically prior to, *F.* Notice, however,

---

[20] Welty, 'Theistic Conceptual Realism' (doctoral thesis), 225; cf. Greg Welty, 'Response to Critics', in *Beyond the Control of God?*, 108.
[21] See Ch. 4, 'Bootstrapping Objection: Vicious Circularity of Absolute Creation'.

that in order to create F, God must have the property of *being able to create a property*. Here is where the trouble begins.[22]

Where the trouble begins for the absolute creationist is where the conceptualist should part company with him. For on divine conceptualism, universals are neither subsistent objects in the world nor constituents in things, but rather thoughts in God's mind. Thus, logically prior to God's conceiving them, there are no universals. That does not imply that, apart from God's conceptions, there are no wise men and no brown dogs, but just no *wisdom* and no *brownness*. Thus, the conceptualist should insist that it is false that in order to conceive a property F, God must have the property *being able to conceive a property*. To be sure, in order to conceive F, God must be able to conceive a property, but He need not have the property *being able to conceive a property* in order to be able to conceive a property.

As we have seen, what is at stake in the bootstrapping objection is not the (causal) dependence of God's thoughts upon God, but rather one's ontological assay of things. Platonism offers an ontological assay of things in terms of substances and properties which are exemplified by those substances. By rejecting the Platonist's ontological assay, the conceptualist may hold coherently that logically prior to His conceptions, God is as He is without standing in an exemplification relation to properties, and that He then produces properties by conceiving them. But, then, as we saw in our discussion of absolute creationism, much of the motivation for realism is undermined.

God's Thoughts as Uncaused Objects

Suppose we do hold, as Welty does, that God's thoughts are uncreated entities. Has the threat of Platonism then really been removed? Have we not merely substituted uncreated, concrete entities for uncreated, abstract entities? Welty does not directly address this worry. He does claim that his theistic conceptual realism violates neither divine sovereignty nor divine aseity. But his defence of that claim fails to satisfy the present worry. With respect to God's sovereignty, Welty

---

[22] Michael Bergmann and Jeffrey E. Brower, 'A Theistic Argument Against Platonism (and in Support of Truthmakers and Divine Simplicity)', in Dean Zimmerman (ed.), *Oxford Studies in Metaphysics*, ii. (Oxford: OUP, 2006), 366.

Divine Conceptualism 81

says: 'Since it is not clear that these thoughts are distinct from God in the sense of being creatures, it is not clear that God's "inability" to think something other than these thoughts—i.e., put these thoughts out of existence—somehow violates his sovereignty (since sovereignty ranges over what God has created).'[23] True, on Welty's model, God's thoughts are not distinct from God in the sense of being creatures because Welty has denied that the relation between God and His thoughts is one of causation or creation, so God's thoughts cannot be creatures. But that is precisely the problem. They are entities which are distinct from God in the sense that they are not identical to God, and yet they are not creatures, but are entities uncreated by God. Even if we agree with Welty that God thinks some of His thoughts necessarily, still we seem to be stuck with a realm of entities which are distinct from God and uncreated by God.

So why does this not violate divine aseity? Welty replies, 'on TCR, abstract objects are not created..., and so the aseity question does not arise. God has (at least some of) the thoughts he has, because of his essential omniscience about himself (in particular, about his power). Thus, the possession of these thoughts by God is rooted in something that has traditionally been ascribed to God.'[24] This response seems to be addressing a quite different worry, namely, why God has the thoughts He essentially has. But the doctrine of divine aseity affirms that God is the only uncreated being. The concern is that, by postulating a realm of concrete entities which are uncreated by God, Welty's conceptualism has violated divine aseity. If that is the case, then the problem which motivates our inquiry remains unsolved.

Still, I think that we have to admit that there remains intuitively a sense, difficult to articulate, in which divine thoughts existing 'inside' God do not seem to violate divine aseity as do uncreated, Platonic, abstract objects existing 'outside' God. But how are we to make sense of the metaphorical, spatial language of 'inside' and 'outside' God? I have spoken of God's being the Creator of everything that exists apart from God. Abstract objects, if they exist, are somehow part of the world in a way that God's thoughts are not. If the world did not exist, there would be neither concrete nor abstract objects in the world, but God and His thoughts would still exist.

---

[23] Welty, 'Theistic Conceptual Realism' (doctoral thesis), 224.
[24] Ibid., 226.

Brian Leftow explicates his claim that God is 'the Source of All that is "outside" him' as follows:[25]

> GSA. For all x, if x is not God, a part, aspect, or attribute of God, or an event, God makes the creating-*ex-nihilo* sort of causal contribution to x's existence as long as x exists.

Unfortunately, Leftow does not define his terms. What counts as a *part* of God? We might take the persons of the Trinity to be parts of God which, though not God in the sense of identity, exist acceptably *a se*. But God's thoughts are not parts of God in that sense. Leftow also does not tell us what an *aspect* is. Could God's thoughts be taken to be aspects of God which exist acceptably *a se*? Perhaps, though Leftow himself takes God's thoughts to be mental *events*.[26] Leftow later walks back his claim that events are exceptions to creation out of nothing.[27] He holds that God's thoughts are, in fact, caused by God. *Attributes* of God would include omnipotence, omniscience, omnipresence, and the like. Oddly, Leftow's statement of GSA might be construed by the Platonist to allow that the abstract entities which are God's properties do exist acceptably *a se*. We saw that absolute creationists Gould and Davis want simply to exempt God's attributes from being created by God in order to stave off the bootstrapping objection and so would be happy with GSA's exempting attributes. Such an interpretation would be contrary to Leftow's intention, but it underlines the difficulty of explaining what it means to differentiate between things 'inside' and 'outside' God.

The anti-realist might plausibly claim that we can cut this Gordian knot by denying that divine thoughts are objects or things that really exist. That is not to deny that God is thinking. Rather, it is to claim that thoughts are just one more example of our inveterate tendency towards nominalization and reification. For example, we are planning to go to the beach tomorrow and so speak of *our plans* for tomorrow, we hunt deer in the fall and so speak of *our deer-hunting* in the fall, we hesitate when learning of the proposed restructuring and so speak of *our hesitations* about the proposal, without thinking that we are thereby ontologically committing ourselves to entities of these sorts. Similarly, God thinks that Columbus discovers the New World in 1492, and so we speak of God's *thought* that Columbus discovers the

---

[25] Brian Leftow, *God and Necessity* (Oxford: OUP, 2012), 20.
[26] Ibid., 302–3.   [27] Ibid., 76–7.

New World in 1492. There is no more reason to add thoughts to our ontological inventory of things than hesitations or plans. If the realist points to our quantifying over divine thoughts and the impossibility of paraphrasing away such quantifying expressions, then, as we shall see, the anti-realist may call into question the customary criterion of ontological commitment that delivers so inflationary an ontology.

The anti-realist will hold that God thinks all the things that the conceptualist says He does, but the anti-realist will not reify God's thinking into objects which exist in addition to God Himself. Anti-realism about God's thoughts removes the need to distinguish between objects which exist 'inside' God and those which exist 'outside' God, since God's thoughts are not objects. Neither are His attributes, of course. Aspects of a thing—like the southern exposure of one's house or a person's health or financial status—are paradigm examples of abstractions that do not really exist. That leaves only undetached parts as things in their own right, and even that is controversial.[28] We can, if we like, leave God's concrete parts as real objects which are exempt from God's creating everything other than Himself without compromising divine aseity. For plausibly, if something creates non-successively all its parts, it creates itself, which, apart from its apparent metaphysical impossibility, would render God a created being if He creates His parts. So God cannot create His parts, and yet, being parts of God, these objects are clearly not examples of things existing *a se* apart from God. If we maintain that undetached parts are not really existing objects, so much the better!

The anti-realist theist may thus espouse a stronger version of (GSA), namely,

> GSA*. For all x, if x is not God or a concrete part of God, God makes the creating-*ex-nihilo* sort of causal contribution to x's existence as long as x exists.

This thesis yields a greater concept of divine aseity and so of God. If we go this route, however, then conceptualism is just misconceived. It foists upon the theist an inflated ontology of mental events which we have no good reason to embrace. Indeed, Welty's own appeal to

---

[28] See Peter van Inwagen, 'The Doctrine of Arbitrary Undetached Parts', *Pacific Philosophical Quarterly*, 62 (1981): 123–37. Van Inwagen is an anti-realist about events in general and thoughts in particular: 'God and Other Uncreated Things', in Kevin Timpe (ed.), *Metaphysics and God* (London: Routledge, 2009), 13–15.

ontological economy would cut against adopting conceptualism, with its added kind of entity, namely, mental events or thoughts.

WORRIES ABOUT CONCEPTUALISM

If the theist feels the force of arguments for realism about mathematical objects, propositions, and so on, conceptualism might seem, in light of the bootstrapping objection, to be a more attractive option than absolute creationism. Still, conceptualism is not entirely worry-free. For the question remains whether mathematical objects and other objects normally taken to be abstract can plausibly be construed as concrete objects, namely, divine thoughts.

Take propositions, for example. How will conceptualists handle false propositions? Conceptualists had better not say that God entertains only true thoughts. Otherwise, only true propositions exist, which is insufficient for the reality of the full range of propositions. We need divine thoughts which stand in for all the false propositions as well. But how is this to be done without attributing to God false beliefs, in contradiction to the doctrine of divine omniscience?

In the case of true thoughts, conceptualists can hold that, for any true proposition p, God thinks that p. But in the case of a falsehood, we cannot let p stand for a false proposition. For to think that p is to believe that p. We might try to avoid the problem by saying that, in the case of false propositions, God thinks that p is false. But the problem here is that God's thought, then, is not p, but the quite different proposition that *p is false*. Thus, ontologically, there really is no thought that p, where p is false, for God would not think such a thing. So there really is, contrary to realism, no proposition p in the case that p is false. But then how can God think that p is false, if there is no such thing?

In response to this worry, the conceptualist can claim that thinking, as he uses the word, encompasses a variety of doxastic attitudes, such as believing, hoping, fearing, and so on. Morris and Menzel, who, as I explained, do not clearly differentiate absolute creationism from conceptualism, distinguish God's *beliefs* from God's *thoughts*: 'We have characterized propositions as God's thoughts. Some of those thoughts are contingently true, some are contingently false.

The latter, of course, are not among God's *beliefs*, since God is omniscient.'[29] Menzel later expands on this distinction:

> God necessarily thinks and conceives, and moreover, necessarily thinks and conceives the same things. Note that this is not to say that God necessarily *believes* (and hence knows) the same things; what God believes will depend in part on contingent facts, e.g., how many people there are at any given moment. However, the *thought* 'There are n people,' for any given n, is conceived by God regardless of whether or not it is true.[30]

This explanation makes it evident that the English idiom 'thinks that' is misleading in the context of conceptualism, for the phrase in ordinary language is virtually synonymous with 'believes that'. 'God conceives that' is less misleading, for we can grasp the propositional content of, for example, questions and commands without believing them. In the case of false propositions, perhaps we should say that God doubts or denies that p. God's denying that p, like His believing that p, thus suffices for the existence of p—assuming, of course, that all one's doubts and beliefs are consciously held.

Aye, but there's the rub! Conceptualism requires that God be constantly entertaining actual thoughts corresponding to every proposition and every state of affairs. But this seems problematic. Graham Oppy complains that 'it threatens to lead to the attribution to God of inappropriate thoughts: bawdy thoughts, banal thoughts, malicious thoughts, silly thoughts, and so forth'.[31] Welty treats this concern somewhat dismissively. He responds,

> An omniscient God has knowledge of the full range of thoughts that we humans can have and will have. We don't surprise Him by our 'bawdy thoughts, banal thoughts, malicious thoughts, silly thoughts, and so forth' (105). His holiness is assured, as He doesn't intend these thoughts as we intend them. He is like the parent who already knows all the ways the child can go astray.[32]

---

[29] Thomas V. Morris and Christopher Menzel, 'Absolute Creation', *American Philosophical Quarterly*, 23/4 (1986): 355.
[30] Christopher Menzel, 'God and Mathematical Objects', in Russell W. Howell and W. James Bradley (eds), *Mathematics in a Postmodern Age* (Grand Rapids, MI: William B. Eerdmans, 2001), 74.
[31] Graham Oppy, 'Response to Greg Welty', in *Beyond the Control of God?*, 105.
[32] Welty, 'Response to Critics', 110.

This response fails to do justice to the objection. The problem, as I understand it, is not that we surprise God by our inappropriate thoughts. Rather, the problem is that if God has the full range of thoughts that we do, then He must imagine Himself, as well as everyone else, to be engaged in bawdy and malicious acts. Moreover, rather than putting such detestable thoughts immediately out of mind as we try to do, He keeps on thinking about them! Of course, God does not intend to do these things; nevertheless, He thinks about them constantly, which does seem to impugn His holiness. The apostle Paul advises, 'whatever is true, whatever is honorable, whatever is just, whatever is pure, whatever is lovely, whatever is gracious, if there is any excellence, if there is anything worthy of praise, think about these things' (Phil. 4.8). Are we really to imagine that God does not exemplify this practice Himself, but also entertains and dwells upon the sorts of thoughts Oppy mentions?

The conceptualist might try to alleviate this difficulty by distinguishing, as Welty does, between the different sorts of thoughts God has. Welty, it will be recalled, distinguished God's thoughts which are propositions from His thoughts which are ways the world might be. Omniscience is normally defined in terms of propositional knowledge: an omniscient person must know every true proposition and believe no false proposition. First-person knowledge is usually taken to be non-propositional knowledge. For example, God does not know or believe that He is Himself Napoleon, even though He knows the same proposition that Napoleon knows when the emperor asserts, 'I am Napoleon'.[33] Thus, the conceptualist is not committed to God's entertaining the bawdy or malicious first-person thought that *I am engaged in* ____, for such first-person, non-propositional knowledge is not demanded by omniscience. At most, He would have the less salacious thought *God is engaged in* ____ and knows that to be false and impossible. What He believes is that *God is not engaged in* ____, which is a true thought and describes an actual state of affairs. Even if God has the first-person belief that *I am not engaged in* ____, the conceptualist need not think that such beliefs are beliefs consciously held by God, since it is only their propositional content which needs

---

[33] See discussion in William Lane Craig, *Divine Foreknowledge and Human Freedom: The Coherence of Theism: Omniscience* (Leiden: E. J. Brill, 1990), 7–9; William Lane Craig, *The Tensed Theory of Time: A Critical Examination* (Dordrecht: Kluwer Academic Publishers, 2000), 40–2, 122–9.

to be a conscious thought of God. In other words, God need not be taken to be actually thinking of these first-person beliefs and states of affairs. That would go some way towards alleviating the worry that conceptualism would require God to be entertaining and dwelling on bawdy or malicious thoughts.

One way of putting this point is to say that what Welty calls the aspectual shape of a thought does not always correspond to the aspectual shape of the proposition expressed by that thought. For example, the thought that *I am making a mess* has a different aspectual shape than the proposition *John Perry is making a mess*. God can know the propositional content of Perry's thought without His thought's having the same aspectual shape as Perry's thought. God need not have the thought that *I am making a mess* in order to grasp the propositional content that Perry grasps when he thinks that *I am making a mess*.

But the fact that thoughts and the propositions which they express can come apart in their aspectual shape raises even deeper problems for the conceptualist. God's thoughts have an aspectual shape that is uniquely His and is plausibly different from their propositional content. But if we say that propositions just are God's thoughts, we are no longer able to distinguish between the aspectual shape of a proposition and the aspectual shape of a divine thought having that propositional content. A first-person divine thought like *I am the God of Israel* is, then, a proposition. Since God has first-person thoughts, identifying God's thoughts with propositions commits us to the existence of purely private propositions which are incommunicable by God to us. At most, we could grasp a proposition like *Yahweh is the God of Israel*; but that is not the same proposition as *I am the God of Israel*. Indeed, God may never entertain the oblique thought that *Yahweh is the God of Israel,* so that there is no such proposition.

First-person beliefs are just the proverbial camel's nose. Paraphrastic strategies for dealing with unwanted ontological commitments, including commitment to abstract objects, major on distinguishing propositional content from the way it comes to expression in our thoughts and language. To take a simple example, the thought *The number of people killed in the attack was 66* and the thought *66 people were killed in the attack* have, on the customary criterion of ontological commitment, different ontological commitments. The former commits us to the reality of the number 66, whereas the latter, using the numerical term adjectivally rather than substantively, lacks such a commitment. So which one is God's thought? If God thinks both, what are His ontological commitments? The ontological commitments of the former cannot be annulled by paraphrasing it as the latter, for the paraphrase cannot be said to give the propositional content of the thought, since according to conceptualism, both divine thoughts just are propositions. Suppose Charles Chihara and Geoffrey Hellman are correct, that the commitment to mathematical objects in the thought *2 + 2 = 4* can be successfully paraphrased away,[34] and suppose that God thinks *2 + 2 = 4*. Then we are stuck with mathematical objects regardless of the success of the paraphrases. The conceptualist might welcome commitment to mathematical objects, but this same approach will wind up committing us to holes, lacks, and other unwanted commitments of ordinary language if God has, indeed, in Welty's words, 'the full range of thoughts that we humans can have and will have'.

In short, distinguishing between the aspectual shape of a proposition and the aspectual shape of thoughts expressing it, as first-person thoughts almost force us to do, is a Trojan Horse for conceptualism, raising all sorts of difficulties that make conceptualism much less attractive than it at first appears. Thoughts may not be well-suited to be identified with propositions and possible worlds after all.

We have been reflecting on the problems raised by the ascription of bawdy and malicious thoughts to God. What about banal and silly thoughts? Here we see another unattractive feature of conceptualism's identification of propositions with God's thoughts. Why in the world should we think that God is constantly thinking the non-denumerable infinity of banal and silly propositions or states of affairs that there are? Take Welty's own illustration of the thought that for any real number r, r is distinct from the Taj Mahal. Why would God hold such inanities constantly in consciousness? Or consider false propositions like *for any real number* r, r *is identical to the Taj Mahal*. Why would God keep such a silly thought constantly in consciousness, knowing it to be false? Obviously, the concern is not that God would be incapable of keeping such a non-denumerable infinity of thoughts ever in consciousness, but rather why He would dwell on such trivialities.

---

[34] See my *God and Abstract Objects* (Berlin: Springer Verlag, 2018), ch. 8, for a discussion of Chihara and Hellman's views.

Welty moves far too hastily from the fact that God is omniscient to the conceptualist view that all that God knows is occurrent in consciousness. He writes, 'if God is omniscient then at the very least, for any possible way something could be, God knows whether or not he could bring it about. This is sufficient for God to have thoughts that match the infinity of propositions that there must be.'[35] God's infinite knowledge is, however, clearly *not* sufficient to guarantee that there are the actual mental events needed by the conceptualist. As Welty rightly puts it, 'This argument assumes, of course, that in God's case <knowing p> entails <thinking or having thoughts that p>.'[36] Oddly, Welty says nothing to justify this crucial assumption. No reason is given for the assumption that in God's case, unlike my case, the knowledge that $2 + 2 = 4$ requires a conscious mental event or thought with that content. Obviously, we know vastly more than we occurrently believe. For example, I know the multiplication table up to 12, but I am not now thinking thoughts like *$2 \times 3 = 6$* or *$7 \times 8 = 56$*. Why should God's case be any different? Now I fully appreciate that God must have a conscious life much different than ours. Still, the proliferation in God's conscious thought of the silly and banal beliefs necessary for divine conceptualism seems pointless and makes conceptualism a less attractive option.

We have been reflecting on the problems posed by identifying propositions and possible worlds with God's thoughts. What about properties? The main reason for construing properties as abstract universals rather than as particulars is the need for an entity that can be wholly located in diverse places.[37] The Platonist's ontological assay of the rose and of the fire truck includes *redness* as an ontological constituent of each. In contrast to property instances (tropes), properties as universals are taken by realists to be wholly present in all the things exemplifying them. The difficulty, then, for conceptualism is that God's thoughts, as concrete objects, are not universals, but particulars, and so cannot be wholly present in spatially separated objects.

---

[35] Welty, 'Theistic Conceptual Realism' (doctoral thesis), 220. [36] Ibid., 222.
[37] See D. M. Armstrong, *Universals and Scientific Realism*, i. *Nominalism and Realism* (Cambridge: CUP, 1978), pp. xiv, 82–3; Armstrong, *Universals: An Opinionated Introduction* (Boulder, CO: Westview Press, 1989), 16, 77, 98–9; J. P. Moreland, *Universals* (Chesham, Bucks.: Acumen, 2001), esp. 100–2.

So Gould and Davis protest:

> For Welty, divine thoughts are not abstract; they are concrete. Therefore, we submit, Welty is a nominalist. By way of contrast, we think being a universal is a *sufficient* condition on being abstract (ontologically speaking), [footnote 4: We think being a universal, being non-spatial, being non-essentially spatio-temporal are *sufficient* conditions for some object X to be abstract] hence it is best to think of divine thoughts (i.e., propositions) and divine ideas (i.e., concepts) as abstract objects.[38]

Gould and Davis certainly represent the mainstream position in saying that concrete objects cannot be universals, in view of the inability of concrete objects to wholly exist simultaneously in different places. It does not follow, however, as they assert, that we should adopt the strange view that God's thoughts are abstract objects.[39] We may, if we wish, take God's ideas or concepts to be the abstract content of God's thoughts, but God's thoughts cannot be abstract objects, since they are mental states or events.

Oddly, Welty seems to concede what I take to be the thrust of Gould and Davis's critique. He asks, 'If another sufficient condition for [abstract object]-status is "being a universal," and that means being "multiply-instantiable," that is, "one and the same object would need to be multiply located," then are divine mental events *multiply located*? I can't make sense of this.'[40] Welty cannot make sense of God's thoughts' being multiply located, which, he seems to admit, excludes them from being universals. How then will the conceptualist make sense of properties as God's thoughts?

Will it help to appeal to exemplification as an account of how properties are constituents of things? J. P. Moreland reports that 'Throughout history, the overwhelming majority of realists have agreed that *qua* universals, properties are the sorts of things that

---

[38] Gould and Davis, 'Response to Welty', 100. NB footnote 4 is Gould and Davis's. Concerning their allegation that Welty is a nominalist, that depends on what one means by 'nominalism'. Welty's conceptualism makes him a nominalist in the sense that he is an anti-Platonist; but he is not a nominalist in the sense of being an anti-realist.

[39] Welty notes, 'Gould/Davis hold that something most everyone else thinks are paradigmatically concrete objects (mental states) are really A[bstract] O[bject]s' (Welty, 'Response to Critics', 108). God's mental states, in particular, are not causally impotent.

[40] Welty, 'Response to Critics', 108.

Divine Conceptualism 91

enter other things by way of the nexus of exemplification.'[41] On this view, 'Universals are literally in their instances, but they are not in the spatiotemporal location of those instances and the former are in the latter by means of a primitive non-spatiotemporal tie of predication.'[42] Indeed, says Moreland, 'it is entirely unclear how a property can be a constituent of a particular (e.g., a concrete particular, a moment, or an event) without doing so by way of exemplification'.[43] On the traditional realist view, properties are abstract objects which exist independently of their instances and exist 'in' their instances, not spatiotemporally, but by being exemplified by particular things.

So could the conceptualist say of divine thoughts what the Platonist says of abstract universals: particulars stand in some sort of relation to God's thoughts in virtue of which particulars are the way they are? An immediate problem for the conceptualist is that, if properties are God's thoughts, then particulars must exemplify God's thoughts. But a concrete object does not seem to be the sort of thing that is exemplifiable any more than it can be a universal, since concrete objects are particulars and particulars are not exemplifiable, but rather exemplify.[44] Accordingly, God's thoughts cannot be properties.

But perhaps the conceptualist could say that divine thoughts can play *the role* of properties. In substituting God's thoughts for properties, Plantinga has suggested that particulars stand to God's thoughts in a relation analogous to exemplification.[45] He appeals to Frege's notion of 'falling under a concept' as the relation in which particulars stand to God's thoughts. Thus, all brown things fall under

---

[41] Moreland, *Universals*, 125; cf. 101–2.   [42] Ibid., 9.   [43] Ibid., 125.

[44] Welty appeals to the example of a city map to show that a concrete object can exemplify something: 'lots of things can be multiply exemplifiable and they're still concrete particulars. Any map or set of directions folded away in my pocket, constituted by spatiotemporal bits of graphite or ink, seems to fit the bill' (personal communication, Greg Welty to Paul Gould, 26 Dec. 2012). It seems to me that this is to confuse representation, which the map certainly does, with exemplification. The map does not exemplify the town. Welty rightly maintains that both abstract and concrete objects can be representations: 'Theistic Conceptual Realism' (doctoral thesis), 71.

[45] For the view that having a property amounts to falling under a concept, see Alvin Plantinga, *Does God Have a Nature?* (Milwaukee, WI: Marquette University Press, 1980), 20–1; Plantinga, *Warranted Christian Belief* (Oxford: OUP, 2000), 15. I am indebted to Welty for these references. Plantinga's full suggestion that falling under a divine concept can be substituted for exemplification of a property was made during discussion of my paper 'In Defense of Conceptualism: A Response to Bergmann and Brower', at the University of Notre Dame.

God's thought of *brown*. Things which are brown resemble each other in virtue of falling under the same concept.

Intriguing as this suggestion might be, it is problematic. In the first place, concepts are not plausibly construed as concrete objects, for they are shared by multiple thinkers in a way that thoughts are not. Concepts seem to be part of the content of our thoughts. As such, they are plausibly abstract objects, if they exist at all.

Moreover, as mental states, thoughts are characterized by intentionality—being about things—not by things' falling under them. My thought of redness is about redness; it is not itself redness, nor do things fall under it. This problem can be generalized. God's thought of the number 2 is about 2. But then His thought is not 2, but something distinct from 2. 2 is what He is thinking about. But He is not thinking about His thought; He is thinking about 2. Therefore, His thought cannot be 2.

Furthermore, substituting the notion of falling under a concept for exemplifying a property seems to get the explanatory order backwards.[46] Things are not brown because they fall under God's concept *brown*, in the way that things are brown because they exemplify *brownness*; rather, they fall under God's concept *brown* because they are brown. Thus, the relation of falling under a concept cannot do the work of exemplification. If this is right, then the conceptualist who wants God's thoughts to play the role of properties still has plenty of work cut out for him, if his view is to commend itself as an attractive option for theists.

Finally, consider mathematical sets. Plantinga suggests that sets be taken to be God's mental collectings.[47] But this raises a problem. If sets are really particular divine thoughts, then how do we have any access to sets?[48] The question here is not whether I have a causal

---

[46] See Armstrong's critique of concept nominalism in *Universals and Scientific Realism*, 27. See further Leftow, *God and Necessity*, 243–4; Leftow, 'God and the Problem of Universals', *Oxford Studies in Metaphysics*, ii (2006): 352.

[47] Plantinga, *Where the Conflict Really Lies*, 289–90. Actually, Plantinga is ambiguous on whether sets are objects formed as a result of God's collectings or just are His collectings. He says, 'It is natural to think of sets as collections—that is, things whose existence depends upon a certain sort of intellectual activity—a collecting or "thinking together"' and later speaks of sets as 'collections, the result of a collecting activity' (289–90). If sets are objects which are not identical to God's mental collectings, then are they abstract objects, as the absolute creationist believes?

[48] Menzel responds to this difficulty by arguing, 'What we do when we construct a set or form a concept is *like* what God does. Hence, our set-like constructions and

connection with sets.[49] Rather, it is that sets, the real sets, are locked away in God's private consciousness, so that what we talk and work with are not sets at all. When I collect into a unity all the pens on my desk, that 'set' of pens is not identical, it seems, with the set constituted by God's collecting activity. Since we have two collectings and since sets are God's particular collectings, the 'set' I form is not identical to the set of all pens on my desk. But if sets are determined by membership, how could they not be identical, since they have the same members?

And again, we might wonder, why would God be constantly collecting things together in the way demanded by the conceptualist? Perhaps the conceptualist might say that God is constantly engaged in such collectings in order to provide the subject matter for the full range of set theoretical truths, including alternative set theories. But what if God merely imagines such collections to exist? As we shall see, a pretence theoretical approach to various set theories is a very plausible interpretation of set theory, one that enjoys support in the community of mathematicians. It has been said that God is a mathematician. Perhaps God is also, in fact, a pretence theorist. Imagining is, after all, a type of thinking. We saw that in order to secure divine thoughts that are false propositions, the conceptualist cannot take 'thinking' to be synonymous with 'believing'. So suppose that God pretends that sets exist in order to provide the subject matter for various set theories. In that case, we can admit that God does have thoughts about all the various set theoretical objects, but we cannot coherently identify His thoughts with sets, for sets on this view do not exist, but are merely imagined to exist. Given the coherence of pretence theory, there is no motivation to move beyond anti-realism to realism about sets as divine thoughts. Indeed, this conclusion can be extended: other abstract objects, especially possible worlds, may be

---

concepts are like His. We thereby gain basic knowledge of mathematical objects in virtue of knowledge of our own perceptions and concepts, and of their similarity to those in the divine mind': 'God and Mathematical Objects', 94. But if our collectings are not God's collectings, then we do not in fact have knowledge of real sets, but only set-like constructions. If we say that we do grasp the same sets as God, then we seem to have given up on conceptualism and reverted to thinking of sets as distinct from, rather than identical with, collecting operations.

[49] As Plantinga thinks; see *Where the Conflict Really Lies*, 291; see further William Lane Craig, 'Critical notice of Alvin Plantinga, *Where the Conflict Really Lies*', *Philosophia Christi*, 14 (2012): 473–7; Plantinga, 'Response to William Lane Craig's Review', 178–9.

plausibly taken to be merely imagined by God. A pretence theoretical approach gives the conceptualist his divine thoughts but precludes our identifying God's thoughts with sets, possible worlds, propositions, properties, and so on.

In short, all sorts of worries arise when we reflect upon the conceptualist identification of objects typically taken to be abstract with God's thoughts. While by no means knock-down objections to conceptualism—indeed, I think that conceptualism remains one option for the theist wrestling with the challenge posed by abstract objects to divine aseity—these worries should motivate the theist to look seriously at the wide variety of anti-realist solutions to the challenge before acquiescing too easily to the traditional conceptualist viewpoint.

CONCLUDING REMARKS

Although the conceptualist view of abstract objects has historically been the mainstream Christian position, it is not incumbent upon us. Even if biblical writers like the author of the prologue to John's Gospel *presupposed* such a view, they did not *teach* such a view as Christian doctrine, any more than they taught, for example, the generally presumed geocentrism. What they taught is that God alone is uncreated and that everything that exists apart from God has been created by Him. The task of articulating a view that does justice to this commitment, while meeting the challenge posed to it by Platonism, is left to the Christian theologian. Moreover, even among the Middle Platonists and Church Fathers who held that abstract objects are ideas in the mind of God, it is far from clear that a heavy metaphysical commitment to objects was intended. We saw that for Philo, the intelligible world may be thought of as either formed by the divine Logos or, more reductively, as the divine Logos itself as God is engaged in creating.[50] The second formulation

---

[50] Recall Philo's words: 'If you would wish to use a formulation that has been stripped down to essentials, you might say that the intelligible cosmos is nothing else than the Logos of God as He is actually engaged in making the cosmos. For the intelligible city too is nothing else than the reasoning of the architect as he is actually engaged in planning the foundation of the city' (*On the Creation of the World* 24).

is quite compatible with an anti-realist view, for the anti-realist does not deny that persons think about numbers, properties, possible worlds, and so on. We also saw that among the Church Fathers, it was sometimes denied that things existing in God's mind have a 'substantial' existence, in contrast to things that exist extra-mentally for God. Anti-realists have no objection to lightweight talk of objects or thoughts in the mind of God.

We saw further that if we do make a metaphysically heavyweight commitment to the reality of divine thoughts as stand-ins for mathematical objects, propositions, properties, and so on, then it is at best unclear that conceptualism succeeds in safeguarding God's status as the sole ultimate reality. For if these objects are held to be causally independent of God, then it would seem that God's status as the sole ultimate reality has been abandoned. If we hold that they are causally dependent on God, then, if we are to avoid the bootstrapping objection, it seems that we must reject the Platonist's ontological assay of things, which tends to remove the motivation for realism.

Finally, we saw that the conceptualist's identification of allegedly abstract objects with divine thoughts is not exactly worry-free. In many cases, God's thoughts seem ill-suited in various ways to play the roles traditionally played by abstract objects.

All this goes to place a question mark behind realism about abstract objects. Why be a realist in the first place? Perhaps absolute creationists and divine conceptualists have been much too uncritical in their acceptance of the Indispensability Argument for realism about mathematical objects and their ilk. Perhaps Christian theists need to take a good look at anti-realist alternatives to Platonism.

6

Making Ontological Commitments (1)

At the heart of the Indispensability Argument for Platonism about mathematical objects, propositions, possible worlds, and the like lies a criterion of ontological commitment, emanating from the late W. V. O. Quine, which comes to expression in the first premiss of that argument:

> I. If a simple sentence (i.e., a sentence of the form 'a is F') is literally true, then the objects that its singular terms denote exist. Likewise, if an existential sentence is literally true, then there exist objects of the relevant kinds; e.g., if 'There is an F' is true, then there exist some Fs.

According to this criterion, singular terms and existential quantifiers are devices of ontological commitment. It is worth noting that such a criterion is not a criterion of existence, telling us what exists. Rather, the criterion is intended to disclose to us the existential commitments of our discourse. It tells us what we must believe exists if we regard certain statements as true. The criterion says, in effect, 'You believe that such-and-such is true? Then you must also believe that the objects referred to by your singular terms and the objects that you say there are actually exist. You're committed to the existence of such entities, so long as you maintain that what you said is true.' If we feel uncomfortable about the ontological commitments of our discourse, we can always avoid such commitments by denying that what we said is true. But we would have to swallow hard before denying, say, that '$2 > 1$' in order to avoid commitment to the reality of numbers.

Now I suspect that the non-philosopher would regard this neo-Quinean criterion of ontological commitment, not only as a piece of linguistic imperialism, but also as a preposterous attempt to read the nature of reality off human language. Why should we think that human language so closely mirrors reality as to allow us to do metaphysics by means of linguistic analysis? Is it not absurd to think that, while the truth of the statement 'Three men entered the tavern' involves no ontological commitment to numbers, the truth of the statement 'The number of men who entered the tavern is three' does?

WHY ACCEPT THE REALIST'S CRITERION OF ONTOLOGICAL COMMITMENT?

I share fully the layman's scepticism about the realist's criterion of ontological commitment. This scepticism ought to motivate us to ask what good reason or argument there is that such a criterion is true. Amazingly, it turns out that virtually no arguments are offered by realists for the truth of their criterion. For example, Peter van Inwagen is a prominent contemporary metaphysician who champions what he calls 'Quine's theses on ontological commitment'.[1] So what are these Quinean theses and why ought we to accept them? In a more recent piece, van Inwagen spells out exactly what he understands by 'Quine's theses on ontological commitment' and explains their role in resolving ontological disputes:

> The parties to such a dispute should examine, or be willing in principle to examine, the ontological implications of *everything they want to affirm.* And this examination should consist in various attempts to render the things they want to affirm into the quantifier-variable idiom (in sufficient depth that all the inferences they want to make from the things they want to affirm are logically valid). The 'ontological implications' of the things they affirm will be precisely the class of closed sentences starting with an existential-quantifier phrase (whose scope is the remainder of the sentence) that are logical consequences of the renderings into the quantifier-variable idiom of those things they want to affirm. Parties to the dispute who are unwilling to accept some ontological implication of a rendering of some thesis they have affirmed into the quantifier-variable idiom must find some other way of rendering that thesis into the quantifier-variable idiom (must find a paraphrase) that they are willing to accept and which does not have the unwanted implication.[2]

---

[1] Peter van Inwagen, 'God and Other Uncreated Things', in Kevin Timpe (ed.), *Metaphysics and God* (London: Routledge, 2009), 19.
[2] Peter van Inwagen, 'Being, Existence, and Ontological Commitment', in David Chalmers et al. (eds), *Metametaphysics: New Essays on the Foundations of Ontology*

So the basic idea is that you must first put what you believe into the form of statements of first-order quantified logic. Then you are ontologically committed by any existentially quantified sentences which are implied by what you believe. If you want to resist those commitments, you are obligated to come up with a paraphrase of your original belief that does not have such implications.

Van Inwagen characterizes Quine's meta-ontological theses as a set of rules or a strategy for settling ontological disputes. Now this is remarkable. Rules or strategies may be useful or effective, but they are not the sort of statements that are true or false. Van Inwagen's characterization implies that Quine's theses are neither true nor false, any more than are rules for the arbitration of labour disputes.

So why should we embrace Quine's meta-ontological method for settling ontological disputes? Van Inwagen answers that it is the 'most profitable strategy to follow to get people to make their ontological commitments clear'.[3] So the suggestion is that we should adopt the method because of its profitability. Van Inwagen illustrates the profitability of Quine's method by appeal to its utility in the ontological dispute over holes. Do holes really exist? Or are some things just holey? In order to avoid quantifying over holes, van Inwagen says, the materialist has to put forward paraphrases of key sentences that are 'bizarre'. 'Certain untoward consequences of a strict nominalistic materialism thus become evident only when one adopts Quine's strategy for clarifying ontological disputes—and it is unlikely that they would otherwise have been noticed.'[4] The general lesson to be drawn from this, he says, is that 'If Quine's "rules" for conducting ontological disputes are not followed, then ... it is almost certain that

---

(Oxford: Clarendon, 2009), 506. These theses are not really expressive of Quine's original criterion of ontological commitment. I shall on occasion mark the difference by calling what passes today as Quine's criterion of ontological commitment the neo-Quinean criterion.

[3] Peter van Inwagen, 'Meta-ontology', in *Ontology, Identity, and Modality* (Cambridge: CUP, 2001), 28; similarly, van Inwagen, 'Being, Existence, and Ontological Commitment', 506; Peter van Inwagen, 'Quantification and Fictional Discourse', in Anthony Everett and Thomas Hofweber (eds), *Empty Names, Fiction, and the Puzzles of Non-Existence* (Stanford, CA: Center for the Study of Language and Information, 2000), 236, where he calls the Lewises' paper on holes 'a paradigm of the application of Quine's strategy'. The paper in question is David Lewis and Stephanie Lewis, 'Holes', *Australasian Journal of Philosophy*, 48/2 (1970): 206–12.

[4] Van Inwagen, 'Meta-ontology', 31.

Making Ontological Commitments (1) 99

many untoward consequences of the disputed positions will be obscured by imprecision and wishful thinking.'[5]

I am far from impressed with this attempt to motivate adoption of Quine's strategy for resolving ontological disputes. Even if Quine's strategy did yield clear answers to ontological disputes, there is no reason to think that those answers are true, since no reason has been given to think that it is true that the ontological commitments of a discourse are disclosed by the criterion in question. Moreover, ironically, the alleged untoward consequences of anti-realism mentioned by van Inwagen are themselves precisely *the result* of adopting Quine's procedure! If one denies that existential quantification is ontologically committing, one will not be troubled by quantifying over holes and other dubious entities, nor will one be forced to offer bizarre paraphrases of one's original statements. The person who rejects Quine's meta-ontological rules will thus not be saddled with the untoward consequences that trouble van Inwagen. The exposure of such consequences thus provides no reason at all for adoption of Quine's procedure. Indeed, Quine's procedure, I think, has the decided drawback that it could force us to embrace all sorts of spurious reifications like, for example, holes. In that sense, Quine's procedure is not at all a profitable strategy to follow to get people to make their ontological commitments clear.

In any case, Quine's meta-ontological procedure does not, in fact, succeed in making the ontological commitments of a discourse clear. Consider van Inwagen's own example of a quantified sentence which supposedly commits the person who asserts it to the existence of properties:

(S) Spiders share some of the anatomical features of insects.

Applying Quine's method, van Inwagen says that if we examine the meaning of this sentence, we find that what it says is this: 'There are anatomical features that insects have and spiders also have', or in the idiom of quantification, 'It is true of at least one thing that it is such that it is an anatomical feature and insects have it and spiders also have it.'[6] Now, if there are anatomical features that insects have and that spiders also have, then it follows that there are anatomical

---

[5] Ibid.
[6] Peter van Inwagen, 'A Theory of Properties', in Dean Zimmerman (ed.), *Oxford Studies in Metaphysics*, i (Oxford: Clarendon, 2004), 113–15.

features that insects have. And if there are anatomical features that insects have, then there are anatomical features—period. An anatomical feature seems to be a property. So, van Inwagen concludes, it follows that properties exist.

But is that really what (S) says? (S) appears to be a universally quantified statement about spiders. But in contrast to existentially quantified statements, such a universally quantified statement makes, on the customary criterion of ontological commitment, no existential commitments, since logically it is a conditional of the form *For any x, if x is a spider, then x has some of the anatomical features of insects.*[7] So (S) carries no ontological commitments.

This *faux pas* on van Inwagen's part raises the very interesting and important question of exactly how to put a sentence acceptably into the idiom of quantification. Van Inwagen himself points out that there is no such thing as the unique translation of some sentence into what he calls 'the quantifier-variable idiom', for two reasons: (i) the quantifier-variable idiom is present in different degrees in various translations of the original sentence, and (ii) there are alternative, creative ways of translating the original sentence into the quantifier-variable idiom.[8]

With respect to (i), van Inwagen gives the example of rendering the sentence 'Every planet is at any time at some distance from every star' into the quantifier-variable idiom of increasing complexity in four successive steps, beginning with the simple 'For any x, if x is a planet, x is at any time at some distance from every star' and finishing with the very complex 'For any x (x is a planet → For any y (y is a star → For any t (t is a time → There is some z (z is a distance & x is at t separated from y by z))))'. How much of the original sentence is put into the quantifier-variable idiom, says van Inwagen, will depend on the purposes of the person who is doing the translation.

This fact raises the question why the anti-realist should not be content to render (S) in the quantifier-variable idiom as simply 'For any x, if x is a spider, then x shares some of the anatomical features of insects', which is ontologically non-committing. Even if we suppose

---

[7] Interestingly, in the version of the argument in his *Metaphysics*, 3rd edn (Boulder, CO: Westview, 2009), 299–300, van Inwagen himself takes a similar sentence to be a universally quantified statement.

[8] Van Inwagen, 'Meta-ontology', 23–4. The quantifier is either the universal or the existential quantifier, and the variable is the x which can take on various values.

Making Ontological Commitments (1) 101

that some individual thing *a* is a spider, so that we may infer that *a* shares some of the anatomical features of insects, we are not committed to the existence of features by the truth of that conclusion. We might simply refrain from quantifying over features.

Van Inwagen himself confronts a similar situation with regard to quantifying over distances in the example about stars. Since he admits that he cannot give a coherent account of such an object as a distance, and the original sentence is intelligible without such objects, van Inwagen says that he is inclined to reject the final translation, which quantifies existentially over distances. So why not just stop short of quantifying over such entities in order to avoid dubious ontological commitments?

Van Inwagen's answer, as we have seen, is that our translating into the quantifier-variable idiom must proceed 'in sufficient depth that all the inferences we want to make from the things we want to affirm are logically valid'. So if we want to draw certain inferences but do not like the entity to be quantified over, we must come up with a paraphrase which avoids quantifying over the dubious entity. So, in the stars example, van Inwagen invents an ingenious paraphrase that avoids mentioning distances but preserves the inferences he wants to make.

Here is where the philosophical creativity alluded to in reason (ii) comes into play, for there is no one right way to paraphrase the relevant sentence. Different paraphrases will leave us with different ontological commitments, and which one we choose to adopt will depend, van Inwagen admits, on personal philosophical and even aesthetic preferences. That undermines the objectivity of one's ontological commitments.

Quine recognized that the application of his criterion of ontological commitment to ordinary language would bring with it all sorts of fantastic and unwanted ontological commitments. So he limited its legitimate application only to an unknown, official, artificial language involving the appropriate logical paraphrases of the statements of our best scientific theories. Van Inwagen is more radical than Quine in that he sanctions the unrestricted use of Quine's criterion even with regard to ordinary language statements in the quantifier-variable idiom and so is prepared to accept the ontological commitments which the lack of acceptable anti-realist paraphrases brings with it.[9]

---

[9] To see how his neo-Quineanism leads him to the bold, if nuanced, affirmation e.g. that fictional characters exist, see van Inwagen, 'Quantification and Fictional Discourse', 235–47. According to van Inwagen, competing ontologies of fiction

But then van Inwagen faces a twofold challenge: first, since he wants to avoid the most bizarre commitments of ordinary language, he needs to provide a general, universally applicable way of paraphrasing ordinary sentences which carry unwanted ontological commitments that eliminates those commitments. Second, he needs to show that anti-realist paraphrases cannot similarly be found for ordinary sentences involving commitment to abstract objects like properties. But van Inwagen admits that he can do neither. With respect to the first task, he says that he would like to be able to show that it is always possible to provide a paraphrase of sentences about various unwanted objects, but 'to do that, I think, it would be necessary to discover a general, universally applicable way of paraphrasing ordinary sentences of the kind we are interested in', which he admits he cannot do.[10] With respect to the second task, he says, 'I cannot hope to provide an adequate defense of this position, for an adequate defense of this position would have to take the form of an examination of all possible candidates for nominalistically acceptable paraphrases of such sentences, and I cannot hope to do that.... My statement "We can't get away with [nominalism]" must be regarded as a promissory note.'[11] But a mere promissory note is plainly inadequate as a defeater of anti-realism.

In light of its lack of objectivity, we might justifiably look at the whole Quinean procedure with a marked scepticism. We still seem to be left with a good deal of 'imprecision and wishful thinking' about

---

should be evaluated by (i) seeing how well they explain our reactions to the whole range of sentences we use to talk about fiction and (ii) our ability to integrate these explanations with (a) an acceptable philosophy of the quantifier and (b) an acceptable general ontology (247). When judged by such criteria, it seems to me very plausible that the implication of our discourse about fictional characters that 'There are fictional characters' is no more ontologically committing than a sentence like 'There's at least one thing that you overlooked: his lack of compassion', i.e. not committing at all.

[10] Peter van Inwagen, *Material Beings* (Ithaca, NY: Cornell University Press, 1990), 108. See further Achille C. Varzi, 'Words and Objects', in Andrea Bottani et al. (eds), *Individuals, Essence, and Identity* (Dordrecht: Kluwer Academic Publishers, 2002), 49–75. Without challenging the Quinean Criterion of Ontological Commitment, Varzi attacks its usefulness in disclosing the ontological commitments of ordinary language speakers. For there is no objective procedure for determining the correct logical form of a sentence, and many paraphrases are simply ingenious attempts to avoid reference. If the paraphrase avoids some of the ontological commitments of the original sentence, how shall we decide which statement to take as true? Varzi charges that van Inwagen's linguistic revisionism involves 'a plain misconstrual' of the statements of ordinary language speakers (65).

[11] Van Inwagen, 'Theory of Properties', 118–19.

ontological disputes. Seeing the dubious entities, like distances, to which the procedure is leading, one might simply decline to make the relevant inferences from the things that one wants to affirm, since so doing would involve dubious reification. Or one might question why ontological commitment should hang so crucially on the availability of a paraphrase, especially given the lack of objectivity of the commitments of the paraphrases and the dubiousness of some of those commitments.[12] Indeed, the relativity of one's ontological commitments, on van Inwagen's view, seems subversive of his meta-ontological method. For if ontological commitment means that one is committed to those entities which must exist if the sentences of a certain class are to be true, then it follows that we have no ontological commitments, since, given the creativity of paraphrase, none of the postulated entities *must* exist.

Even more fundamentally, however, one might simply reject the view that existential quantifiers and singular terms are devices of ontological commitment. That is not to say that we have no means in English of indicating our ontological commitments. Rather, it is to say that the use of existential quantification and singular terms in sentences we take to be literally true does not inevitably commit us to the existence of the things we refer to or say there are. So let us look more closely at each of the devices taken by proponents of the Indispensability Argument to be ontologically committing.

EXISTENTIAL QUANTIFICATION AND ONTOLOGICAL COMMITMENT

Consider first the allegedly ontologically committing nature of existential quantification. Quine claimed that his criterion was 'scarcely contestable' because the formal logical quantifier ($\exists x$) is explained by the words 'there is an object x such that'.[13] Notwithstanding, many

---

[12] Van Inwagen's paraphrase for distances e.g. quantifies over numbers, so that the original statement, which made no mention whatsoever of numbers, winds up committing us to the reality of not just stars and planets, but an infinity of numbers! Is ontology really that easy?

[13] W. V. O. Quine, *Philosophy of Logic*, 2nd edn (Cambridge, MA: Harvard University Press, 1986), 89.

anti-realists dispute the claim that the existential (or particular) quantifier is ontologically committing to whatever x stands for. Prominent among these are neo-Meinongians and neutralists (Figure 1).

Neo-Meinongianism and Neutralism

Richard Routley (who later changed his name to Sylvan) was a maverick Australian philosopher who helped to revive the views of the late nineteenth-century Austrian philosopher Alexius Meinong. Meinong became famous—or perhaps 'infamous' would be the better word—for his theory of objects, according to which there are not only existing objects, but also non-existent objects. Meinong's most radical contention was that non-existent objects, like existing objects, have properties. Pegasus, for example, has the property of being a winged horse, and the round square has the properties of being round and of being square. Meinong's most famous statement was his aphorism: 'There are objects of which it is true that there are no such objects.'[14] Now, obviously, if Meinong took the existential quantifier to be a device of ontological commitment, his statement would be flatly self-contradictory, as many unsympathetic interpreters have taken it to be. But Meinong took the existential quantifier to be ontologically neutral in its commitments. Given an ontologically neutral interpretation of the existential quantifier, it is unobjectionable to assert that there are things that do not exist. In this neutral sense, it seems obvious that there are things that do not exist—unicorns, centaurs, Zeus, for example—and the Quinean claim that everything exists seems, by contrast, bizarre.

Routley is willing to affirm that traditional quantificational logic is, as he puts it, 'existentially loaded'.[15] So, in order to signal the difference in his interpretation of the quantifier, Routley proposed calling

---

[14] Alexius Meinong, 'The Theory of Objects' ('*Über Gegenstandstheorie*', 1904), tr. Isaac Levi et al., in Roderick M. Chisholm (ed.), *Realism and the Background of Phenomenology* (Atascadero, CA: Ridgeview, 1960), 83. In German: 'Es gibt Gegenstände, von denen gilt, daß es die gleichen Gegenstände nicht gibt.' See discussion in J. N. Findlay, *Meinong's Theory of Objects and Values*, 2nd edn (Oxford: Clarendon, 1963), 44–50.

[15] Richard Routley, *Exploring Meinong's Jungle and Beyond: An Investigation of Noneism and the Theory of Items* (Canberra: Australian National University Research School of Social Sciences, 1979), 56.

the neutral quantifier the particular quantifier, symbolized as 'P', to be read 'for some...', in contrast to the existentially loaded existential quantifier ∃. So the statement 'Some things do not exist' would be symbolized (Px) (¬Ex), where 'E' stands for the predicate 'exists'. Tufts University philosopher Jody Azzouni, though no neo-Meinongian, agrees with Routley's ontologically neutral logic and is the most prolific proponent of neutralism today.[16] The main difference is that, whereas Routley substitutes the neutral particular quantifier for the existentially loaded existential quantifier, Azzouni denies that the existential quantifier is existentially loaded and so sees no need of a substitute. Azzouni thinks that the reason Quine just took it as obvious that the existential quantifier is ontologically committing is because Quine thought that the ordinary language idiom 'there is/are' carries ontological commitment and that this idiom is straightforwardly represented by the existential quantifier. Azzouni sharply challenges the claim that the ordinary language expressions codified by the existential quantifier inevitably imply the mind- and language-independent existence of the items quantified over. On Azzouni's view, *no* idiom—even 'exists'—in ordinary language is ontologically committing.[17] As evidence of the ontologically non-committing nature of 'there is/are' phrases in the vernacular, Azzouni adduces various examples of what he calls 'ontically irrelevant' uses:[18]

(1) No mouse—not Mickey Mouse, not Minnie Mouse—has ever been depicted in movies as a plumber, although there are several that have been depicted as pirates.
(2) There is a certain position in society that I deserve, but because of certain unscrupulous people, I've failed to procure it.
(3) There is a certain imaginary woman that Jane and Heather dream about regularly.
(4) There are many ways of getting around this.
(5) There are as many goddesses as gods in Greek mythology.

Moreover, there is evidence of a similar sort that 'exist' is also ontically neutral in the vernacular:

---

[16] I am grateful to Jody Azzouni for extensive personal discussion of neutralism.
[17] Jody Azzouni, 'Ontological Commitment in the Vernacular', *Noûs* 41/2 (2007): 220 n. 4.
[18] Jody Azzouni, 'Ontology and the Word "Exist": Uneasy Relations', *Philosophia Mathematica*, 18/1 (2010): 77–84.

(6) Strategies for circumventing anger exist.
(7) Although waltzes designed to last more than ten hours exist, people rarely dance unexpurgated versions of them.

Azzouni believes that the ordinary speaker would be quite surprised to learn that his use of 'there is/are' with respect to fictional characters, dream figures, ways of going about something, and so on, oblige him to acknowledge the reality of such things or to offer paraphrases to avoid such 'there is/are' statements. Ordinary language speakers sense no obligation to offer paraphrases of such sentences if challenged concerning their ontological commitments; rather, they just clarify that such statements were not to be taken in an ontologically committing way.[19] 'Ordinary speakers find the philosopher's charge of ontic commitment in many cases as *silly* because ontic commitment (and ontology) seems irrelevant.'[20]

Azzouni agrees that we often do use 'there is/are'—and even more frequently 'exist'—in ontically relevant ways to assert our belief in the mind- and language-independent reality of some thing.[21] But the linguistic phrases themselves are not ontologically committing simply in virtue of their meaning. The linguistic meaning of 'exists' does not change with its ontically relevant or irrelevant uses. The locutions are neutral in and of themselves, and different users on different occasions may use the same 'there is/are...' phrases with different ontological commitments in mind. The way ordinary language speakers indicate or deny ontological commitment is by such devices as tone of voice, addition of words like 'really', or contrastive use of 'exist' with 'there is/are.' In Azzouni's view, then, there just are no idioms in the vernacular which, by virtue of their meanings alone, are ontologically committing. Ontological commitment is thus a varying, person-relative matter.

Prospects of Neutralism

So one way the theist who wants to defeat the Platonist's Indispensability Argument can do so is by advocating a neutral view of

---

[19] Azzouni, 'Ontological Commitment in the Vernacular', 224 n. 38.
[20] Azzouni, 'Ontology and the Word "Exist"', 78–9.
[21] Ibid., 89. Azzouni thinks that mind- and language-independence is, in fact, the criterion of existence which ordinary language speakers have collectively adopted, though the criterion cannot be established by conceptual analysis or philosophical argument.

Making Ontological Commitments (1) 107

quantificational logic. Not only do I find such a view to be tenable—which is all the theist need contend in order to undercut the Indispensability Argument—but I am persuaded that it is correct.

There are two ways in which existential quantification has been thought to be ontologically committing: first, through the semantic theory of logical quantification and, second, through the linguistic meaning of the quantifiers. Let us look at each in turn.

Semantics for Quantificational Logic

Objectual Semantics

According to so-called objectual semantics for quantificational logic, the variables (like x, y, and z) which lie within the scope of our quantifiers range over a specified domain of objects to pick out various objects in the domain. In order for a universally quantified statement to be true, that statement must be true no matter which object in the domain is plugged in for the variable. In order for an existentially quantified statement to be true, at least one of the objects in the domain, when plugged in for the variable, yields a true statement. Now some theorists, including Quine, have maintained that such objectual semantics for sentences we take to be true commits us ontologically to all or at least some of the objects in the domain.

This claim is misconceived. There is no reason to limit one's domain of quantification to existing objects or to think that it must include existing objects. We are at liberty to quantify over anything we choose, whether it exists or not. For example, a historian may quantify over past US Presidents, asserting truly that some of them were born outside the United States. It would be a metaphysical extravagance to think that merely quantifying over past US Presidents commits one to a tenseless theory of time, according to which temporal becoming is illusory and past, present, and future entities are ontologically on a par. Or again, we may quantify over courses of action which we are contemplating, assessing which of them would likely lead to disaster. In this case, the courses of action which are not chosen as a result of such deliberation never do exist. Or again, we may quantify over hobbits in Tolkien's novels, asking how many of them are said to live underground, without committing ourselves to the existence of hobbits. And in everyday matters, we quantify over things like holes, Fridays, problems, needs, and so on, without thinking that we are thereby committing ourselves to the reality of such things. As Azzouni points out, whether one is ontologically committed to objects said to be in the domain depends entirely on whether the quantifiers in the second-order language (or metalanguage) used to establish the domain are themselves devices of ontological commitment.[22] Without that presupposition, talk of objects' being in a domain no more commits us to anything real than do the ground-level assertions. If I choose to quantify over Fridays in 2014, I am no more committed to the existence of Fridays by such a decision than I am by my assertion 'There are five Fridays in October'.

Substitutional Semantics

Azzouni reminds us that there is another semantics for quantificational discourse which is admitted on all sides not to be ontologically committing to objects in a domain, namely, so-called substitutional quantification. On a substitutional understanding of quantification, one does not take the variables within the scope of the quantifier to range over a domain of objects; rather, we take the variables as dummy letters which may be replaced by linguistic expressions in order to form sentences. A universally quantified statement is true just in case the substitution of any term for the variable in the sentence following the quantifier yields a true sentence. An existentially quantified statement is true just in case the substitution of at least one term for the variable in the sentence following the quantifier yields a true sentence. So, for example, 'All cats are mammals' is true just in case any singular term plugged into 'If x is a cat, then x is a mammal' is true; and 'Some cats are black' is true just in case at least one singular term, when plugged into 'x is a cat and x is black', yields a true sentence. Since one is simply substituting words for the variables, no objects in a domain even come into view.

Early proponents of substitutional semantics, like Ruth Barcan Marcus, therefore considered it superior to what they took to be the ontologically inflationary objectual semantics championed by Quine.[23] Quine himself recognized how alien to ordinary language

---

[22] Jody Azzouni, *Deflating Existential Consequence: A Case for Nominalism* (Oxford: OUP, 2004), 54.

[23] Ruth Barcan Marcus, 'Quantification and Ontology', *Noûs*, 6/3 (1972): 245. This article includes some wonderful illustrations of the ontologically inflationary character of objectual semantics if it is taken to be ontologically committing.

objectual semantics is, when construed as carrying ontological commitments, and he also conceded that substitutional semantics would avoid such ontological commitments.[24] Quine's main objection to substitutional quantification was that many things in the world over which we want to quantify do not have singular terms, like names, denoting them. But for the theist that presents no problem. The theist will insist that God is able to name any object that exists. 'He determines the number of the stars and calls them each by name' (Ps. 147: 4). I am reminded of Wilfrid Sellars's appeal to 'the language of omniscience', in which every object has a name.[25] The truth conditions for substitutional quantification may be successfully stated relative to the language of omniscience, even if many, or most, objects have not yet received names in English.[26]

Some philosophers have sought to avoid ontological commitment to abstract objects by construing the semantics for abstract discourse substitutionally, rather than objectually.[27] But Azzouni's point is more modest. The lesson to be learned from substitutional quantification, he thinks, is that a semantics for quantificational discourse need not involve ontological commitment to objects.[28] Apart from a stipulation that the quantifiers of one's meta-level language are ontologically committing, even the objectual semantics for ground-level quantificational discourse is just neutral.[29]

---

[24] W. V. O. Quine, *The Roots of Reference* (LaSalle, IL: Open Court, 1973), 89, 135–6. Quine sought to avoid such unwanted commitments by restricting his criterion of ontological commitment to an artificial language somehow purged of the offending expressions.

[25] Wilfrid Sellars, 'Realism and the New Way of Words', *Philosophy and Phenomenological Research*, 8/4 (1948): 604–5.

[26] See discussion in Michael J. Loux, 'Ontology', in C. F. Delaney (ed.), *The Synoptic Vision: Essays on the Philosophy of Wilfrid Sellars* (Notre Dame, IN: University of Notre Dame Press, 1977), 66–7; cf. Loux, 'Rules, Roles, and Ontological Commitment: An Examination of Sellars' Analysis of Abstract Reference', in Joseph C. Pitt (ed.), *The Philosophy of Wilfrid Sellars: Queries and Extensions* (Dordrecht: D. Reidel, 1978), 247.

[27] Dale Gottlieb, *Ontological Economy: Substitutional Quantification and Mathematics* (Oxford: OUP, 1980).

[28] Azzouni, *Deflating Existential Consequence*, 57. Note the difference between Azzouni's view and Dale Jacquette's neo-Meinongian view that the domain is expanded to comprise both existent and non-existent objects. Jacquette, 'Meditations on Meinong's Golden Mountain', in Nicholas Griffin and Dale Jacquette (eds), *Russell vs. Meinong: The Legacy of 'On Denoting'* (London: Routledge, 2009), 195–6.

[29] Azzouni himself takes meta-level claims about domains, quantifiers, and the like to be merely metaphorical, not literal: Azzouni, 'Ontological Commitment in the Vernacular', 222 n. 18; similarly, Jody Azzouni, 'A New Characterization of Scientific

The fundamental point is that there is no reason to treat the quantifiers of the metalanguage setting up the domain as ontologically committing, unless it is so stipulated. The debate on ground-level quantifiers thus replays itself on the meta-level, and the neutralist sees no reason to take the metalanguage quantifiers, any more than the ground-level language quantifiers, as carrying ontological commitments. Azzouni summarizes:

> The lesson should be clear: Objectual quantifiers have 'objects' to range over only relative to a body of claims in a metalanguage that itself gains access to these 'objects,' if at all, via what its own quantifiers range over. And if *those* (metalanguage) quantifiers do *not* carry ontological commitment, then neither do the objectual quantifiers that the metalanguage quantifiers help provide objectual semantics for. A slogan: *One can't read ontological commitments from semantic conditions unless one has already smuggled into those semantic conditions the ontology one would like to read off.*[30]

Only if the Quinean were able to show that the informal quantifiers of ordinary language which are codified by the formal quantifiers of objectual semantics are ontologically committing could he justifiably insist that formal quantifiers are ontologically committing. That forms a segue to the second way in which it has been claimed that quantification is a device of ontological commitment.

Linguistic Meaning of Quantificational Expressions

A neo-Quinean like van Inwagen makes no appeal to objectual semantics to justify taking the existential quantifier to be a means of ontological commitment. Rather, he proceeds simply on the basis of the linguistic meaning of quantificational expressions in ordinary language which the formal quantifier abbreviates.

Saul Kripke, whose pioneering work in modal semantics made him one of the twentieth century's brightest philosophical luminaries, insists that the objectual (or, as he calls it, referential) quantifier

---

Theories', *Synthèse*, 191/13 (2014): 2993–3008. Azzouni's appeal to a metaphorical metalanguage is an emphasis associated with figuralist or pretence theoretical views of abstract discourse, to be discussed in Chapters 9 and 10.

[30] Azzouni, *Deflating Existential Consequence,* 55.

derives its meaning entirely from ordinary language quantificational expressions:

> We did *not* learn quantification theory as our mother tongue. Somehow or other the weird notation '(∃x)' was explained to us, by teachers or books, either by such examples as ' "(∃x) Rabbit (x)" means *"there is an x* which is a rabbit"', or by a formal definition of satisfaction, couched in English.... And the quantifiers will be said to range over a *non-empty* domain *D*, where the technical term 'non-empty' is explained by saying that *D* is non-empty iff *there is an element in D*, or the equivalent. *If* the interpretation of the English 'there are' is completely in doubt, the interpretation of the formal referential quantifier, which depends on such explanations, must be in doubt also; perhaps the explanation the teacher used when he taught it to us was couched in a substitutional language, and we spoke such a language when we learned his interpretation!... Nonsense: we speak English, and the whole interpretation of the referential quantifier was *defined* by reference to 'there are' in its standard employments.[31]

Kripke thinks the assertion 'There are rabbits' undoubtedly commits us to the existence of rabbits; but he himself acknowledges that there are English uses of 'there is/are' which are not ontologically relevant, as in 'There is a good chance' or 'There are three feet in a yard'. Kripke's disagreement is merely with 'anyone who doubts or denies that English has any resources for making genuinely existential assertions'[32]—a position to which no neutralist ascribes.

Kripke and the neutralist concur on the overriding point: if the existential quantifier is defined in terms of the ordinary English 'there is/are', then if the latter is not ontologically committing, neither is the former. Van Inwagen agrees that it is so defined: 'The meaning of the quantifiers is given by the phrases of English ... that they abbreviate. The existential quantifier therefore expresses the sense of "there is" in ordinary English.'[33] The problem for van Inwagen is that such a sense does not seem to be ontologically committing. Consider Thomas Hofweber's list of some of the things we ordinarily say there are:

- something that we have in common
- infinitely many primes

---

[31] Saul Kripke, 'Is there a Problem about Substitutional Quantification?', in Gareth Evans and John McDowell (eds), *Truth and Meaning: Essays in Semantics* (Oxford: Clarendon, 1976), 379.
[32] Ibid., 380.
[33] Van Inwagen, 'Quantification and Fictional Discourse', 239.

- something that we both believe
- the common illusion that one is smarter than one's average colleague
- a way you smile
- a lack of compassion in the world
- the way the world is
- several ways the world might have been
- a faster way to get to Berkeley from Stanford than going through San Jose
- the hope that this dissertation will shed some light on ontology
- the chance that it might not
- a reason why it might not[34]

It would be fantastic to think that there are real objects answering to these descriptions. There is no evidence that the ordinary language speaker labours under the delusion that there are.

Van Inwagen does not directly engage neutralism, which denies that ordinary language quantificational expressions are ontologically committing. All van Inwagen really offers for thinking that quantificational expressions are ontologically committing is the synonymy in ordinary language of 'there is/are' and 'there exist(s)'. Synonymy is really beside the point, however, for the neutralist denies that either expression is ontologically committing in ordinary language. It is worth emphasizing, in view of van Inwagen's insistence that 'existence' is not only synonymous with 'being', but univocal as well,[35] that the non-committing character of 'there is/are' and 'there exists' in ordinary language is not, according to neutralism, due to any equivocation of such expressions, as though there were one meaning which is ontologically committing and another which is not. Rather, on Azzouni's view, these expressions in the vernacular just do not force ontological commitments in virtue of their meaning.

Robert Adams thinks that the English word 'exists' is univocal in its various uses but observes that it is metaphysically lightweight in ordinary language. He writes,

---

[34] Thomas Hofweber, 'Ontology and Objectivity' (Ph.D. dissertation, Stanford University, 1999), 1–2.

[35] See e.g. van Inwagen, 'Being, Existence, and Ontological Commitment', 482–92.

I believe that the meaning of 'exist' and of (informal) quantifiers is metaphysically light in natural languages. I think we speak sincerely and literally, but without meaning to commit ourselves on deep metaphysical issues, when we say, as we do, that there are rocks as well as roosters, shapes and sizes, numbers and theorems, molecules composed of several atoms, amoebas and other living cells that split in two, cities and states, laws and agreements, properties and relations, words that are spoken and written, books that exist in both printed and electronic forms—and so on. I suppose that few if any of us would say that all of those objects are fundamental metaphysically.[36]

I think that Adams's observation about the lightweight nature of existence predications and informal quantifiers in ordinary language is obviously correct. We commonly say that there are, for example, shades of grey, differences in height, angles from which something can be seen, principles, hostilities, prospects for success, primes between 2 and 12, hours before dawn, dangerous excesses, drawbacks to the plan, and so on, without imagining that there are mind-independent objects of these sorts.[37]

In Adams's view, what is asserted to exist in a metaphysically light sense is a matter of linguistic conventions and one's personal interests. It is in this light sense, I think, that a lightweight Platonist like John Burgess affirms the existence of abstract objects, as well as most other things.[38] Adams's claim that the sense of 'exists' in ordinary language is very lightweight accords well with Azzouni's claim that existential quantification and 'exists' are not ontologically committing in the vernacular.

Disadvantages of Existentially Loaded Quantifiers

Intentional Statements

Furthermore, there are decided disadvantages to taking formal and informal quantificational expressions to be ontologically committing. First, we should be logically hamstrung when it comes to dealing with

---

[36] Robert Adams, 'The Metaphysical Lightness of Being', paper presented to the Philosophy Department colloquium at the University of Notre Dame, 7 Apr. 2011.

[37] See Gerald Vision, 'Reference and the Ghost of Parmenides', in Rudolf Haller (ed.), *Non-Existence and Predication* (Amsterdam: Rodopi, 1986), 297–326.

[38] Recall Ch. 1, 'Terminological Clarifications: Platonism'.

intentional statements. Routley is especially emphatic about there being true intentional statements in which things that do not exist are referred to or quantified over, for example:

1. Ponce de Leon was searching for the Fountain of Youth.
2. Some people don't believe in any of Meinong's non-existent objects.
3. An actual person sometimes wants something that doesn't exist.
4. A cyclone, code-named Thales, is expected to form in the Coral Sea.
5. Some mathematicians mistakenly think that every consistent item exists.

Since intentionality results in intensional, as opposed to extensional, contexts, he observes: 'The overwhelming part of everyday, and also of extraordinary, of scientific and of technical discourse is intensional.'[39] Statements of this sort are universally regarded as true. But they are not generally regarded as genuine statements about things that do not exist because intensional contexts are 'opaque', that is to say, one cannot quantify into such contexts or refer to the objects which are the denotations of the singular terms appearing in those contexts.

But why not? This exemption is simply the unpleasant consequence of adopting the customary criterion of ontological commitment, if that criterion is to be at all plausible. Exempting intensional frameworks might well be seen as an ad hoc adjustment aimed at saving an otherwise implausible criterion. On a neutral logic, quantifying into intensional contexts is not ontologically committing and so need not result in ontological extravagances. So from (1) above, one may validly infer

6. There is something that Ponce de Leon was searching for,

meaning merely that the explorer was not aimlessly rambling about, but had an object in mind, for which he was looking. This is not to say that in certain situations the assertion of a statement like (6) does not convey and would not be taken to convey the speaker's conviction about the real existence of something. It is merely to insist that quantificational phrases are not, in virtue of their meaning, ontologically committing.

---

[39] Routley, *Exploring Meinong's Jungle*, 8. He presents his theory of objects as the key to intentionality.

Van Inwagen exploits the situational relativity of neutral quantificational phrases to try to make the neo-Meinongian position look silly:

> One day my friend Wyman told me that there was a passage on page 253 of volume IV of Meinong's *Collected Works* in which Meinong admitted that his theory of objects was inconsistent. Four hours later, after considerable fruitless searching, I stamped into Wyman's study and informed him with some heat that there was no such passage. 'Ah,' said Wyman, 'you're wrong. There is such a passage. After all, you were looking for it: there is something you were looking for. I think I can explain your error; although there *is* such a passage, it doesn't *exist*. Your error lay in your failure to appreciate this distinction.' I was indignant.
>
> My refusal to recognize a distinction between existence and being is simply my indignation, recollected in tranquility and generalized.[40]

In this admittedly funny story, Wyman, presumably an adherent of neutral logic, is prepared to quantify into an intensional context without ontological commitment: after all, van Inwagen was not just browsing through Meinong; there was something he was intent on finding. By contrast, van Inwagen, a meta-ontological Quinean, knows that, given his own criterion of ontological commitment, quantifying into such a context would lead to an ontological falsehood, so van Inwagen exempts intensional contexts from the quantifier's reach.

But with what justification? The implication of the joke is that neutral logic would lead us into egregious misunderstandings. But that is surely not the case. Any neutralist would recognize that Wyman's original assertion would be taken to imply that upon turning to page 253 of volume IV, one might read Meinong's confession, and that van Inwagen's indignant protest that there is no such passage was intended to convey the opposite. Everyone knows that 'there is' is often used in ordinary language to express the existence of real world objects—but, according to the neutralist, not always and

---

[40] Peter van Inwagen, *Ontology, Identity, and Modality: Essays in Metaphysics* (Cambridge: CUP, 2001), 16. As the name 'Wyman' reveals, what we have here represented is the caricature of Meinongianism given by Quine in his influential essay 'On What There Is', *Review of Metaphysics*, 2 (1948): 21–38, not genuine Meinongianism. See comments by Graham Priest, *Towards Non-Being: The Logic and Metaphysics of Intentionality* (Oxford: Clarendon, 2005), 108.

automatically. There are contextual clues and rhetorical devices by means of which we can make our intentions clear. Ironically, in his discussion of neo-Meinongianism, van Inwagen himself uses italics to signal an ontologically relevant use of 'there is': 'There *is* no nonexistent poison in the paranoid's drink. There *is* no such thing as his uncle's malice.'[41] Thus, by double italicizing Wyman's statement 'there *is* such a passage, but it doesn't *exist*', van Inwagen fosters the desired appearance of contradiction. As his closing remark indicates, van Inwagen misinterprets the neo-Meinongian's advocacy of neutral logic as the attempt to draw a distinction between being and existence.[42] But neo-Meinongians like Routley regard 'being' and 'existence' as synonymous but lightweight and, therefore, not ontologically committing.

Van Inwagen is assuming his own meta-ontological criterion of ontological commitment when he issues the following challenge to the neo-Meinongian: 'If you think there are things that do not exist, give me an example of one. The right response to your example will be either, "That does too exist," or "There is no such thing as that".'[43] Here the two prongs of the 'right response' make it evident that van Inwagen is assuming that 'there is' carries ontological commitment, so that the second prong, 'There is no such thing as that', means to deny that the thing in question does exist. So if I, in response to his challenge, say, 'the hole in my shirt', a retort by van Inwagen, 'That does, too, exist', seems ontologically extravagant; while the retort, 'There is no such thing as that', means only that the hole in my shirt does not exist in a metaphysically heavy sense, which is precisely what I already affirmed! On a neutral logic, I can quantify over holes in my shirt without ontological commitment to holes as existing things. To return to the subject of intensional contexts, given a neutral logic, I can quantify into an intensional context like 'Peter contemplated the two holes in my shirt' by asserting 'There are two holes in my shirt which Peter contemplated' without ontological commitment to holes, whereas an existentially loaded logic will be hobbled in its permitted

---

[41] Van Inwagen, *Ontology, Identity, and Modality*, 16; cf. Van Inwagen, 'Fiction and Metaphysics', *Philosophy and Literature* 7/1 (1983): 68.

[42] See also van Inwagen, 'Theory of Properties', 129; Van Inwagen, 'Being, Existence, and Ontological Commitment', 480.

[43] Van Inwagen, *Ontology, Identity, and Modality*, 16; similarly, van Inwagen, 'Theory of Properties', 129; Van Inwagen, 'Being, Existence, and Ontological Commitment', 481.

inferences by the presupposition of the neo-Quinean criterion of ontological commitment.

Tensed Statements

A second respect in which existentially loaded quantification is markedly disadvantageous concerns tensed statements about no longer existent or not yet existent individuals. Routley is a presentist, who denies that the past and future are on an ontological par with the present. I have elsewhere argued at length in favour of such a tensed view of time and consider it a natural concomitant of theism.[44] Even if some partisans of tensed time deny that future contingent statements are true or false, nonetheless, very few have the temerity to deny that past-tense statements about individuals who do not presently exist are true.[45] For example, it seems indisputably true that 'There have been forty-four US presidents'. The non-existence of most of them is no impediment to our quantifying over past US presidents. To infer from the truth of such statements that time is, in fact, tenseless and that past and future individuals are on an ontological par with present individuals would be to draw a breathtaking metaphysical inference on the basis of the slim reed of the neo-Quinean criterion of ontological commitment.

It is noteworthy that in debates over presentism, tenseless time theorists tend simply to presuppose without argument that quantification is ontologically committing, and so our ability to quantify over past/future individuals in true sentences is taken to commit us to their existence.[46] Thus, Theodore Sider muses, 'Since ordinary talk and

---

[44] See my *The Tensed Theory of Time: A Critical Examination* (Dordrecht: Kluwer Academic Publishers, 2000) and my *The Tenseless Theory of Time: A Critical Examination* (Dordrecht: Kluwer Academic Publishers, 2000).

[45] Ulrich Meyer is right: 'Caesar did cross the Rubicon; that's what started the civil war. Any philosophical view that forces us to deny claims like [that] is for that reason unacceptable': 'The Presentist's Dilemma', *Philosophical Studies*, 122/3 (2005): 223.

[46] See, e.g. David Lewis, 'Tensed Quantifiers', *Oxford Studies in Metaphysics*, i (2004): 3–14. Notoriously, Lewis also presented a similar quantificational justification for belief in modal realism on the grounds that there are ways the world might have been. Not only is such a metaphysical commitment to the reality of other worlds extravagant, but by the same token, there are also, then, impossible worlds, ways the world could not have been—Margery Bedford Naylor, 'A Note on David Lewis's Realism about Possible Worlds', *Analysis*, 46/1 (1986): 28–9; Takashi Yagisawa, 'Beyond Possible Worlds', *Philosophical Studies*, 53/2 (1988): 175–204—which reduces modal realism to absurdity.

thought are full of quantification over non-present objects, presentists are in a familiar predicament: in their unreflective moments they apparently commit themselves to far more than their ontological scruples allow.'[47] In fact, the only person in a predicament here is the presentist who also accepts the neo-Quinean criterion of ontological commitment. It never seems to occur to tenseless time theorists that our ability to quantify over purely past/future individuals in true sentences might be a good reason to reject the criterion of ontological commitment which they unquestioningly presuppose. Sider himself thinks that the presentist should adopt a sort of fictionalism: sacrifice the truth of past- and future-tense statements in favour of their quasi-truth or verisimilitude. There is no reason the presentist should accept such a fool's bargain, for it is far more obvious that, for example, the statement 'Some medieval theologians wrote in Latin' is true than that the neo-Quinean criterion of ontological commitment is true. Sider notwithstanding, we *do* speak as if presentism is true, but we do *not* speak as if quantification is a device of ontological commitment. That is why we quantify freely over merely past objects without thinking that such objects therefore exist.

The tensed time theorist can hardly be blamed if he elects to deny the neo-Quinean criterion of ontological commitment rather than surrender his view of time. Of course, if we had strong independent grounds for preferring a tenseless view of time, then Routley's argument would be void. But we have, in my view, no such grounds.[48]

The case of tensed truths serves as just another illustration of Routley's first point about logic's inability to handle intensional contexts when the quantifiers are taken to be existentially loaded. From 'Aristotle was born at Stagira', for example, we cannot infer that 'Someone was born at Stagira', since that would involve quantification over a non-existent. The advantage of neutral logic is that it allows us to quantify into such intensional contexts without the need for elaborate paraphrase or committing ourselves to the existence of the things quantified over.

---

[47] Theodore Sider, 'Presentism and Ontological Commitment', *Journal of Philosophy*, 96/7 (1999): 325.

[48] See further Trenton Merricks, *Truth and Ontology* (Oxford: Clarendon Press, 2007), who challenges the argument that past- and future-tense truths require the tenseless existence of truthmakers of such statements.

Modal Statements

A third and related respect in which existentially loaded quantification threatens to lead to metaphysically outrageous conclusions concerns modal discourse. Oxford logician Timothy Williamson has argued on purely logical grounds for the radical thesis that everything that exists exists necessarily.[49] Williamson calls this view necessitism. Contingentism is just the denial of this view, namely, the view that some things exist contingently.

In order to accommodate the apparent fact that many concrete objects do not exist necessarily, Williamson maintains that such objects could have been, and, indeed, once were or will be, abstract objects (or, at least, non-concrete objects).[50] So, for example, I, as a necessary being, could have been and once was a non-concrete object. I existed prior to my conception—not, of course, as a concrete, spatiotemporal object, but as a non-concrete object which later became concrete. What sort of object was I? I was once a merely possible person, an impersonal thing which could be and did become a concrete person, and in worlds in which I never exist as a person, I remain a merely possible person.[51] So on Williamson's view, I am not essentially a person.

Most people (including professional metaphysicians!) find necessitism to be an outrageously implausible thesis which we should, if at all possible, avoid. It is therefore noteworthy that Williamson's arguments for necessitism depend crucially on taking the quantifiers of first-order logic to be devices of ontological commitment. For example, he compares favourably arguments for necessitism with Lewis and Sider's arguments against presentism based upon quantification over past realities:

---

[49] Timothy Williamson, *Modal Logic as Metaphysics* (Oxford: OUP, 2013).

[50] Williamson recoils from calling objects which are contingently non-concrete 'abstract' because they do not fit in with paradigmatic abstract objects like mathematical objects (ibid., 7). But abstract objects come in a bewildering variety, and by the definition of 'abstract' as 'causally impotent', such non-concrete objects qualify as abstract objects. So it is not unfair, I think, to say that on Williamson's view, I could have been and, indeed, once was, an abstract object.

[51] Williamson rejects the predicative reading of 'possible person', according to which a possible person is a kind of person, in favour of the attributive reading, according to which a possible person is something that could have been a person (ibid., 10–12). Cf. Williamson's correction of A. N. Prior for referring to a merely possible person as 'someone' rather than 'something' (ibid., 68).

David Lewis challenges presentists to analyse in their terms sentences such as 'There have been infinitely many kings named John' (compare 'There are infinitely many possible stars'), in order to cast doubt on the truth of presentism. Ted Sider challenges sceptics who claim that the dispute between presentism and eternalism is merely verbal to analyse in presentist terms sentences of the form 'Half the objects from all of time that are Ks are Ls' (compare 'There are at least as many possible planets as possible stars').[52]

These lame arguments for a tenseless theory of time, depending as they do on the assumption that existential quantification is ontologically committing, ought, in my opinion, to cast more doubt on the neo-Quinean criterion of ontological commitment than on presentism.

As the parenthetical comparisons in the quotation suggest, Williamson considers the non-paraphrasability of certain quantified modal truths like 'There are uncountably many possible stars' to indicate ontological commitments on the part of the person who asserts them. The same assumption underlies his boast that necessitists (unlike contingentists) can straightforwardly use quantification over possible worlds.[53]

Williamson makes no attempt at all to justify the assumption that first-order quantification is existentially loaded. He merely explains:

> By definition, ontology concerns what there is. Claims of the form 'There is a G' are naturally paraphrased by first-order sentences of the form $\exists x\, Gx$. The quantification in 'There is a G' is not into predicate position, even if 'G' is replaced by 'property', 'relation', or 'concept'. Ontology is part of metaphysics. The content of the ontological commitment is true if there is a G and false otherwise. Its truth value depends on how the mostly non-linguistic world is, as characterized in first-order terms.[54]

The problem is that sentences of the form 'There is a G' or even 'G exists' have a very light sense in ordinary English, and so some justification is needed for taking the formal quantifiers that abbreviate them as involving metaphysically heavy commitments.

---

[52] Ibid., 368; cf. 150. The references are to David Lewis, 'Tensed Quantifiers', *Oxford Studies in Metaphysics*, i (2004): 3–14; Theodore Sider, 'Quantifiers and Temporal Ontology', *Mind*, 115/457 (2006): 75–97.
[53] Williamson, *Modal Logic as Metaphysics*, 376.   [54] Ibid., 261.

Williamson's deductive formulations of his arguments for necessitism make it especially clear that he takes first-order quantifiers to carry ontological commitments,[55] for the arguments will typically involve some premiss in which it is asserted that $(\exists x)\,(x = y)$, leading to a necessitist conclusion like

NNE.$\Box((\forall x)(\Box(\exists x)(x = y)))$.

That is to say, necessarily, for any x, necessarily there is an object to which x is identical. But on a neutral logic, (NNE) is itself innocuous. Of course, necessarily, everything is necessarily identical to something, namely, itself; but that does not imply that that thing exists. So, for example, Allah is identical to Allah, but Allah is not identical to Zeus, whether or not either one exists.

Necessitism illustrates the sort of metaphysical debacle which the neo-Quinean criterion of ontological commitment helps to generate.[56] Williamson declares, 'what we want is not a weak modal logic, neutral on the relevant metaphysical questions. Rather, we want a strong modal logic that answers those metaphysical questions.'[57] I should think that precisely the opposite is true. We want a modal logic that is neutral as to ontological commitments. Williamson complains in another context that 'Metaphysics based on weak logic wastes its time taking crank theories seriously.'[58] To the contrary, basing metaphysics on an existentially loaded, metaphysically strong modal logic helps to generate a theory like necessitism, which is about as cranky as they get.

Mereological Statements

Finally, a fourth area where the disadvantages of existentially loaded quantification become evident is mereology, or the study of parts and wholes. Contemporary debates in mereology have focused upon the

---

[55] Ibid., 288–96.
[56] See Takashi Yagisawa, 'Critical notice of *Modal Logic as Metaphysics*, by Timothy Williamson,' *Notre Dame Philosophical Reviews* (15 Oct. 2013), <http://ndpr.nd.edu/news/43612-modal-logic-as-metaphysics>.
[57] Williamson, *Modal Logic as Metaphysics*, 429. Boldly asserting that 'Logic has no metaphysically neutral core', Williamson affirms that 'on the standard objectual interpretation of the first-level quantifiers, the semantics cannot "serve as a neutral device for exploring alternative views about possible objects"' (146).
[58] Ibid., 226.

so-called special composition question, namely, what conditions have to be met in order for a plurality to compose an object.[59] The predominant answer to that question among contemporary metaphysicians is mereological universalism. This view assumes a principle of unrestricted mereological composition (UMC), according to which any plurality whatsoever composes an object:

> UMC. Necessarily, whenever there are some things, then there is a fusion of those things.

So Lewis, on the basis of (UMC), holds that there is such a thing as a trout-turkey, a fusion, for example, of the front half of a particular trout and the back half of a particular turkey.[60] Given (UMC), there are even objects like the sum of me and $\sqrt{2}$. 'Though the view presents a wildly counterintuitive description of reality,' Ross Inman observes, 'there are surprisingly powerful arguments in its favor, which partly explains its widespread appeal among many contemporary metaphysicians.'[61] That appeal is so strong that Hud Hudson can write, 'the view becoming (if not already) the orthodoxy among those writing in mereological metaphysics is that composition is absolutely unrestricted; any plurality whatever has a mereological sum or fusion'.[62]

Does (UMC) force us to include such wildly counter-intuitive objects as trout-turkeys in our ontological inventory? No; it is only the conjunction of (UMC) with the neo-Quinean criterion of ontological commitment that would foist such commitments upon us. Hence, some theorists have sought to soften the impact of (UMC) by denying that it involves ontological commitment to any object in addition to the plurality of objects summed together. Lewis gives the following assurance:

> To be sure, if we accept mereology, we are committed to the existence of all manner of mereological fusions. But given a prior commitment to cats, say, a commitment to cat-fusions is not *a further* commitment.

---

[59] For what follows, I am indebted to Ross Inman, 'On Christian Theism and Unrestricted Composition', paper presented at the annual meeting of the Evangelical Philosophical Society, Milwaukee, WI, Nov. 2012.

[60] David Lewis, *Parts of Classes*, with an Appendix by John P. Burgess, A. P. Hazen, and David Lewis (Oxford: Basil Blackwell, 1991), 80.

[61] Inman, 'Christian Theism and Unrestricted Composition'.

[62] Hud Hudson, 'Confining Composition', *Journal of Philosophy*, 103/12 (2006): 633.

The fusion is nothing over and above the cats that compose it. It just *is* them. They just *are* it.... In general, if you are already committed to some things, you incur no further commitment when you affirm the existence of their fusion. The new commitment is redundant, given the old one.[63]

Lewis's back-pedalling is eloquent testimony to the implausibility of so bloated an ontology as that apparently sanctioned by (UMC). The difficulty for Lewis is that he accepts the neo-Quinean criterion of ontological commitment, so that his meta-ontology commits him, in spite of himself, to the existence of objects over and above the plurality of objects composing the fusion.[64] He says, 'Only if you speak with your quantifiers wide open must you affirm the trout-turkey's existence. If, like most of us all the time and all of us most of the time, you quantify subject to restrictions, then you can leave it out. You can declare that there just does not exist any such thing— *except*, of course, among the things you're ignoring.'[65] But, Lewis concedes, 'Once you've said "there is" your game is up.'[66]

Hardier advocates of (UMC) do not shrink from admitting the additional objects into their ontology. Thus, an obviously discomfited Lynne Rudder Baker writes,

> So, are sums objects or not?... Since I have endorsed universalism, I must (hold my nose and) say that sums are objects. However, the unpalatability of commitment to arbitrary sums is mitigated by the fact that the ontological difference that sums make is negligible: the only ontological effect of holding that sums are objects is to increase the number of existing objects.[67]

We can, however, avoid the noxious smell of mereological universalism simply by abandoning the neo-Quinean criterion of ontological commitment. Given neutral quantifiers, we can talk freely about

---

[63] Lewis, *Parts of Classes*, 81–2.
[64] Phillip Bricker rightly protests Lewis's claim to 'ontological innocence', commenting, 'If I am ontologically committed to A and to B, then I am thereby ontologically committed to [the mereological sum] A+B. For that reason I don't need to list A+B as a separate item in my ontology. But it is a separate item in this sense: it is not identical to any of the other items in my ontology. It really (literally, altogether) exists.' Phillip Bricker, personal correspondence, cited by Lynne Rudder Baker, *The Metaphysics of Everyday Life: An Essay in Practical Realism* (Cambridge: CUP, 2007), 192.
[65] Lewis, *Parts of Classes*, 80.   [66] Ibid., 81.
[67] Baker, *Metaphysics of Everyday Life*, 193. She says this only after futilely trying to differentiate sums from genuine objects.

mereological sums without ontological commitment. Existentially loaded quantification is a positive impediment to mereology and, hence, to metaphysics, an assumption which the discipline would be well without.

CONCLUDING REMARKS

The foregoing considerations are sufficient, in my opinion, to warrant rejection of the neo-Quinean view of formal and informal quantifiers. But that conclusion may remain moot. What is important for our purposes, rather, is that these considerations, coupled with the want of any arguments for the truth of the neo-Quinean meta-ontological rules, certainly suffice to show that the neo-Quinean criterion of ontological commitment is far from incumbent upon us and that therefore the theist may plausibly reject it. Alex Orenstein wisely reminds us that 'There are fashions in philosophical explications', one of which is today taking metaphysically heavy existence assertions to be expressed by the first-order existential quantifier.[68] It is perfectly reasonable to buck the fashion trend in this regard. So doing opens the door for affirming truths like 'There is a prime number between 2 and 4' without commitment to the existence of mathematical objects.

---

[68] Alex Orenstein, 'Is Existence What Existential Quantification Expresses?', in Robert B. Barrett and Roger F. Gibson (eds), *Perspectives on Quine* (Oxford: Basil Blackwell, 1990), 266. Orenstein follows neutralists in introducing an existence predicate instead in order to express existential claims.

7

Making Ontological Commitments (2)

Although Quine thought that it is only through quantification that we make ontological commitments, neo-Quineans think that singular terms are also devices of ontological commitment. This conviction comes to expression in the first part of premiss (I) of the Indispensability Argument for abstract objects:

> I. If a simple sentence (i.e. a sentence of the form 'a is F') is literally true, then the objects that its singular terms denote exist.

Here the truth of 'a is F' is said to require the existence of some object which is the referent of the singular term 'a'.

What is at stake here is one's theory of reference. Must singular terms refer to something in order for a sentence featuring them to be true, and does successful reference imply that there is something in the world which is the referent (or denotation) of the relevant term? Proponents of the Indispensability Argument answer 'Yes' to both of these questions.

FREE LOGIC, NEUTRALISM, AND NEO-MEINONGIANISM

In contrast to neo-Quineans, so-called 'free' logicians and neutralists challenge the claim that the use of singular terms in sentences we take to be true is ontologically committing. One might also think that this claim is repudiated by neo-Meinongians. For example, Routley holds that the sense of 'refer' in ordinary English is ontologically neutral, although the word has become existentially loaded in philosophical usage:

> The word 'refer' is used in everyday English (see *OED*), in the relevant sense, to indicate merely the subject or topic of discourse, or subject-matter, or even more loosely what such discourse touched upon or what was drawn attention to or mentioned. *Any* subject of discourse can count as referred to, including nonentities of diverse kinds; in this sense there is not commitment to existence. Superimposed on this non-theoretical usage we have a philosophers' usage which embodies theoretical assumptions about language, according to which the reference of a subject expression is some existing item (or extensionally characterised entity) in the actual world.[1]

Because the word 'refer' has become so loaded with existence assumptions among philosophers, Routley thinks that we have little choice but to reserve the word 'refer' for the relation between a singular term and an existing entity. So he concedes that a singular term '*a*' has reference only in the case that the object *a* exists. Nevertheless, even if *a* does not exist, '*a*' can still be 'about' or 'signify' or 'designate' *a*. Reference can be defined in terms of aboutness: to say that '*a*' refers to *b* is to say that '*a*' is about *b*, and *b* exists. 'Then "refers to" is existentially loaded and can do the classical work of "hooking language onto the world" . . . '[2] But we can still use '*a*' irreferentially as the proper subject of a true sentence.

Appearances notwithstanding, however, Routley, along with other neo-Meinongians, remains, in a sense, deeply committed to referentialism with respect to singular terms. For he construes reference as a relation between words and objects. Indeed, neo-Meinongianism is a kind of hyper-referentialism, in that it takes there to be objects correlated with *every* singular term, whether occurring in a true sentence or not. Meinong held that there are non-existent objects correlated with singular terms like 'the golden mountain' and even with contradictory terms like 'the round square'.[3] Routley concedes

---

[1] Richard Routley, *Exploring Meinong's Jungle and Beyond: An Investigation of Noneism and the Theory of Items* (Canberra: Australian National University Research School of Social Sciences, 1979), 53. The *OED* is, of course, the *Oxford English Dictionary*.

[2] Routley, *Exploring Meinong's Jungle*, 617.

[3] Alexius Meinong, 'The Theory of Objects' ('*Über Gegenstandstheorie*', 1904), tr. Isaac Levi et al., in Roderick M. Chisholm (ed.), *Realism and the Background of Phenomenology* (Atascadero, CA: Ridgeview, 1960), 82.

that for Meinong, every term designates an object, but Routley insists that on Meinong's view, not every such object exists.[4] Granted; but Routley is able to deny that such terms successfully refer to their correlative objects only by taking reference to be existentially loaded. Inasmuch as there are, indeed, such correlative objects, no singular terms are truly vacuous or empty, even if they are, in Routley's peculiar, existentially loaded sense, irreferential. Neo-Meinongianism accepts wholeheartedly the assumption that successful reference is a relation in which words stand to certain objects, and even goes so far as to say that no singular terms fail to stand in such a relation.

The conviction that there are objects standing in relation to singular terms sets neo-Meinongianism apart from neutralism, which denies that successfully referring terms require correlative objects. When we assert '2 is an even prime number', the anti-realist neutralist and neo-Meinongian agree that we have spoken truly, despite the fact that 2 does not exist. But whereas the neutralist holds that my having successfully said something about 2 does not require that there is any object answering to the term '2', the neo-Meinongian holds that there is, indeed, such an object, though it does not exist.

Free logic is more of a mixed bag. Developed only since the 1950s, free logic accepts that the quantifiers of first-order logic are ontologically committing, but it denies that singular terms are devices of ontological commitment. As John Nolt explains, free logic can be semantically characterized as a formal logic whose quantifiers are interpreted objectually with respect to a specified domain D—which is usually taken to be the class of existing objects—but whose singular terms may either refer to objects outside of D or fail to refer at all.[5] Free logic employs an existence predicate 'E' in order to distinguish terms that refer to members of D from those that do not. For any singular term t, 't exists' is true if and only if t refers to a member of D.

---

[4] Routley, *Exploring Meinong's Jungle*, 490.
[5] John Nolt, 'Free Logic', *The Stanford Encyclopedia of Philosophy*, 5 Apr. 2010, <http://plato.stanford.edu/entries/logic-free>, §1.1. For a wonderfully limpid exposition of this semantical approach, see John Nolt, 'Free Logics', in Dale Jacquette (ed.), *Handbook of the Philosophy of Science*, v. *Philosophy of Logic* (Amsterdam: Elsevier, 2006), 1023–60.

Empty or vacuous singular terms are simply terms that fail to refer to a member of *D*.

As Nolt indicates, singular terms which do not refer to an existing object may be regarded either as irreferential (not referring to anything at all) or as referring to something not in the domain *D*. In order to allow reference to something outside *D*, one can provide a dual domain semantics, as Nolt explains:

> In a single-domain semantics *the* domain typically represents the class of the existing things, and empty singular terms have no referents.... In a dual-domain semantics... singular terms may refer to objects outside the quantificational domain. These outlying objects are collected into a second or *outer* domain, in contrast to which the usual quantificational domain is described as *inner*. The inner domain typically represents the class of existing things; the outer, correlatively, includes nonexistents. Thus on a dual-domain semantics all singular terms refer, but not all refer to existing things; the term 'empty' is therefore not equivalent to 'non-referring' or 'non-denoting', as it is in single domains semantics.[6]

Dual domain semantics sounds very much like neo-Meinongianism, unless one adopts a pretence theoretical approach to the outer domain and its members, whereas single domain semantics is akin to neutralism with respect to singular terms.

Advocates of so-called positive (as opposed to negative or neutral) free logic maintain that certain sentences can be truly asserted even though they contain singular terms that do not refer to any existing objects. But because free logic, unlike neutral logic, takes the first-order quantifiers to be ontologically committing to existing objects, free logic must impose restrictions on the rules of inference known as Existential Generalization (EG) and Universal Instantiation (UI), so that they hold only for things to which the existence predicate applies. So, for example, from the truth of 'Sherlock Holmes is the most famous detective of English fiction', we cannot infer that $\exists x \, (x = $ the most famous detective of English fiction). By the same token, from the arithmetic truth that $3 < 5$ we cannot infer that $\exists x \, (x < 5)$. By contrast, the neutralist welcomes such inferences, since on neutral logic, in contrast to free logic, the quantifier $\exists$ is not a device of ontological commitment.

---

[6] Nolt, 'Free Logics', 1025; cf. his 'Free Logic', §3.

SINGULAR TERMS AND ONTOLOGICAL COMMITMENT

So how shall we assess the neo-Quinean's claim that the use of singular terms in sentences we take to be true commits us to the existence of the things referred to? Azzouni points out that the majority tradition, which opposes the minority neo-Meinongian tradition, remains deeply conflicted about how to understand vacuous singular terms. Azzouni identifies four powerful, conflicting intuitions that serve to divide the majority tradition:

1. *Aboutness.* When we talk or think about something, we often do so in a singular way.
2. *Normality.* Thoughts and statements about non-existents have the same form and structure as ordinary statements about existents.
3. *Truth.* Thoughts and statements about non-existents have specific truth values.
4. *Nonexistence.* There are no objects serving as referents of vacuous singular terms.

Azzouni's neutralism aspires to satisfy all these intuitions.

Azzouni denies the crucial assumption underlying both neo-Meinongian and neo-Quinean views that statements involving singular terms 'are true and false on the basis of the properties had by objects referred to by the singular terms appearing in those statements'.[7] He distinguishes between reference^R (or aboutness^R), which is a relation between a term and an object, and reference^E (or aboutness^E), which is not a relation, but a characterization that applies to empty singular terms in a discourse.[8] This distinction allows Azzouni to maintain that the use of singular terms is ontologically neutral: 'the ordinary words "about" and "refer" are neutral between uses of them that indicate genuine relations between language and thought and the world, and pseudo-relations: terms that have the appearance of relations but aren't'.[9] Azzouni differentiates his view from those of the

---

[7] Jody Azzouni, *Talking about Nothing: Numbers, Hallucinations, and Fictions* (Oxford: OUP, 2010), 58. Azzouni continues: 'or that fall within the range of one or another kind of quantifier appearing in those statements'.

[8] Ibid., 24. Azzouni actually uses blindingly tiny, lower case superscripts, for which I have substituted more visible upper case letters.

[9] Ibid., 44.

neo-Quinean and the neo-Meinongian, who are united in construing reference and aboutness as in every case a relation to an object, whether existent or nonexistent. For Azzouni, reference^E and aboutness^E are object-directed, in the sense of being intentional, but they are not relations to an object of any sort.[10] So, for example, the singular term '2' does not, in Azzouni's view, refer^R to anything, for there is no object to which this term stands in a relation; but '2' is about^E the number 2, in that one's thoughts are 2-directed. Azzouni is even willing to say, using the ontologically neutral quantifier, that there is something to which we refer^E and about^E which we speak.[11] But by such an ontologically irrelevant assertion, he means to indicate merely the object-directedness of our thought and discourse. Azzouni thus offers a nuanced account of reference, according to which not all singular terms in true statements need have real-world referents.

It seems to me that Azzouni is on the right track here. As Routley observed, it is a datum of ordinary language that we frequently assert true statements which contain singular terms which do not denote existing objects. Consider the following examples:

- The weather in Atlanta will be hot today.
- Sherrie's disappointment with her husband was deep and unassuageable.
- The price of the tickets is ten dollars.
- Wednesday falls between Tuesday and Thursday.
- His sincerity was touching.
- James couldn't pay his mortgage.
- The view of the Jezreel Valley from atop Mt Carmel was breathtaking.
- Your constant complaining is futile.
- Spassky's forfeiture ended the match.
- He did it for my sake and the children's.

It would be fantastic to think that all of the singular terms featured in these plausibly true sentences have objects in the world corresponding to them.

---

[10] Cf. Jody Azzouni, 'Singular Thoughts (Objects-Directed Thoughts)', *Proceedings of the Aristotelian Society Supplementary Volume*, 85/1 (2011): 45–61, where he contrasts objects-directed thoughts with descriptive thoughts and equates 'about' with 'in mind'.

[11] Azzouni, *Talking about Nothing*, 45.

Making Ontological Commitments (2)   131

Examples like these are legion. In fact, I suspect that singular terms which refer to real-world objects may actually be the *exception* rather than the rule in ordinary language. Consider the following paragraph quoted by the British philosopher Michael Dummett from a London daily:

> Margaret Thatcher yesterday gave her starkest warning yet about the dangers of global warming caused by air pollution. But she did not announce any new policy to combat climate change and sea level rises, apart from a qualified commitment that Britain would stabilize its emissions of carbon dioxide—the most important 'greenhouse' gas altering the climate—by the year 2005. Britain would only fulfil that commitment if other, unspecified nations promised similar restraint.

Nothing unusual about such discourse—but, as Dummett observes, 'Save for "Margaret Thatcher," "air" and "sea," there is not a noun or noun phrase in this paragraph incontrovertibly standing for or applying to a concrete object....'[12] A lightweight Platonist, Dummett is unfazed about postulating objects as referents for such terms; but those who have a more robust sense of reality will be very hesitant about augmenting the world's population so profligately.[13]

It is noteworthy that several of Dummett's examples have to do with socially constructed realities like policies, commitments, and nations. On the influential analysis of Berkeley philosopher John Searle, socially constructed realities involve our assigning some function or status to a mind-independent object, according to the schema *X counts as Y in C*, where *C* is some social context.[14] For example, in our social context, a certain object counts as a screwdriver. Given human intentionality and civilization, it should come as no surprise that our discourse is pervaded by talk of such socially constructed objects. But, arguably, the only existing objects in such cases are the mind-independent *X*s, which are seen as *Y*s.

Money, for example, arguably does not exist, except in a metaphysically light sense. At most, what exist are things like pieces of

---

[12] Michael Dummett, *Frege: Philosophy of Mathematics* (Cambridge, MA: Harvard University Press, 1991), 231.

[13] Now, of course, neo-Quineans will claim that such sentences can be paraphrased in ways so as to avoid untoward ontological commitments. But then not only are these thinkers saddled with the two seemingly impossible tasks noted in the last chapter near the end of the section 'Why Accept the Realist's Criterion of Ontological Commitment?', but they are also stuck with the implausible view that *these* sentences, at least, do commit us to such ontological *grotesqueries*.

[14] John Searle, *The Construction of Social Reality* (New York: Free Press, 1995).

metal or paper, which in a certain social context count as money. If some South Pacific islanders decide to use cowrie shells as currency, the shells count as money in their society. If a disease were to wipe out the population of the island, the shells would still exist without any intrinsic change, but there would no longer be any money. The shells are not identical to the money, since they have different properties (for example, the shells antedated the money). But neither are there monetary objects distinct from the shells, since the shells are rightly taken to be money. It is better to say with Searle that socially constructed reality involves human beings' imposing functions on objects. Once this is done, social or institutional facts can contain symbolic elements which transcend the objects.

Consider, for example, a touchdown's being worth six points. Searle comments, 'The expression "six points" does not refer to some language-independent objects in the way that the expressions "the man," "the ball," "the line,"... refer to language-independent objects. Points are not "out there" in the way that... men, balls, and lines are out there.'[15] Once the appropriate conventions are in place, we can refer successfully to the touchdown scored at the end of the first quarter, even though objectively there is no such thing. There can thus be objective facts about social reality without the existence of the object referred to. Searle is therefore inclined to speak of social (or institutional) facts rather than objects.

So how does God see things? Searle notes, 'God could not see screwdrivers, cars, bathtubs, *etc.*, because intrinsically speaking there are no such things. Rather, God would see *us treating* certain objects as screwdrivers, cars, bathtubs, *etc.*'[16] The implication of socially constructed reality is that our discourse is pervaded by singular terms which do not refer to existents.

THE NATURE OF REFERENCE

How is it that we are able to assert truly sentences with empty singular terms? In order to get at this question, we first need to address the question, do vacuous singular terms refer? And in order to answer

---

[15] Ibid., 68.   [16] Ibid., 12.

that question, we need to ask what it is to refer, or what is the nature of reference? This question is largely neglected by contemporary theorists. Almost all contemporary theories of reference are actually theories about how to *fix* reference, rather than theories about the nature of reference itself.[17] The unspoken assumption behind most contemporary theories of reference is the presupposition that reference is a word–world relation, so that terms which refer must have real-world objects as their denotations. The very title of Quine's influential book *Word and Object* betrays this assumption.[18] Back in 1969, John Searle could assert that it is a 'generally accepted axiom' concerning reference and referring expressions that whatever is referred to must exist.[19] Searle regarded this axiom as a tautology, since it says only that one cannot refer to a thing if there is no such thing to be referred to. Searle just took it for granted that reference is or involves a word–world relation.

This underlying assumption remains widespread. In a standard philosophical encyclopedia, Timothy Williamson calls reference 'the central relation between language or thought and the world'.[20]

---

[17] Symptomatic is Marga Reimer's article 'Reference', in *The Stanford Encyclopedia of Philosophy,* 20 Jan. 2003, <http://plato.stanford.edu/entries/reference>. She simply takes for granted that 'Reference is a relation that obtains between expressions and what speakers use expressions to talk about.' So 'the central question' concerning reference then becomes 'How do words refer? What is the "mechanism" of reference?' Oblivious to intentionality, she thinks that 'certain types of words "hook onto" things in the world', as though words had such an ability in themselves. She even says that proper names themselves 'purport to refer' to particular things, as if they were intentional agents.

[18] See his remarks on vacuous names in W. V. O. Quine, *Word and Object* (Cambridge, MA: MIT Press, 1960), 177.

[19] John R. Searle, *Speech Acts: An Essay in the Philosophy of Language* (Cambridge: CUP, 1969), 77. Ironically, Searle's own construal of referring as a speech act strongly motivates a theory of reference that defeats the axiom, as we shall see. Significantly, Searle's subsequent study of socially constructed reality seems to have convinced him that successful reference does not, in fact, require the existence of real-world objects as the referents of referential terms, for reference comes into play only *after* we have created certain mind-dependent ontological categories which make it possible to refer or fail to refer to e.g. the touchdown scored at the end of the fourth quarter, even though there is no language-independent object referred to by the relevant expression (Searle, *Construction of Social Reality*, 68, 76).

[20] Timothy Williamson, 'Reference', in Donald Borchert (ed.), *Encyclopedia of Philosophy*, 2nd. edn (New York: Thomson-Gale, 2006). Joseph Margolis thinks that in the analytic tradition nearly everyone writing on the topic has assumed that reference is a relationship of some sort: 'Reference as Relational: *Pro* and *Contra*', in Rudolf Haller (ed.), *Non-Existence and Predication* (Amsterdam: Rodopi, 1986), 341. Diane Proudfoot and B. Jack Copeland observe that the thesis that reference is a

Williamson is right about the importance of reference; but the assumption that reference is a relation begs the question against certain theories of reference. In distinguishing reference^R, which is, indeed, a word–world relation, from reference^E, which is a non-relational sort of reference, Azzouni challenges this widespread assumption.

It seems to me, however, that Azzouni's evolving views on reference have not yet come to the most satisfactory form. For his reference^R is simply what most theorists take reference to be, and his reference^E remains unexplicated and mysterious. We are left wondering what it is and how it works.

It therefore behoves us to look more deeply into the nature of reference. It is an experiential datum that referring is a speech act carried out by an intentional agent.[21] Words in and of themselves engage in no such activity. Lifeless and inert, words are just ink marks on paper or sounds heard by a percipient. Absent an agent, shapes or noises do not refer to anything at all. If, for example, an earthquake were to send several pebbles rolling down a hillside which randomly came to rest in the configuration JOHN LOVES SUSIE, the names—if we would even call them names—would not refer to anybody.[22] As Searle argues, 'Since sentences...are, considered in one way, just objects in the world like any other objects, their capacity to represent is not intrinsic but is derived from the Intentionality of the mind.'[23]

---

relation, though deeply problematic, is entrenched in philosophy, psychology, linguistics, cognitive science, and artificial intelligence: 'Wittgenstein's Deflationary Account of Reference', *Language and Communication,* 22/3 (2002): 331–2.

[21] A fact emphasized by Searle, *Speech Acts,* 27; cf. Searle, *Construction of Social Reality,* 228. If Searle is correct that, in affirming that people have mental states which are intrinsically intentional, he has broken company with many, perhaps most, of the currently influential views in philosophy of mind—Searle, *Intentionality: An Essay in the Philosophy of Mind* (Cambridge: CUP, 1983), p. viii—then it is little wonder that contemporary theory of reference is in such turmoil! Look at the philosophical dead end reached by Alex Rosenberg, whose physicalism in philosophy of mind, coupled with his recognition that no physical object exhibits intentionality, lead him to deny that we ever think about anything, to claim that sentences are therefore meaningless, and to affirm that no sentence, including all the sentences in his own book, is true: Rosenberg, *The Atheist's Guide to Reality* (New York: W. W. Norton, 2011), 43, 170–93, 235, 309.

[22] Observing that it is 'evident that it [object-directedness] is a property which no non-mental entity could possibly possess', J. N. Findlay wryly remarks that, if stones refer to objects, then 'they undoubtedly have, or are, minds': *Meinong's Theory of Objects and Values,* 2nd edn (Oxford: Clarendon, 1963), 6.

[23] Searle, *Intentionality,* p. vii. 'A sentence is a syntactical object on which representational capacities are imposed' (pp. vii–viii). Language relates to reality in virtue

An interpreting agent uses his words as a means of referring to something.[24] Referring is thus an intentional activity of persons, and words are mere instruments. It is the great merit of the Swedish philosopher Arvid Båve's new deflationary theory of reference that he takes truly seriously the fact, given lip service everywhere, that it is *persons* who refer to things *by means of* their words, so that words at best refer only in a derivative sense, if at all.[25] As obvious as this point is, theorists of reference remain strangely oblivious to the fact. Reference continues to be very widely construed as a relation obtaining between words and objects in the world. This is the case with all of the deflationary theories of reference critically surveyed by Båve—whether disquotational (S. Leeds, H. Field, P. Horwich), propositional (P. Horwich), or anaphoric (R. Brandom). The neglect of persons in favour of words is also the crucial shortcoming of Azzouni's theory. Although Båve does not do so, he might have indicted all of the foregoing theories

---

of the fact that speakers so relate it in their performance of linguistic acts. '"How does language relate to reality?" is only a special case of "How does the mind relate to reality?"' (197). Searle therefore regards philosophy of language as a branch of the philosophy of mind. That reference does not belong primarily to the category of language is evident from the fact that mental reference precedes linguistic reference: R. M. Sainsbury, *Reference without Referents* (Oxford: Clarendon, 2005), 216. We sometimes refer to something by merely gesturing or glancing, which underlines the fact that reference springs from intentionality, not language.

[24] This is the answer to Horwich's question, 'How is it possible for those intrinsically inert ink marks (or some associated state of the brain) to reach out into the world and latch on to a definite portion of reality...?' Horwich, *Meaning* (Oxford: Clarendon, 1998), 1. For a nice statement of the answer, see Alvin Plantinga, 'Against Materialism', *Faith and Philosophy*, 23/1 (2006): 3–32, esp. 16–17; see also Dallas Willard, 'Knowledge and Naturalism', in William Lane Craig and J. P. Moreland (eds), *Naturalism: A Critical Analysis* (London: Routledge, 2000), 39–41. Searle points out that intentionality is more fundamental than language, since babies and even animals have intentional states. 'Only someone in the grip of a philosophical theory would deny that small babies can literally be said to want milk and that dogs want to be let out or believe that their master is at the door' (Searle, *Intentionality*, 5). Mental states are intrinsically (even if not always) intentional; intentionality cannot be reductively analysed, but is a ground floor property of the mind. By contrast, referring speech acts have a physical level of realization that is not intrinsically, but derivatively intentional (ibid., 27). According to Barry Loewer, it is today widely held that the semantic properties of natural language expressions are derived from the semantic properties of mental states: 'A Guide to Naturalizing Semantics', in Bob Hale and Crispin Wright (eds), *A Companion to the Philosophy of Language* (Oxford: Wiley-Blackwell, 1997), 108.

[25] Arvid Båve, 'A Deflationary Theory of Reference', *Synthèse*, 169/1 (2009): 51–73. I am very grateful to Arvid Båve for extended discussion of Båve's theory.

simply for their neglecting to construe reference primarily in terms of the speech acts of persons. Båve's significant contribution to our understanding reference is that he furnishes a central schema formulated in terms of the referring activity of persons. Båve provides the following schema for reference:

(R) *a* refers to *b* if and only if *a* says something (which is) about *b*,

where '*a*' always stands for a speaker. Though formulated in terms of persons rather than words, this account is truly deflationary because it does not attempt to tell us anything about the nature of reference itself. It leaves it entirely open whether reference is a relation (as Gottlob Frege and Alexius Meinong assumed) or whether it is an intentional property of a mind (as held by Franz Brentano and Edmund Husserl).

Taking reference to be a relation between a speaker and some object does make (R) ontologically committing to either existing or non-existing objects which are the referents of which one speaks. But no such commitment is involved for someone who, like Azzouni, stands in the tradition of Brentano and Husserl in thinking of reference as an intentional activity of agents which may or may not be correlated with real-world objects.[26] J. N. Findlay indicts Meinong primarily for his failure to appreciate his mentor Brentano's insight into the nature of reference:

> Meinong assumes throughout his treatment that an object is in some sense a logical *prius* of a conscious reference or intention: for there to be a conscious reference or intention there must in some wide sense *be* something which that reference or intention is 'of'.... Since this is

---

[26] Brentano insisted upon the uniqueness of mental phenomena as object-directed or intentional. The object-directedness of mental reference does not imply that intentional objects exist in the external world. 'All it means is that a mentally active subject is referring to them.' Franz Brentano, 'The Distinction between Mental and Physical Phenomena', tr. D. B. Terrell from *Psychologie vom empirischen Standpunckt* (1894), vol. i, bk. 2, ch. 1, repr. in Roderick M. Chisholm (ed.), *Realism and the Background of Phenomenology* (Atascadero, CA: Ridgeview, 1960), 50–1; Brentano, 'Genuine and Fictitious Objects', tr. D. B. Terrell from *Psychologie vom empirischen Standpunckt*, Supplementary Essay 9 (1911), repr. in *Realism and the Background of Phenomenology*, 71. For Husserl, by contrast, intentional objects are real-world objects about which one is thinking; but he denied that all intentional activity has intentional objects associated with it. Rejecting Meinongianism, Husserl held that, when no object exists, then the intentional activity exists without any object: *Logical Investigations*, 2 vols., tr. J. M. Findlay (New York: Humanities Press, 1970), ii. 595–6.

obviously not true in an ordinary sense in the case of *some* conscious intentions, there must, Meinong thinks, be a subtle sense or senses in which there *are* objects of such conscious intentions.... What should be seen is that this whole line of argumentation is wrong:... what our usage shows is that 'thinking' and its cognates are not relational expressions like 'above', 'before', 'killing', 'meeting', &c., nor can they be said to express relations.... We cannot therefore validly take an object of thought out of its object-position in a statement and make it an independent subject of reference: from 'X thinks of a Y as being Z' it does not follow that there is a Y which is being thought of by X, nor even that a thought-of Y really is Z....

That intentionality is not a relation but 'relation-like' (*relativliches*) is, of course, an insight of Brentano's: Meinong, who frequently surpassed his master, in this respect certainly lagged behind him. He could only conceive intentional references in terms of objects logically prior to them, on which they necessarily depended: hence, the many absurdities of his theory of objects.[27]

As an illustration of a property that is merely relation-like, Findlay gives *to-the-east-of-China*.[28] If China is really a constituent of this property, he says, then China must inhere, in all its solid immensity, in the Philippine Islands, which is absurd. Similarly, with respect to intentionality, if I think of X, my *thinking-of-X* is a mental relational property of which X is not a constituent. My state of mind has the relational property of *being-directed-to-X*, whether or not X exists. Of course, talk of properties here is just a useful *façon de parler*. We are simply engaged in the intentional activity of thinking-of-X or referring-to-X.

So on Båve's account, if I assert '$1+1=2$,' then I have said something about 2; it follows from (R) that I have thus referred to 2. But it does not follow that there is some such object, whether existent or nonexistent, as the number 2. One has the option of avoiding the inference to 'There is something to which I have referred' by restricting, with the free logicians, Existential Generalization, or the option of granting the inference but rendering it harmless by denying, with neutralism, that the existential quantifier is ontologically committing. Hence,

---

[27] Findlay, *Meinong's Theory of Objects*, 343–4.
[28] Ibid., 40–1. See also Margolis, 'Reference as Relational', 327–57; R. Scott Smith, *Naturalism and our Knowledge of Reality* (Farnham: Ashgate, 2012), esp. ch. 2, where he interprets Fred Dretske, Michael Tye, and William Lycan as endorsing a view of intentionality which construes it as a property, not a relation.

Båve recognizes the neutrality of his theory for the debate between realists and anti-realists.

Given (R), we now ask, what does it mean to say that *a* says something 'about' *b*, as stipulated by (R)? Båve proposes to 'analyse the expression "about", and then explain "refer" in terms of it'.[29] He offers the following schema as implicitly defining 'about':

(A) That $S(t)$ is about t,

where $S(\ )$ is a sentence context with a blank slot for singular terms. Again, Båve's account of aboutness is extraordinarily deflationary. It does not tell us what aboutness is, but simply provides a schema for determining what a that-clause containing a singular term (or, presumably, terms) is about. So, for example, that Ponce de Leon sought the Fountain of Youth is about Ponce de Leon and about the Fountain of Youth because the singular terms 'Ponce de Leon' and 'the Fountain of Youth' fill the blanks in the sentence context '____ sought ____.'

Now since (A) is so deflationary, I do not think we should take (A) as providing an *analysis* of aboutness or serving as an *explanation* of reference, as Båve claims. Indeed, taking (A) to explain (R) seems to get things exactly backwards. The reason why that $S(t)$ is about t is because '*t*' is used by some person to refer to *t*. On an account like Båve's, so-called 'speaker's reference'—what the speaker has in mind—becomes paramount, for, given schema (R), the only genuine referring is that done by the speaker.[30] Rather, schema (A) merely tells us when someone has said something about something, so as to meet the condition laid down by (R).

---

[29] Båve, 'Deflationary Theory of Reference', 63.

[30] Saul Kripke, 'Speaker's Reference and Semantic Reference', in Peter A. French et al. (eds), *Contemporary Perspectives in the Philosophy of Language* (Minneapolis: University of Minnesota Press, 1979), 6–27. Kripke recognized that words alone do not refer and so tried to explain the difference between what he took to be the semantic reference of the words and what the speaker meant to refer to by contrasting the speaker's general intentions with his specific intentions. But Kripke neither provided an explication of this vaguely characterized difference nor showed its plausible application to actual practice. As Searle notes, Kripke's distinction is not really about reference at all, since referring is something only speakers do, but is about the difference between the speaker's meaning and the linguistic meaning of the relevant expressions. Searle, *Expression and Meaning: Studies in the Theory of Speech Acts* (Cambridge: CUP, 1979), 155; Searle, *Speech Acts*, ch. 4. But the linguistic meaning of the words is beside the point, so far as reference is concerned.

Båve recognizes that schema (A) is no more ontologically committing to objects than (R): '(A) itself is neutral on how to conceive of the position following "about" in the instances of (A), so that we *could* deny the validity of the inference to "There is something such that I have a certain belief about it".'[31] So if I assert, 'Ponce de Leon sought the Fountain of Youth', I have said something which is both true and about the Fountain of Youth (as well as about Ponce de Leon); but we are not entitled to infer with Meinong that there is a non-existent object called the Fountain of Youth which this sentence is about. I can, therefore, say things about non-existents like Pegasus, the accident that was prevented, holes, or numbers without committing myself to there being objects of which I am speaking. This accords with the nature of intentionality, since intentional states of mind are not always about real-world objects.[32]

By construing, not just some, but all reference in terms of the referring activity of persons and understanding aboutness in terms of intentionality, we make an advance over Azzouni's views to arrive at a more satisfactory neutralist account. This account is consistent with anti-realism because successful singular reference does not require that there be objects in the world which stand in some sort of relation to a speaker's words. Of course, sometimes objects answering to the terms we use do exist. But in a surprisingly large number of cases, as our earlier illustrations showed, there are no such objects. That does not stop us from talking about them or referring to them, for these activities are, at least in such cases, purely intentional activities.

---

[31] Båve, 'Deflationary Theory of Reference', 71. Or, with the neutralist, we could grant the inference but deny that it is ontologically committing.

[32] Searle, *Intentionality*, 4. In Searle's view, as in Husserl's, not every intentional state has an intentional object. Every intentional state consists of an intentional content (which may or may not be propositional) in a psychological mode (such as fearing, desiring, believing, etc.) (*Intentionality*, 11–12). Since he takes intentional objects to be just real-world objects towards which one's mental states are directed, it follows that in the case of intentional states which have no real-world objects, one has an intentional content without there being an intentional object. So e.g. when Johnny fears the bogeyman, Johnny has an intentional content associated with 'bogeyman' in a psychological mode of fearing. Searle's view is in contrast with those who take intentional objects to be mere 'notional objects', i.e. what we think about, whether or not there are real-world objects correlated with such thoughts. The bogeyman is a notional object of Johnny's thoughts. Peter Lamarque and Stein Haugom Olsen, *Truth, Fiction, and Literature* (Oxford: Clarendon, 1994), 183–4, see the idea of notional objects as continuous with Brentano's understanding of intentional objects.

DISADVANTAGES OF TAKING SINGULAR TERMS TO BE ONTOLOGICALLY COMMITTING

Not only does the use of singular terms in sentences we take to be true seem to be non-committing ontologically, but, just as there are disadvantages to taking first-order quantification to be existentially loaded, so there are disadvantages to taking reference in true sentences to carry existential implications.

Karel Lambert, one of the pioneers of free logic, complains that, although modern logic in the late nineteenth century shed itself of various existence assumptions implicit in Aristotelian logic with respect to the use of general terms,[33] modern logic remains infected with existence assumptions with respect to the use of singular terms, assumptions that should not characterize a purely formal discipline.[34] For we have at the deepest level 'a primordial intuition that logic is a tool of the philosopher and ideally should be neutral with respect to philosophical truth.... So if there are preconditions to logic that have the effect of settling what exists and what does not exist, they ought to be eliminated because they corrupt the ideal of logic as a philosophical tool.'[35]

These existence assumptions regarding singular terms surface dramatically in the way in which standard modern logic handles identity

---

[33] These include the assumptions that in the traditional 'square of opposition', A-statements like 'All men are mortal' imply I-statements like 'Some man is mortal', while E-statements like 'No men are immortal' imply O-statements like 'Some man is not immortal'. Modern sentential logic strips Aristotelian logic of these existence assumptions by interpreting universally quantified statements to have the logical form of conditionals, e.g. 'If something is a man, then it is mortal', which carries no commitment to the existence of a man. Just as modern sentential logic aspires to be free of existence assumptions with respect to general terms, so free logic aspires to go one step further, to be free of existence assumptions when it comes to singular terms. According to Lambert, *Free Logic: Selected Essays* (Cambridge: CUP, 2003), 143–4, the central question posed by the free logician is why the assumption of existential import should be rejected for general terms but accepted for singular terms.

[34] See Karel Lambert, 'Existential Import Revisited', *Notre Dame Journal of Formal Logic*, 4/4 (1963): 288–92; Lambert, 'The Nature of Free Logic', in Lambert (ed.), *Philosophical Applications of Free Logic* (Oxford: OUP, 1991), 3–12; Lambert, *Free Logic*, 17–24; so also Rolf Schock, *Logics without Existence Assumptions* (Stockholm: Almqvist & Wiksell, 1968), 7–15. Nolt observes that, because the domain of quantification cannot be empty, contemporary standard logic treats many existential claims as logical truths: 'Free Logics', 1025.

[35] Karel Lambert, *Meinong and the Principle of Independence* (Cambridge: CUP, 1983), 98–9.

Making Ontological Commitments (2) 141

statements. For such statements cannot be true, according to standard logic, unless the referents of the singular terms employed in such statements exist. In other words, identity statements are ontologically committing for anyone who asserts them. But it seems bizarre to think that from a seemingly trivial truth of the form $t = t$, where t is some singular term, it follows that the thing denoted by t actually exists. Nevertheless, this is what standard logic requires. For from the truth of the predication 'a is F' it follows by Existential Generalization that $\exists x\ (Fx)$, or that something is F. So if we let 'F' be the predicate '$= a$', it follows from the identity statement $a = a$ that $\exists x\ (x = a)$, or that something is identical with a. The reader will recognize that this implication is troubling only if we take the quantifier to be existentially loaded. The neutral logician is unfazed by the inference that something is identical to a, since he does not take such a statement to carry a heavy metaphysical commitment. But for neo-Quineans and free logicians, with their existentially loaded quantifiers, $\exists x\ (x = a)$ just is the symbolization of 'a exists'.

Lambert takes this ontological implication of mere identity statements to be absurd. For it would follow from the fact 'Vulcan = Vulcan' that there is some object identical with Vulcan, that is to say, that Vulcan exists. Standard logic avoids this untoward result by treating all identity statements with vacuous singular terms as false. So standard logic must regard a statement like 'Vulcan = Vulcan' as false, even though it appears to be a tautology which is necessarily true. Standard logic cannot therefore distinguish the truth value of identity statements like 'Zeus = Zeus' and 'Zeus = Allah'. Yet, the first seems to be necessarily true and the second obviously false. Nor can standard logic affirm the truth of 'Aristotle = Aristotle' or 'Lincoln = Lincoln', since Aristotle and Lincoln no longer exist and so there are no things with which they can be identified. As I said before, it would be the height of ontological presumption to claim that the truth of such seemingly trivial statements implies a tenseless theory of time, according to which all persons throughout time are equally existent. Such an inference would only underscore the free logician's claim that modern logic is still infected with inappropriate existence assumptions.

As a result of its existence assumptions with respect to singular terms, standard logic becomes limited in its application to certain inferences and does not permit us to discriminate between inferences where the referentiality of the terms is crucial and those where it is not.³⁶ This violates the intuitive distinction between arguments whose validity does require existence assumptions and those which do not. For example, we are prohibited from inferring, 'Lincoln was the Great Emancipator; Lincoln brooded; therefore, the Great Emancipator brooded', an inference whose obvious validity should not be dependent on Lincoln's existing. Standard logic also cannot be applied to a statement like 'The object at position P on which no external forces are acting maintains a constant velocity' because there is no such object. Moreover, one might think that the methods of logic should apply to reasoning involving singular terms which, for all we know, may or may not refer to existing objects, as was the case for astronomers who used 'Vulcan' for the suspected planet between Mercury and the Sun before knowing whether such a planet existed or not. Nolt observes that the obligation to confirm the existence of things before naming them is so irksome that 'even mathematicians routinely flout it.... They get away with this, usually, only by being discreetly inexplicit about the underlying logic—which is, in consequence, not rigorously classical.'³⁷

Advocates of positive (as opposed to negative or neutral) free logic maintain that certain sentences can be truly asserted even though they contain irreferential singular terms. This feature of positive free logic strikes me as well-motivated and eminently plausible. The truth of identity statements involving vacuous singular terms is of a piece with the evident truth of many sentences which feature vacuous singular terms.³⁸ Free logic's denial that the use of singular terms in sentences we take to be true is ontologically committing for their user is, I think, a step in the right direction. But because free logic takes the existential quantifier of first-order logic to carry existence commitments, it cannot avoid the Platonistic commitments of much abstract object talk, such as 'There are prime numbers greater than 100'. Better to adopt a consistent neutralism, according to which

---

[36] Lambert, *Free Logic*, 143–4.   [37] Nolt, 'Free Logics', 1023.

[38] E.g. Henry Leonard complains that the object languages of traditional logical systems cannot meaningfully contain such attributions as 't is fictitious', since the truth of such an attribution requires that t exists, in which case, t is not fictitious after all. Thus, 't is fictitious' is false if t does exist and false if t does not exist, in contradiction to ordinary English. Henry S. Leonard, 'Essences, Attributes, and Predicates', *Proceedings and Addresses of the APA*, 37 (1963–4): 29–30. To escape this dilemma, neo-Quineans sometimes resort boldly to affirming the existence of fictitious entities as abstract objects.

first-order quantifiers are also not ontologically committing. Such a neutral logic will not, technically speaking, be a free logic; but as Alex Orenstein asks: 'Isn't a logic which disassociates the quantifiers from existence a paradigm of a logic that is free of existence assumptions, indeed freer of existence assumptions than Lambert's variety?'[39]

In sum, given a logic featuring existentially loaded quantifiers, the existence assumptions underlying the use of singular terms are going to force revisions in classical logic, like the restriction of Existential Generalization and Universal Instantiation, if plausible assignment of truth values to various sentences is to be preserved. We can avoid such major revisions by adopting a thoroughgoing neutral logic.

CONCLUDING REMARKS

In my opinion, the criterion of ontological commitment that comes to expression in premiss (I) of the Indispensability Argument is not only false, but, I should say, obviously false and wholly implausible. It is a meta-ontological thesis for which there is no good argument, and the linguistic evidence is overwhelmingly against it. Its assumption hinders logical reasoning. Most significantly for our purposes, it is outrageously inflationary ontologically, saddling us not only with innumerable abstract objects, but fantasies of almost every sort.

But never mind; for the purposes of our study, our conclusion may be much more modest: simply that the criterion does not rationally impose itself upon us. One need not *refute* premiss (I) of the Indispensability Argument in order to defeat it; one need only *undercut* it by showing that it has not been proven. The theist is entirely rational to align himself with the many philosophers and logicians who rationally challenge this criterion.

---

[39] Alex Orenstein, 'Is Existence What Existential Quantification Expresses?', in Robert B. Barrett and Roger F. Gibson (eds), *Perspectives on Quine* (Oxford: Basil Blackwell, 1990), 265.

8

Useful Fictions

In the previous two chapters, we saw that the criterion of ontological commitment that lies at the heart of the Indispensability Argument for Platonism has been plausibly challenged, in part or in whole, by neo-Meinongians, neutralists, and free logicians, so that it can hardly be said to be incumbent upon the classical theist. Premiss (I) of that argument may therefore be plausibly rejected. This fact alone suffices to defeat the Indispensability Argument for Platonism.

But what about premiss (II) of that argument?

II. There are literally true simple sentences containing singular terms that refer to things that could only be abstract objects. Likewise, there are literally true existential statements whose existential quantifiers range over things that could only be abstract objects.

If there are plausible ways of regarding such sentences as not literally true, then the Indispensability Argument will be doubly defeated, so to speak. In the next three chapters, we shall examine three anti-realisms which challenge premiss (II), namely, fictionalism, figuralism, and pretence theory (Figure 1). Fictionalism holds that abstract object talk is not true. Figuralism holds that abstract object talk is figurative and therefore not literally true. Pretence theory holds that abstract object talk is a matter of make-believe and therefore need not be taken to be true.

In this chapter, we want to explore the boldest of these three views, fictionalism. Fictionalists flatly deny that mathematical sentences and other abstract sentences are true, period. Statements involving quantification over or reference to abstract objects are false (or at least untrue). Abstract objects are merely useful fictions; that is to say, even though no such objects exist, it is useful to talk as though they did. Hence, the name fictionalism.

CONTEMPORARY FICTIONALISM

Although contemporary fictionalism has historical precursors, particularly Jeremy Bentham's 'theory of fictions' and Hans Vaihinger's 'philosophy of "as if"',[1] the fount of contemporary fictionalism is Hartry Field's *Science without Numbers* (1980). Field questions why we should regard standard mathematics as a body of truths. The fact that the theorems of mathematics are logically derived from a consistent body of axioms does not guarantee their truth, for we may still ask, 'why regard the axioms as *truths,* rather than as fictions that for a variety of reasons mathematicians have become interested in?'[2] Since the truth of mathematical theories, taken at face value, would commit us to the existence of a variety of abstract objects, 'an anti-platonist', Field advises, 'should embrace fictionalism about mathematics—or at least fictionalism about mathematics-taken-at-face-value'.[3]

Field's brand of fictionalism is thus compatible with views like figuralism, which treats mathematical statements as figurative discourse. The figuralist agrees that taken literally, or at face value, mathematical statements are not true, but he denies that they should be taken literally. A good many fictionalists, however, would say that mathematical statements should be understood as literal assertions, not as figurative discourse. Mark Balaguer thinks that fictionalism enjoys an advantage over other anti-realist views precisely because it shares with Platonism a common and customary semantics for abstract discourse.[4] Fictionalists agree with Platonists that sentences involving either quantification over or singular terms referring to

---

[1] On some early figures, see Gideon Rosen, 'Problems in the History of Fictionalism', in Mark Eli Kalderon (ed.), *Fictionalism in Metaphysics* (Oxford: Clarendon Press, 2005), 14–64. For Bentham, see C. K. Ogden, *Bentham's Theory of Fictions* (New York: Harcourt, Brace, & Co., 1932). For Vaihinger, see H. Vaihinger, *The Philosophy of 'As If'* (1911), 2nd edn, tr. C. K. Ogden (London: Routledge & Kegan Paul, 1949).
[2] Hartry Field, *Science without Numbers: A Defence of Nominalism* (Princeton: Princeton University Press, 1980), p. viii.
[3] Hartry Field, *Realism, Mathematics, and Modality* (Oxford: Basil Blackwell, 1989), 2.
[4] See Mark Balaguer, 'Fictionalism in the Philosophy of Mathematics', *The Stanford Encyclopedia of Philosophy,* 16 Sept. 2011, <http://plato.stanford.edu/entires/fictionalism-mathematics>. Strictly speaking, Balaguer is not himself a fictionalist because he thinks that the case for fictionalism and the case for Platonism are of comparable weight.

abstract objects, if true, are ontologically committing; but they differ from Platonists in thinking such sentences to be untrue.

What would be the consequences for physical science of taking mathematical sentences to be untrue? Field thinks that the falsity of mathematical sentences does not undermine natural science because mathematics is ultimately dispensable for science. Balaguer thinks that the falsity of mathematical sentences does not undermine natural science because what he calls the nominalistic content of scientific theories is independent of and, hence, unaffected by the falsity of their Platonistic, mathematical content. Balaguer is willing to concede Quinean claims about the indispensability of mathematics to physical science, but he maintains that while the nominalistic content of empirical science is (mostly) true, its Platonistic content is not. Because abstract objects are causally unconnected to the physical world, there must be a nominalistic content of scientific theories, which, even if inexpressible by us due to mathematics' indispensability, is made true by the physical world wholly independently of whether abstract objects exist. Thus, says Balaguer, while Field's claim that mathematics is scientifically dispensable is 'highly controversial', the claim that empirical science has a nominalistic content that captures its complete picture of the physical world 'is no more controversial than the claim that abstract objects (if there are such things) are causally inert'.[5]

In support of the plausibility of nominalistic scientific realism, Balaguer defends the thesis

(TA) Empirical theories use mathematical object talk only in order to construct *descriptive frameworks* in which to make assertions about the physical world.

Balaguer takes it to be obvious that mathematics does function in the way described by (TA) in physical theories. Consider, for example, the use of mathematics in quantum mechanics (QM):

it seems entirely obvious that (TA) applies to QM, that is, the reason we refer in QM to things like vectors and subspaces and real numbers is that this provides us with a convenient way of describing quantum phenomena. (Indeed, what else could we say here? We certainly

---

[5] Mark Balaguer, *Platonism and Anti-Platonism in Mathematics* (New York: OUP, 1998), 135.

Useful Fictions 147

wouldn't want to claim that we refer to these objects in QM because we simply want to state facts about them, or because we think they are partly responsible for the operation or state of the quantum level of the physical world. It just seems obvious that the reason we refer to these objects is that this provides us with an easy way of saying what we want to say about quantum phenomena.)[6]

Whether or not mathematics is dispensable to physical theory, (TA) accurately describes, in Balaguer's view, the function of mathematics in scientific theories. But such a role is perfectly compatible with fictionalism because descriptive aids can be useful without being genuinely referential. We could use mathematical object talk to depict accurately the physical world even if no mathematical objects existed. In short, 'the reason nominalistic scientific realism is a sensible philosophy of science is that the nominalistic content of empirical science is all empirical science is really "trying to say" about the world. Its platonistic content is something it "says incidentally" in its effort to say what it really "wants to say".'[7]

So fictionalists may regard Platonistic mathematics as either dispensable (Field) or indispensable (Balaguer) to physical science. What unites them is their conviction that mathematical sentences, whether pure or applied, are not true.

THE OBVIOUS TRUTH OF ELEMENTARY MATHEMATICS

The most evident objection to fictionalism is that some mathematical statements, like '2 + 2 = 4,' are just obviously true. Indeed, they seem to be necessarily true. Therefore, fictionalism is simply ruled out.

Field tries to soften fictionalism's blow by holding that '2 + 2 = 4' is true according to standard mathematics:

> A fictionalist needn't (and shouldn't) deny that there is *some* sense in which '2 + 2 = 4' is true; but granting that it is true in some sense does not commit one to finding any interesting translation procedure that takes acceptable mathematical claims into true claims that don't postulate mathematical entities. Rather, the fictionalist can say that the sense

[6] Ibid., 139. [7] Ibid., 141.

in which '2 + 2 = 4' is true is pretty much the same as the sense in which 'Oliver Twist lived in London' is true: the latter is true only in the sense that it is true *according to a certain well-known story,* and the former is true only in the sense that it is true *according to standard mathematics.*[8]

By appealing to truth according to standard mathematics, Field can differentiate between commonly accepted mathematical falsehoods like '2+2=4' and outrageous mathematical falsehoods like '2+2=5.' The latter are obviously not true according to standard mathematics.

But this response fails, I think, to alleviate our misgivings. For the point is surely that the standard model of arithmetic is correct. It is inconceivable, given the meaning of the symbols 0, ', and + in the logical language of arithmetic, that $0'' + 0'' \neq 0''''$.[9] The elementary truths of arithmetic impose themselves upon us, along with the axioms from which these truths are derived.

Field reacts to the claim that a mathematical assertion like '2 + 2 = 4' must be true simply as a consequence of the meaning of its terms by saying that this claim cannot be right because analytic truths cannot have existential implications. He grants that

> the claim 'If there are numbers then 2 + 2 = 4' has some claims to count as an analytic truth, indeed one so obvious that its denial is unintelligible.... But... it can't be an analytic or purely conceptual truth that there *are* objects 1, 2, 3, 4 etc. obeying such laws as that 2 + 2 = 4. An investigation of conceptual linkages can reveal conditions that things must satisfy if they are to fall under our concepts; but it can't yield that there are things that satisfy those concepts.[10]

Field rightly contends that we cannot infer the existence of things from merely definitional truths. But it is only the unquestioned presupposition of the neo-Quinean criterion of ontological commitment that leads the fictionalist to think that a statement like '2 + 2 = 4' has existential implications. Deny that criterion and one is not forced into the awkward position of denying that 2 + 2 = 4.

Mary Leng, in response to the obviousness of elementary mathematics, boldly denies that any arithmetical propositions are obviously

---

[8] Field, *Realism, Mathematics, and Modality*, 2–3.
[9] '0' is the name of a number, "'" a one-place function symbol for the successor relation, and '+' a two-place function symbol for addition. For discussion of standard and non-standard models of the Peano Axioms of arithmetic, see George Boolos and Richard Jeffrey, *Computability and Logic* (Cambridge: CUP, 1974), esp. ch. 17.
[10] Field, *Science without Numbers*, 5.

true. For, she points out, if it is obvious that there is, for example, an even prime number, then it is likewise obvious that there are numbers. But the debate over the reality of numbers has been raging for over two thousand years, so 'surely the mere existence of a debate over this matter speaks against the claim that the truth of the arithmetic propositions in question is genuinely obvious?'[11]

Leng's response assumes that the neo-Quinean criterion of ontological commitment has the same obviousness as the truths of elementary arithmetic, which is absurd. People have not been debating for two thousand years whether there is an even prime number or whether $2+2=4$, but rather the ontological implications of such truths. It has only been within the past century that a criterion of ontological commitment has evolved that takes such truths to be ontologically committing. The millennia-long debate, especially the contemporary debate, over the reality of numbers ought to make us dubious, I think, not of the obviousness of arithmetic, but of the obviousness of the assumed criterion of ontological commitment.

Leng herself confesses that '$2 + 2 = 4$' is 'difficult to doubt', even for fictionalists.[12] Remarkably, however, rather than reject the neo-Quinean criterion of ontological commitment, she tries instead to explain away the apparent obviousness of '$2 + 2 = 4$'! She suggests, 'Perhaps what is obvious to us is just that certain propositions, including the proposition that $2 + 2 = 4$, follow from the assumption that there are numbers satisfying the Dedekind-Peano axioms.'[13] Such a suggestion seems to me outrageous, since these axioms were formulated only in the late nineteenth century, and yet people have believed since the most primitive times that $2 + 2 = 4$. Even today, most people would not have a clue how to derive the truths of elementary arithmetic from the Peano Axioms.

Leng acknowledges that, long before people knew much number theory, it seemed obvious that $2 + 2 = 4$, but she entertains sympathetically the claim that the apparent obviousness of basic arithmetic is due to our childhood conditioning, which 'might create an illusion of obviousness'.[14] I should have thought, to the contrary, that the reason we teach elementary arithmetic to our children in the first place is because we find it, upon reflection, to be evidently true. Leng agrees that we could not have found different number-theoretic

---

[11] Mary Leng, *Mathematics and Reality* (Oxford: OUP, 2010), 91.
[12] Ibid., 92.   [13] Ibid.   [14] Ibid.

statements like '2 + 2 = 5' to be obviously true. But she insists that the salient point is that

> Our early training in basic arithmetic conditions us to accept claims about numbers as true without regard to the ontological commitments they bring with them, so that by the time we come to consider matters of *ontology*, we find it hard to take seriously the possibility that there may not be any numbers.[15]

This claim strikes me as both false and irrelevant. The first clause seems nearly right, though it would have been better to speak of '*alleged* ontological commitments'. Such ontological concerns are doubtless absent from primary school instruction in arithmetic. But the last clause following the word 'ontology' should have been 'we are astonished to learn that some philosophers think that the truths of basic arithmetic commit us to the existence of numbers as mind-independent objects'. It is the disclosure that our childhood belief that 2 + 2 = 4 commits us to the reality of 4 that is hard to take seriously at first. In any case, even if, as Leng thinks, we were conditioned against anti-realism from childhood, this is irrelevant to the obviousness of arithmetic. Statements of elementary arithmetic are still obviously true. So why not call into question the criterion of ontological commitment which has been surreptitiously drilled into us?

Finally, Leng suggests more plausibly that the reason $2+2=4$ seems obvious is due to our experience of counting objects:

> When we say that it is obvious that 2 + 2 = 4, it is plausible that we sometimes mean, not that it is obvious that *number theory implies that* 2 + 2 = 4, but rather, that it's obvious that if I correctly count exactly two objects of one sort... and exactly two objects of another sort..., then taking these together I will be able to count exactly four objects that are either of the first sort or the second sort.[16]

'But,' she adds, 'this just makes adjectival use of the natural numbers, and such uses can be formalized without quantification over natural numbers.'[17] Let us suppose that Leng is right, that our experience of counting goes to explain the obviousness of elementary arithmetic and that adjectival use of numbers suffices to capture such experience. Upon being told that nominal use of the number 2 is ontologically committing in a way that adjectival use is not, should we react by

---

[15] Ibid., 93.   [16] Ibid.   [17] Ibid.

doubting the truth of elementary arithmetic vouchsafed to us by counting? Should we not rather doubt the criterion of ontological commitment which requires that my belief that 'Ten is the number of my fingers' commits me to a mind-independent, abstract object, while 'I have ten fingers' does not? To doubt instead the truth of elementary arithmetic would be to display a misplaced confidence in the criterion of ontological commitment. Any criterion of ontological commitment will always be less obvious than the truths of elementary arithmetic.

In short, one's attitude towards the objection from the obviousness of elementary arithmetic is probably going to depend on one's attitude towards the neo-Quinean criterion of ontological commitment. If with the fictionalist we are convinced that quantification and singular terms are devices of ontological commitment, then we shall find upon reflection that the sentences of elementary mathematics, if taken literally, are anything but obvious. For we shall come to see that statements which we have unhesitatingly accepted as true since childhood are, in fact, radical ontological assertions about the existence of mind-independent abstract objects. As such, they are not at all obviously true. We come to realize that we have, in fact, misunderstood them all these years; we literally did not understand what we were asserting.

On the other hand, if we find sentences of elementary arithmetic to be obvious because we do not take them to be ontologically committing, then we shall be led to reject the neo-Quinean criterion of ontological commitment which would saddle us with such commitments. This seems to me the obvious course to take. After all, the sentences of elementary mathematics are much more obviously true than any criterion of ontological commitment, and so should be more tenaciously held and less quickly surrendered than the neo-Quinean criterion of ontological commitment.

Platonists and fictionalists might try to force us to choose against the obvious truth of mathematical statements by simply stipulating that they are using 'there is/are' in a metaphysically heavyweight sense, so that in that sense the anti-realist is forced to say things like 'There is no number greater than 3' or 'There are no prime numbers less than 100', which sounds absurd.[18] Neutralism is thus said to collapse into

---

[18] Balaguer makes such a move in trying reduce our options to Platonism or fictionalism ('Fictionalism in the Philosophy of Mathematics' § 1.3).

fictionalism once we make clear that we are talking about existence in a metaphysically heavyweight sense.[19]

Neutralist Jody Azzouni takes a very dim view of this sort of move on the part of the neo-Quinean, characterizing it as a kind of philosophical chicanery:

> 'There are fictional mice that talk,' one says, during a discussion about talking fictional animals. 'Oh, so you believe fictional mice *really exist*?' the philosophical trickster responds. 'I didn't say that,' one responds. 'Yes, you sure did—you said *"there are* fictional mice that talk"*.* What do you think "there is" means?'... But what's happened is that the philosophical trickster has (implicitly) switched on *usage*—now one is speaking so that 'there is' (at least for the time being) *does* convey onticity; and the ordinary person isn't sophisticated enough to see how he or she has been duped.[20]

In all fairness, the 'trickster' seems to be doing just what Azzouni advises: using tone of voice and qualifying words like 'really' to make it clear that he is talking about existence in a metaphysically heavyweight sense. The trick here would be his pretending that he is sticking with ordinary usage of quantificational expressions, with the intention of embarrassing the anti-realist. The trickster puts the ordinary person in an awkward situation only by changing the way in which informal quantifiers are used.

Neo-Quinean Theodore Sider is more candid: 'Ontological realism should not claim that ordinary quantifiers carve [reality] at the joints, or that disputes using ordinary quantifiers are substantive. All that's important is that one can introduce a fundamental quantifier, which can then be used to pose substantive ontological questions.'[21] We just stipulate explicitly that we are using 'there is/are' in a metaphysically heavyweight sense. When we do so, says Sider, we are no longer speaking ordinary English, but 'a new language—"Ontologese"— whose quantifiers are *stipulated* to carve [reality] at the joints'.[22] If

---

[19] Balaguer, *Platonism and Anti-Platonism*, 101–4.
[20] Jody Azzouni, 'Ontological Commitment in the Vernacular', *Noûs*, 41/2 (2007): 224 n. 38.
[21] Theodore Sider, *Writing the Book of the World* (Oxford: Clarendon, 2011), 171. 'Carving reality at its joints' is a metaphor for correctly determining ontology, stating accurately what objects there really are. Compare our comments on mereological universalism in Ch. 6.
[22] Sider, *Writing the Book of the World*, 172. Even if the neutralist 'is right about natural language quantifiers, ontologists could always relocate to the metaphysics

one stipulates that 'there is/are' is being used to indicate ontological commitments, then, of course, the anti-realist will regard a statement like 'There are odd numbers' as false. But anti-realism has not thereby been thrust into an embarrassing position, for in a metaphysically heavyweight sense it is anything but obvious that there are numbers.

What this discussion reveals is that the correct logic for Ontologese, or metaphysically heavyweight discourse, should be a positive free logic. For we have already argued for a neutral theory of reference in Chapter 7. Since free logic takes quantification to be ontologically committing but does not take singular terms to be devices of ontological commitment, we may deny the truth of 'There are numbers,' while—the fictionalist notwithstanding—affirming the truth of '2 + 2 = 4.' There do not need to be objects which are the denotations of the singular terms '2 + 2' and '4' in order for '2 + 2 = 4' to be true. So the anti-realist need not and should not be a fictionalist about the statements of arithmetic, even if he is a fictionalist when it comes to statements quantifying over mathematical objects.

INDISPENSABILITY/UTILITY OF MATHEMATICS

If, as the fictionalist claims, sentences quantifying over or involving reference to mathematical objects are not true, then how can they be so useful and, indeed, indispensable to modern science in describing the physical world? The issue that arises here is why mathematical statements in scientific theories cannot be taken merely instrumentally, just as many other statements in scientific theories are. The philosopher of mathematics Penelope Maddy provides some engaging illustrations:

> If we open any physics text with these questions in mind, the first thing we notice is that many of the applications of mathematics occur in the company of assumptions that we know to be literally false. For example, we treat a section of the earth's surface as flat, rather than curved, when we compute trajectories; we assume the ocean to be infinitely deep when we analyze the waves on its surface; we use continuous functions to

---

room, and conduct their dispute in Ontologese' (197). Of course, no one really speaks Ontologese, and it would be a delusion of philosophers to think that they do. They just determine to use selected English expressions in a metaphysically heavy way.

represent quantities like energy, charge, and angular momentum, which we know to be quantized; we take liquids to be continuous substances in fluid dynamics, despite atomic theory. On the face of it, an indispensability argument based on such an application of mathematics and science would be laughable: should we believe in the infinite because it plays an indispensable role in our best scientific account of water waves?[23]

Why should we not take mathematical sentences to be false though useful?

Azzouni acknowledges that scientists often do take an instrumentalist attitude towards their theories, and so he inquires how we can tell when a theory is being treated instrumentally. How does the difference in attitude towards sentences presumed to be true and those which are taken merely instrumentally manifest itself? 'The answer is that if a theory (or sentence) is one we think true, then we must also include in our body of beliefs (at least implicitly) *all* of its implications... if we really do take the theory *only* as an instrumental device..., then we ignore or quarantine the other implications of the theory from our communal body of beliefs.'[24] In Azzouni's view, this manifestation condition is both a necessary and sufficient condition of a theory's being construed instrumentally.

In response to Maddy, Azzouni insists, 'implications of applied mathematical doctrine are never placed in quarantine in the way that (instrumentally construed) implications of empirical doctrine are'.[25] He concludes:

> the Quinean claim, that an indispensable empirical theory *must be* regarded as true, has been *qualified*, because such isn't the case in ordinary scientific practice if certain implications of such theories are placed in quarantine....
>
> Nevertheless,... this qualification offers little solace to instrumentally inclined philosophers—those, anyway, who urge us to take applied mathematical doctrine or fundamental scientific laws to be false—because in these cases scientists do *not* engage in the practice of placing in quarantine (some of) the implications of such theories, and so

---

[23] Penelope Maddy, *Naturalism in Mathematics* (Oxford: OUP, 1997), 143.
[24] Jody Azzouni, *Deflating Existential Consequence: A Case for Nominalism* (Oxford: OUP, 2004), 35.
[25] Ibid., 46.

philosophers have no grounds to regard such theories as false, or even grounds to be agnostic regarding the truth of such theories.[26]

Now all sorts of questions might be raised concerning the justification for Azzouni's manifestation condition. But let that pass. There is a more glaring lacuna in the argument, or at least so it seems. Azzouni claims that scientists never place any of the implications of the mathematical doctrine applied in their theories in quarantine. But the fictionalist will contend that such a claim is patently mistaken.[27] They will say that scientists most certainly *do* place into quarantine implications of the mathematical statements used in or presupposed by scientific theories. For example, given the neo-Quinean criterion of ontological commitment, it is an implication of '2 + 3 = 5' that there is a mind-independent object designated by the singular terms '2 + 3' and '5'. This is, to be sure, not a *mathematical* implication, that is to say, a mathematical theorem; rather, it is, as Maddy says, an *ontological* implication. It is with such an ontological conclusion that Maddy is concerned when she protests against believing in the infinite because of the indispensable role it plays in our best theory of ocean waves. Mathematics can play its indispensable role in scientific theories, even as its ontological implications are ignored, so long as all the mathematical implications hold.

Quarantining, according to Azzouni, involves simply ignoring some of the implications of a theory, that is to say, not including those implications in our (communal) body of beliefs. I think it highly improbable that Platonism is included in the body of beliefs of the scientific community! Even in the absence of a sociological survey, it seems safe to say that most scientists simply ignore any alleged ontological commitments following from the mathematical statements used in their theories.

Even the Platonists John Burgess and Gideon Rosen acknowledge evidence in favour of instrumentalism concerning mathematical objects, namely, the *lightheartedness* with which novel mathematical entities are introduced, the *indifference* when it comes to questions of

---

[26] Ibid., 47.
[27] On Azzouni's own view of how we make ontological commitments, the manifestation condition is not fulfilled. For Azzouni is a neutralist concerning quantification and reference, and so does not think that the truth of pure mathematical statements has any ontological implications. But the question before us is the tenability of mathematical instrumentalism on a fictionalist view.

identifying mathematical objects such as the number 2 with other objects such as {{∅}} or {0, 1}, and the *varying reactions* of practitioners when pressed by philosophers about the ontological commitments of their theorems.[28] Although Burgess and Rosen try to diminish the force of this evidence, these considerations do, I think, supply strong grounds for suspecting that mathematicians and scientists are not concerned about the ontological implications of mathematical sentences.

If this is correct, the manifestation condition has been met, and the fictionalist is entirely within his rights in construing the indispensable mathematical content of scientific theories instrumentally. In that case, the indispensability of mathematics to empirical science fails to defeat the fictionalist claim that such mathematical statements are false. As Field puts it, mathematics need not be true to be good.

We are thus brought back to the same choice we confronted when dealing with the objection to fictionalism from the obvious truth of elementary arithmetic. It does seem bizarre to deny, as the fictionalist does, that the sentence 'The number of Mars' moons is two' is true. But the *only* reason the fictionalist denies the truth of this statement is because he takes it to be equivalent to the claim that 'A mind-independent, abstract object exists which numbers the moons of Mars as two.' Other anti-Platonists join the fictionalist in rejecting such a claim. The question anti-Platonists face is whether it is more plausible to deny the truth of the neo-Quinean criterion of ontological commitment which gives rise to so extraordinary a claim or to deny the truth of the common-sense assertion about the number of Mars' moons. It seems to me evident that given the prima facie truth of the common-sense assertion, there is properly a presumption of its truth which can be overturned only by the demonstration that the neo-Quinean criterion of ontological commitment is even more obviously true than the common-sense assertion. If this is right, then fictionalism should be the last resort of the anti-realist, to be entertained only after all attempts to affirm the truth of statements of applied mathematics without commitment to abstract objects have proved themselves futile.

---

[28] Gideon Rosen and John P. Burgess, 'Nominalism Reconsidered', in Stewart Shapiro (ed.), *The Oxford Handbook of Mathematics and Logic* (Oxford: OUP, 2005), 526–7.

It seems to me, therefore, that while the indispensability/utility of mathematics to science might justifiably lead us to call into question the neo-Quinean devices of ontological commitment, the determined fictionalist, like the instrumentalist, can consistently take such mathematical sentences to be literally false. Such an instrumentalist attitude is manifested by placing some of the implications of the mathematical statements used in science in quarantine.

IS FICTIONALISM SELF-DEFEATING?

The fictionalist claim that abstract objects such as numbers are merely useful fictions occasions a deeper question: do useful fictions exist? Surely not, for a useful fiction would be an abstract object, and fictionalism denies that there are abstract objects. But then it is strictly false to say that numbers and the like are useful fictions, which seems to make fictionalism self-defeating.

Now at first blush, this problem might seem easy to solve. Strictly speaking, according to fictionalism, there are no fictions. But when fictionalists say that something is a useful fiction, what they mean is merely that the singular terms allegedly referring to such an entity are vacuous but may nevertheless be usefully employed in our scientific theorizing. Thus, we are not committed to the reality of useful fictions.

The problem, however, is not so easily dismissed. For fictionalists want to distinguish between useful falsehoods like '2 + 2 = 4' and outrageous falsehoods like '2 + 2 = 5'. They do so, as we have seen, by saying that the former is true according to the standard model or story of arithmetic, while the latter is not. But then the fictionalist seems to have committed himself to the reality of models or stories, which are abstract objects. So the fictionalist has to say that his claim that '"2 + 2 = 4" is true in our standard story of arithmetic' is, strictly speaking, false, which seems to make fictionalism self-defeating. The difficulty is that fictionalism itself, wedded as it is to the neo-Quinean criterion of ontological commitment, seems to be committed to the reality of abstract objects.

At this point, the sensible anti-realist might conclude that such an impasse gives good grounds for jettisoning the criterion of ontological commitment assumed by the fictionalist, which results in his being committed to abstract entities like models or stories. But in order to give fictionalism a full run for its money, let us ask what the fictionalist might say in response to the objection.

Paradox and Linguistic Frameworks

The most daring response would be to say that, due to the indispensability of abstract terminology, paradox is inevitable. We inevitably have to recur to abstract terminology in order to express our views, so that we find ourselves trapped by our language into making paradoxical assertions.

Such a response does not strike me as absurd. This fictionalist rejoinder can be made to appear less radical by appealing to Carnap's distinction between internal and external questions relative to a linguistic framework.[29] Carnap, it will be remembered, drew a fundamental distinction, which he took to be of paramount importance, between what he called 'internal questions', that is to say, questions posed within a linguistic framework, and 'external questions', that is, questions posed from a vantage point outside that framework. Despite the widespread rejection of Carnap's verificationism, many philosophers find his distinction between external and internal questions relative to a linguistic framework to be intuitive and helpful. Øystein Linnebo puts his finger on Carnap's fundamental insight when he writes:

> In fact, many nominalists endorse truth-value realism, at least about more basic branches of mathematics, such as arithmetic. Nominalists of this type are committed to the slightly odd-sounding view that, although the ordinary mathematical statement
>
> (1) There are prime numbers between 10 and 20.
>
> is true, there are in fact no mathematical objects and thus in particular no numbers. But there is no contradiction here. We must distinguish between the language L_M in which mathematicians make their claims and the language L_P in which nominalists and other philosophers make theirs. The statement (1) is made in L_M. But the nominalist's assertion that (1) is true but that there are no abstract objects is made in L_P. The nominalist's assertion is thus perfectly coherent.[30]

---

[29] Recall Ch. 3 under 'Responses to the Indispensability Argument'.
[30] Øystein Linnebo, 'Platonism in the Philosophy of Mathematics', *The Stanford Encyclopedia of Philosophy*, 21 Sept. 2009, § 1.4, <http://plato.stanford.edu/entries/

Statements made in the mathematical language L_M correspond to Carnap's internal questions, and statements made in the philosophical language L_P correspond to external questions. External questions are meaningful and have objective answers, but those answers may be quite different than the answers to similar questions posed internally. If the claim 'There are prime numbers between 10 and 20' is expressed in L_M, then the fictionalist will accept the claim as stated in L_M while denying, in L_P, that there are numbers.

By distinguishing between internal and external questions concerning abstract objects, the fictionalist could circumscribe the neo-Quinean criterion of ontological commitment. We are at best ontologically committed by quantification and singular terms in L_P, the language in which external questions are posed; but use of quantification and singular terms in L_M, the language in which internal questions are posed, is not ontologically committing. Certain statements made internally are to be regarded as fictionally true, even though these statements, when considered externally, are false. Thus, '2 + 2 = 4' is fictionally true, whereas '2 + 2 = 5' is fictionally false, though neither of these statements is true outside the framework.

The pickle in which the fictionalist may find himself is that, for whatever reason, he is able to express certain external claims *only by using the language of the framework L_M*. For example, talk of linguistic frameworks is itself in the language of L_M. The fictionalist may explain that he is unfortunately forced by the exigencies of language to express some of his external claims using the language of the framework L_M. His fundamental view that no abstract objects exist and therefore no sentence involving putative quantification over or singular terms referring to such objects is true can be expressed externally and coherently in L_P; but his views on the difference between statements like '2 + 2 = 4' and '2 + 2 = 5' require him to speak in the language of L_M, thereby generating the appearance of self-referential incoherence.

platonism-mathematics/>. Linnebo unfortunately limits the range of anti-realist solutions unnecessarily. Linnebo has in mind Geoffrey Hellman's translations of mathematical statements into counterfactual conditionals, so that the mathematical truths affirmed in L_P will look or sound quite different than those truths as stated in L_M. That leaves out of account anti-realisms like fictionalism, which regards statements in L_M as fictionally true and similar statements in L_P as false, as well as anti-realisms which, unlike fictionalism, call into question the criterion of ontological commitment underlying indispensability arguments for Platonism.

It is not clear to me that such a position is untenable; indeed, it seems plausible that we could find ourselves in such an awkward situation. Accordingly, this response provides the fictionalist a not unreasonable way out of self-defeat.

Counterfactual Paraphrases

A second, and different, response to the spectre of self-defeat is to abandon the self-referentially incoherent claims in favour of paraphrases that are consistent with anti-realism about abstract objects. Recall that the present difficulty is the result of the fictionalist's attempt to distinguish between outrageous falsehoods like '2 + 2 = 5' and falsehoods vital to our getting along in the world like '2 + 2 = 4'. The fictionalist says that one is true in our standard story of mathematics, while the other is not, which, given his criterion of ontological commitment, leaves him with abstract objects like stories on his hands.

One way the fictionalist could avoid ontological commitment to things like stories is by employing counterfactual claims to explicate fictional truth. Counterfactual statements are conditionals in the subjunctive mood, such as 'If there were unicorns, narwhals would not be the only single-horned mammals' or 'If a rigid rod were placed in uniform motion through the aether, it would contract in the direction of motion'. Since the neo-Quinean criterion of ontological commitment applies only to extensional contexts,[31] it does not apply when quantification and singular terms are employed in an intensional context like a counterfactual statement. So, for example, the fictionalist could coherently claim that what is right about '2 + 2 = 4', in contrast to '2 + 2 = 5', is that, if there were numbers, then '2 + 2' and '4' would refer to the same number. The correctness of our story of mathematics lies in the fact that, if there were numbers, that is what they would be like. The fictionalist can employ counterfactuals in order to meet the challenge of distinguishing outrageous falsehoods from falsehoods which are commonly accepted as mathematical truths: in the one case, one says, 'If there were numbers, then it would be the case that...', and in the other case, 'If there were

---

[31] Recall our discussion of "Singular Terms" in Ch. 3 under 'Premiss (I): A Criterion of Ontological Commitment'.

numbers, it would not be the case that . . . ' We do not need abstract entities like stories, fictions, or whatever, to express the difference between sentences like '2 + 2 = 4' and '2 + 2 = 5'.

So in response to the charge of self-defeat, the fictionalist may explain that, in affirming that certain sentences are true in the standard story of mathematics, he means to affirm that, if there were numbers, then things would be as the sentences say. Certain sentences in our best scientific theories, namely, sentences involving quantification and reference only to physical realities, may be taken as true, while sentences involving indispensable quantification over or reference to mathematical objects are to be regarded as false but fictionally true, that is to say, they would be true if the objects in question existed.

Deflationism and Mathematical Utility

Hartry Field's deflationary view of truth suggests yet a third way of escape for the fictionalist from self-defeat. To begin with, Field maintains that what distinguishes commonly accepted mathematical falsehoods from outrageous falsehoods is simply the utility of the former. He explains:

> What makes the mathematical theories we accept better than . . . alternatives to them is not that they are true and the modifications not true, but rather that they are more *useful*: they are more of an aid to us in drawing consequences from those nominalistic theories that we are interested in. If the world were different, we would be interested in different nominalistic theories, and in that case some of the alternatives to some of our favorite mathematical theories might be of more use than the theories we now accept.[32]

Unfortunately, by appealing to the utility of our mathematical theories to distinguish commonly accepted falsehoods from unhelpful falsehoods, Field appears to be ontologically committed to the reality of theories, which are abstract objects. Gideon Rosen asks pointedly:

---

[32] Field, *Science without Numbers*, 15. Field apparently thinks that it is a contingent matter that numbers do not exist. But even given that numbers, if they exist, do so necessarily, there is no objection, I think, to the non-vacuous truth of counterfactuals involving impossible antecedents, e.g. 'If God did not exist, the world would not exist.'

When Field says that set theory is false but useful,... what precisely does he mean by 'set theory'? A scattered mass of ink and chalk? A theory shaped region of spacetime? The general worry is that on a wide range of restrictive ontological views, theories turn out to be among the entities the theorist professes not to believe in. And whenever this is the case, the fictionalist way out is simply not available.[33]

Given that a theory, if it existed, would be an abstract object, the fictionalist must say that it is false that accepted mathematical theories are more useful than alternatives, which seems to be self-defeating.

Field's deflationary view of truth, however, enables him to evade this objection. On a deflationary view, the truth predicate 'is true' is merely a device of semantic ascent, whereby we talk *about* a claim rather than simply *make* the claim itself. For example, rather than asserting, 'Hitler was an evil man', we may ascend semantically and say, 'It is true that Hitler was an evil man.' The first assertion is about Hitler; the second assertion is about the first assertion, namely, that it is true.

Similarly, instead of saying that a mathematical theory is useful, the fictionalist may make use of a deflationary schema like

(CONC) The concrete world is so structured that it is useful to assume that _____

where the '_____' is to be filled by the axioms of the mathematical theory in question. Since the completed sentence does not *mention* or *refer to* the theoretical axioms, but is merely completed by inserting the relevant words into the blank, such a sentence would make no ontologically committing reference to theories. The fictionalist will assert such a sentence when the blank is filled by the axioms of a standard mathematical theory like Peano arithmetic, but he will not make such an assertion when the axioms of some non-standard theory fill the blank.

Such a deflationary approach to theories enables the fictionalist to avoid self-referential incoherence in the statement of his position. Contrary to Rosen, the fictionalist will not assert that set theory—or any other mathematical theory—is useful though false. On a deflationary view, one will not ascend semantically to talk of the truth or

---

[33] Gideon Rosen, 'What is Constructive Empiricism?', *Philosophical Studies,* 74/2 (1994): 169.

Useful Fictions 163

utility or consistency of scientific or mathematical theories. One will simply affirm of the concrete world that it is so structured that it is useful to assume that [stick in the axioms here].

Of course, that raises the question as to *why* the physical world is so structured as to make mathematical sentences useful in describing the world—what physicist Eugene Wigner famously referred to as 'the unreasonable effectiveness of mathematics'.[34] This is the question, not of mathematics' indispensability, but of its applicability. Neither the Platonist nor the fictionalist as such has much to contribute towards the explanation of mathematics' applicability.

As Leng points out, for the Platonist, the fact that physical reality behaves in line with the dictates of acausal mathematical entities existing beyond space and time is 'a happy coincidence'.[35] This is simply to reiterate that abstract objects are causally inert. The idea that Platonism somehow accounts for the applicability of mathematics 'is actually very counterintuitive', muses Balaguer. 'The idea here is that in order to believe that the physical world has the nature that empirical science assigns to it, I have to believe that there are causally inert mathematical objects, existing outside of spacetime', an idea which is inherently implausible.[36]

But the fictionalist is no better off. Philosopher of science Tim Maudlin muses, 'The deep question of why a given mathematical object should be an effective tool for representing physical structure admits of at least one clear answer: because the physical world literally has the mathematical structure; the physical world is, in a certain sense, a mathematical object.'[37] Leng says that there is no happy coincidence on anti-realism, since mathematical relations just mirror the relations among things in the physical world. This explanation of mathematics' applicability in fact falls short, as Mark Steiner emphasizes in his groundbreaking *The Applicability of Mathematics as a Philosophical Problem*;[38] but never mind. Even in cases where

---

[34] Eugene P. Wigner, 'The Unreasonable Effectiveness of Mathematics in the Natural Sciences', *Communications on Pure and Applied Mathematics*, 13/1 (1960): 1–14.
[35] Leng, *Mathematics and Reality*, 239.
[36] Balaguer, *Platonism and Anti-Platonism in Mathematics*, 136.
[37] Tim Maudlin, 'On the Foundations of Physics', 5 July 2013, <http://www.3ammagazine.com/3am/philosophy-of-physic>.
[38] Mark Steiner, *The Applicability of Mathematics as a Philosophical Problem* (Cambridge, MA: Harvard University Press, 1998). Steiner focuses on examples of mathematical applicability in which the physical world in no way has the

mathematical structure does mirror the structure of the physical world, what remains wanting is an explanation *why* the physical world exhibits so complex and stunning a mathematical structure in the first place. Balaguer admits that he has no explanation why, on fictionalism, mathematics is applicable to the physical world or why it is indispensable in empirical science. He just observes that the Platonist cannot answer such 'why' questions either. That answer must be sought elsewhere.

It seems to me that, whether one is a realist or an anti-realist about mathematical objects, the theist enjoys a considerable advantage over the naturalist in explaining the uncanny success of mathematics. On the one hand, the theistic realist can argue that God has fashioned the world on the structure of the mathematical objects. This is essentially the view that Plato defended in his dialogue *Timaeus*. God looks to the realm of mathematical objects and models the world on it. The world has mathematical structure as a result. Thus, the realist who is a theist has a considerable advantage over the naturalistic realist in explaining why mathematics is so effective in describing the physical world.

On the other hand, the theistic anti-realist also has a ready explanation of the applicability of mathematics to the physical world: God has created the world according to a certain blueprint which He had in mind. He might have chosen any number of blueprints. The world exhibits the mathematical structure it does because God has chosen to create it according to the model He had in mind. This was the view of Philo of Alexandria, who maintained in his treatise *On the Creation of the World* that God created the physical world on the mental model in His mind. Thus, the theist—whether he be a realist or an anti-realist about mathematical objects—has the explanatory resources to account for the mathematical structure of the physical world and, hence, for the otherwise unreasonable effectiveness of mathematics—resources which the naturalist lacks.

To return, then, to the objection that fictionalism is self-defeating, it seems to me that fictionalists can escape this charge. At worst, even

---

mathematical structure which proves so useful in discovering facts about the physical world, such as e.g. the applicability of Hilbert space to quantum mechanics. Steiner concludes, 'The world, in other words, *looks* "user friendly." This is a challenge to naturalism' (176). The user friendliness of the physical world in cases like Steiner's powerfully underscores the argument I give in what follows for the advantage enjoyed by theism.

if fictionalism cannot be thoroughly explicated without use of abstract object talk of stories, theories, models, and the like, the fictionalist can, by distinguishing between internal and external questions, coherently hold that, due to the indispensability of abstract object talk, we are stuck with explicating at least some external questions only by using vocabulary belonging to the abstract linguistic framework, thus giving the appearance of incoherence. But it is far from clear that the fictionalist is, in fact, stuck in such an awkward position. For even if abstract object talk is indispensable to scientific theorizing and, indeed, life in general, still it seems that the central claims of fictionalism can be coherently explicated by dispensing with reference to stories, theories, models, and the like in favour of either counterfactual claims about what mathematical entities would be like were they to exist or else deflationary claims about what is useful to assume.

CONCLUDING REMARKS

I have not in this chapter argued that theists should embrace fictionalism, but have simply examined its tenability as an option for the classical theist. The three objections to fictionalism which I have discussed—namely, the obvious truth of elementary arithmetic, the indispensability/utility of mathematics, and the self-referential incoherence of fictionalism—are, I think, the principal objections that have been raised against it in the literature. We have seen that, insofar as these objections cast doubt on the fictionalist's claim that mathematical statements are false, they cast doubt, not on anti-realism, but on the criterion of ontological commitment assumed by the fictionalist, which would force on us Platonistic ontological commitments as a result of seemingly innocuous truths. Nevertheless, granted the neo-Quinean criterion, fictionalist claims about the falsehood of such statements seem not only coherent, but even plausible.

This conclusion is important because, even if we adopt a neutralist perspective on quantification and reference, as I have advocated, or even if abstract object talk is taken to be figurative or merely prescribed to be imagined, as figuralists and pretence theorists maintain, still there are occasions on which we shall want to speak Ontologese in order to make metaphysically heavyweight assertions like 'There are no abstract objects' or 'There are no mathematical objects and, hence, no numbers'. We shall then adopt a fictionalist take on such quantificational discourse. But, contrary to the fictionalist, we still want to be able to assert truly that $2 + 2 = 4$ or that $3 < 5$. That implies that what we want is a positive free logic for our metaphysically heavyweight assertions. A positive free logic will enable us to use singular mathematical terms in sentences we take to be true without ontological commitment to real-world denotations of those terms, and at the same time, to deny with the fictionalist that there are mathematical and other abstract objects.

9

Figuratively Speaking

In the previous chapter, we explored the view of fictionalists that abstract discourse is not true. In this chapter, we want to examine the view of anti-realist thinkers who maintain that abstract object sentences like mathematical sentences, though true, are not *literally* true. According to these theorists, such abstract talk is figurative language and, therefore, contrary to premiss (II) of the Indispensability Argument, not to be taken literally. Representative of this view is MIT philosopher Stephen Yablo, who began as a fictionalist but eventually found 'a path through fictionalism' to a view he calls figuralism.[1]

ABSTRACT DISCOURSE AS FIGURATIVE

Yablo observes that figurative language is a pervasive feature of ordinary language, indeed, so much so that we often do not even realize that we are speaking figuratively. In fact, Yablo believes that literal talk is actually the exception rather than the rule.[2] He observes that this fact presents a serious problem for Quine's project of determining the ontological commitments of our discourse. For Quine recognized that since figures of speech should not be taken literally, his criterion of ontological commitment could not be applied to such discourse. The problem is that we have no criterion for identifying an expression as literal or metaphorical. The boundaries of the literal, Yablo maintains, are so unclear that there is no way to

---

[1] Stephen Yablo, 'Go Figure: A Path through Fictionalism', in Peter A. French and Howard K. Wettstein (eds), *Figurative Language* (Oxford: Blackwell, 2001), 72–102.
[2] Ibid., 85.

tell in the most controversial cases whether our assertions are to be taken literally or not. The more controversial philosophical claims about things' existence are in the boundaryland between the literal and the figurative in a way that Quine's method is powerless to address.[3] 'To determine our ontological commitments, we have to ferret out all traces of non-literality in our assertions; if there is no sensible project of doing that, there is no sensible project of Quinean ontology.'[4]

Talk of abstract objects is a case in point. In Yablo's view, talk of abstract objects involves the use of what he calls 'existential metaphors', that is to say, metaphors 'making play with a special sort of object to which the speaker is not [ontologically] committed'.[5] For example, when we say something like 'John's luck had finally run out', the singular term 'John's luck' is an existential metaphor, not a term denoting a real object in the world. Numerical terms are similarly existential metaphors. Such terms, though metaphorical, are nonetheless useful, and sometimes indispensable, for expressing truths about the real world. Yablo provides the following illustration:

> Much as we make as if, e.g., people have associated with them stores of something called 'luck,' so as to be able to describe some of them metaphorically as individuals whose luck is 'running out,' we make as if pluralities have associated with them things called 'numbers,' so as to be able to express an (otherwise hard to express because) infinitely disjunctive fact about relative cardinalities like so: The number of Fs is divisible by the number of Gs.[6]

Given our finitude, we cannot express infinite disjunctions like 'There is one star and one planet, or there are two stars and one planet, or ...' and so have no choice but to resort to number talk in order to talk, in this case, about stars and planets. 'It is only by making *as if* to countenance numbers, that one can give expression in English to a fact having nothing to do with numbers, a fact about stars and planets and how they are numerically proportioned.'[7]

---

[3] Stephen Yablo, 'Does Ontology Rest on a Mistake?', *Proceedings of the Aristotelian Society* (Supplement), 72 (1998): 255, 259.

[4] Ibid., 229. Cf. Stephen Yablo, 'A Paradox of Existence', in Anthony Everett and Thomas Hofweber (eds), *Empty Names, Fiction, and the Puzzles of Non-Existence* (Stanford, CA: Center for the Study of Language and Information, 2000), 304–5.

[5] Yablo, 'Paradox of Existence', 293.

[6] Stephen Yablo, 'The Myth of the Seven', in Mark Eli Kalderon (ed.), *Fictionalism in Metaphysics* (Oxford: Clarendon Press, 2005), 98.

[7] Yablo, 'Paradox of Existence', 295.

Figuratively Speaking 169

Yablo draws a number of fascinating parallels between figurative talk (construed as talk about make-believe objects (MBOs)) and talk about what he calls Platonic objects[8] (POs):

Paraphrasability

- MBOs are often paraphrasable away with no felt loss of subject matter, e.g. 'That was her first encounter with the green-eyed monster' goes to 'That was her first time feeling envious.'
- POs are often paraphrasable away with no felt loss of subject matter, e.g. 'There is a possible world at which S' goes to 'It is possible that S'.

Impatience

- One is unmoved, even impatient, when someone suggests we should get worried about the fact that an MBO may not really exist. 'I wasn't thinking there was *really* a green-eyed monster.'
- One is unmoved, even impatient, when someone suggests that a PO or type of PO may not really exist. 'So what if the models peter out above such and such a cardinality?'

Translucency

- About the best one can do with 'What if there is no green-eyed monster?' is to hear it as the (bizarre) suggestion that no one is ever really envious.

---

[8] It should be noted that Yablo has an idiosyncratic understanding of what a Platonic object is. Normally, a Platonic object is taken to be an abstract object. But Yablo defines an object as Platonic relative to an area of discourse, just in case the discourse depends on how that object behaves, even though the discourse is not really about that object. For example, someone who expresses concern about the number of starving people in the world is concerned about people, not some abstract mathematical object. Notice that even though Yablo does not identify Platonic objects as abstract objects, nevertheless, most of the objects which he identifies as Platonic are plausibly construed to be abstract objects. In fact, Yablo himself says, 'the existence of abstract objects is straightforwardly deducible from premises that few would think to deny' (Yablo, 'Paradox of Existence', 276). Since our interest is in the existence of abstract objects, I shall take Yablo's Platonic objects to be abstract.

- About the best one can do with 'What if there are no God-worlds?' is to hear it as the suggestion that God is not really possible.

Insubstantiality

- Unlike ordinary objects, MBOs tend to have not much more to them than what flows from our conception of them. The green-eyed monster has no 'hidden substantial nature'; neither do the real estate bug, the blue meanies, the chip on my shoulder, etc.
- Unlike ordinary objects, POs often have not much more to them than what flows from our conception of them. All the really important facts about the numbers follow from (second-order) Peano's Axioms. Likewise, mutatis mutandis for sets, functions, etc.

Indeterminacy

- Unlike ordinary objects, MBOs can be 'indeterminately identical'. There is no fact of the matter as to the identity relations between the fuse I blew last week and the one I blew today, or my keister and my wazoo ('I've had it up to the keister/wazoo with this paperwork'). The relevant game(s) leave it undecided what is to count as identical to what.
- Unlike ordinary objects, POs can be 'indeterminately identical'. There is no fact of the matter as to the identity relations between the natural numbers and the Zermelo numbers, or the possible worlds and the maximal consistent sets of propositions, or the events and the property instantiations. It is left (partly) undecided what is to count as identical to what.

Silliness

- MBOs invite 'silly questions' probing areas the make-believe does not address, e.g. we know how big the average star is, where is it located? You say I have risen in your esteem, by how many inches? Do you plan to *drop*-forge the conscience of your race in the smithy of your soul?
- POs invite questions that seem similarly silly. What are the intrinsic properties of the empty set? Is the event of the water's

boiling itself hot? Are universals wholly present in each of their instances? Do relations lead a divided existence, parcelled out among their relata?

Expressiveness (Representationality)

- MBOs show a heartening tendency to boost the language's power to express facts about other, more ordinary, entities. 'The average taxpayer saves an increasing fraction of his income.'
- POs show a strong tendency to boost the language's power to express facts about other, more ordinary, entities. 'This line here is p times as long as that line there.'

Irrelevance

- MBOs are called on to 'explain' phenomena that would not on reflection suffer by their absence. Even if the average taxpayer had not existed, the savings rate would still have increased.
- POs are called on to 'explain' phenomena that would not on reflection suffer by their absence. If all the one-one functions were killed off today, there would still be as many left shoes in my closet as right.

Disconnectedness

- MBOs have a tendency not to do much *other* than expressive work. As a result, perhaps, of not really existing, they tend not to push things around.
- POs have a tendency not to do much *other* than expressive work; numbers et al. are famous for their causal inertness.

Availability (Apriority)

- MBOs' lack of naturalistic connections might seem to threaten epistemic access—until we remember that 'their properties' are projected rather than detected.

- POs' lack of naturalistic connections are widely thought to threaten epistemic access—the threat evaporates if 'their properties' are projected, not detected.

These parallels serve as evidence that abstract object talk is a kind of figurative language.[9]

Platonic objects, Yablo points out, are deducible by what he calls overly easy existence proofs. Such overly easy proofs of the existence of Platonic objects trivialize the task of metaphysics. Yablo gives the following illustrations of discovering unexpected objects in statements' truth conditions:

the truth value of:	is held to turn on:
argument A is valid	the existence of *countermodels*
it is possible that B	the existence of *worlds*
there are as many Cs as Ds	the existence of 1-1 *functions*
there are over five Es	the *number* of E's exceeding five
he did it F-ly	the *event* of his doing it being F
there are Gs which ____	there being a *set* of Gs which ____
she is H	her relation to the *property* H-ness

The entities denoted by the italicized terms in the right-hand column are said to be Platonic because the sentences in the left-hand column are not really about them.[10] The italicized expressions on the right are therefore best taken as existential metaphors. Yablo claims that additional evidence for the metaphorical character of such abstract talk is that so construing it is the best explanation of why such overly easy existence proofs fail.

Ultimately, Yablo thinks that the decision to embrace Platonism or figuralism depends upon the answers to the following comparative questions:

(1) What does Platonism/figuralism help us to explain?
(2) What explanatory puzzles does Platonism/figuralism generate?

Consider, first, the explanatory puzzles generated respectively by each view. Yablo thinks that anti-Platonists have relied too heavily on the explanatory puzzles generated by Platonism (such as how we

---

[9] Yablo, 'Paradox of Existence', 302–4; cf. Yablo, 'Go Figure', 89–90; Stephen Yablo, 'Abstract Objects: A Case Study', in Ernest Sosa and Enrique Villanueva (eds), *Realism and Relativism* (Boston: Blackwell, 2002), 227–30.

[10] Yablo, 'Paradox of Existence', 277.

could have epistemic access to abstract objects) as justification for anti-Platonism. But, unsurprisingly, Yablo takes no cognizance of the theological puzzle that drives our inquiry, namely, how the supposed existence of abstract objects can be reconciled with divine aseity and *creatio ex nihilo*. Given our theological commitments, some sort of anti-Platonism must be true.

As for explanatory puzzles generated by figuralism, the only problem that Yablo is aware of is the objection to pretence theory (to be discussed in Chapter 10) that abstract object talk and particularly mathematical discourse are not plausibly a matter of make-believe. This objection, however, is really an objection to a pretence theoretical analysis of figurative language, not to the fundamental figuralist claim that abstract object talk is figurative. Consideration of such a puzzle is therefore better reserved for our discussion of pretence theory in Chapter 10. So with respect to the explanatory puzzles generated by Platonism/figuralism, Platonism clearly comes out with the short end of the stick.

So what about the explanatory benefits of Platonism/figuralism respectively? We have already seen the explanatory advantages which Yablo finds in figuralism's handling of Platonic objects and overly easy existence proofs. That leaves the explanatory benefits of Platonism to be considered. The principal merit claimed on behalf of Platonism is that it provides a basis for the objective truth of mathematics.[11] The assumption here is that mathematical objects must exist in order for mathematical statements to be true. But why think that? Figuralism also affirms the truth of mathematical sentences, but since such sentences are figurative speech, they do not imply ontological commitment to objects. Just as 'It's raining cats and dogs!' may be true without there being animals falling from the sky, so the truth that '1 + 1 = 2' does not require the reality of numbers.

Still, we may wonder what the objective basis of mathematical truths is, if not the reality of the objects referred to or quantified over in such statements. Yablo maintains that what he calls the real content of mathematical truths is logical truths, which require no ontological foundation: 'Arithmetic is, at the level of real content, a body of logical truths—specifically, logical truths about cardinality—while set theory consists at the level of real content, of logical truths of

---

[11] Yablo, 'Go Figure', 88; Yablo, 'Paradox of Existence', 286–90.

a combinatorial nature.'[12] Since there are no numbers, the literal content of arithmetical truths is false; nevertheless, their real content is true by definition. When it comes to non-numerical mathematical statements such as are comprised by set theory, Yablo takes the figurative language of sets to express certain combinatorial logical truths, that is, truths about what one gets when combining objects in different ways. Yablo recognizes that certain parts of set theory, for example, the Continuum Hypothesis, can at most be said to be relatively true, that is, true in some nice-looking models while false in others, but he thinks that the axioms of Zermelo-Fraenkel set theory are true in virtue of their real contents. Alternative set theories which do not represent sets as forming a cumulative hierarchy may also have real contents which are logical truths and therefore necessary and a priori; but such theories are not really about sets as we understand them. In sum, the realist has no advantage over the anti-realist in accounting for the objectivity of mathematical truth, since the real content of metaphorical statements about such imaginary entities as numbers and sets is logical truths. So once again, figuralism shows itself to be the superior view vis-à-vis Platonism in terms of its explanatory benefits.

Generating fewer explanatory puzzles while enjoying greater explanatory benefits than Platonism, figuralism is thus the preferable view.

OBJECTIONS TO FIGURALISM

How have Platonists responded to Yablo's figuralism? The predominant complaint in the literature is that such a view either grossly misrepresents mathematical discourse or advocates without sufficient justification a radical revision of mathematical discourse. This complaint is rooted in a familiar distinction drawn by John Burgess and Gideon Rosen between what they call hermeneutic nominalism and

---

[12] Yablo, 'Myth of the Seven', 99; Yablo, 'Abstract Objects', 230–2. For example, the real content of arithmetical truths like $2 + 3 = 5$ is the first-order logical truth $(\exists_2 x Fx \,\&\, \exists_3 y Gy \,\&\, \neg \exists z \,(Fz \,\&\, Gz)) \rightarrow \exists_5 u \,(Fu \lor Gu)$. This states that, if there are two things that are F and three things that are G, and there is nothing that is both F and G, then there are five things that are either F or G.

revolutionary nominalism.[13] Hermeneutic nominalism aims to offer an exegesis of mathematical discourse in order to determine what mathematicians and scientists themselves mean by their mathematical assertions. The hermeneutic nominalist claims that the experts do not really take their assertions to be literally true and so ontologically committing to abstract objects. The revolutionary nominalist, by contrast, grants that mathematicians and scientists do take mathematical discourse to be literally true but offers in place of the standard interpretation a novel reinterpretation of such discourse which is not Platonistic and which the experts ought to adopt instead. Burgess and Rosen's objection is that neither hermeneutic nor revolutionary nominalism is plausible, and therefore both should be rejected in favour of the literal interpretation, which is taken to be ontologically committing to abstract objects.

Anti-realists have typically repudiated Burgess and Rosen's distinction between hermeneutic nominalism and revolutionary nominalism as concocted in order to set up straw men as targets for criticism. Most anti-realists do not claim to know, in the absence of a sociological study, whether the majority of mathematicians and scientists take their statements to be Platonistic assertions about the existence of mathematical objects, nor would anti-realists be so audacious as to recommend a reform of mathematical practice predicated upon a new interpretation of mathematical discourse.[14] Their claim, rather, is that mathematical discourse *can* be understood in a non-literal way which is ontologically non-committing and that such an interpretation is unobjectionable.

Still, Yablo does affirm that his project is hermeneutical in nature and that taking abstract object talk figuratively may well give the most plausible account of our practice.[15] Two points may be made about his contention.

---

[13] See John P. Burgess, 'Why I Am Not a Nominalist', *Notre Dame Journal of Formal Logic*, 24/1 (1983): 93–105; John P. Burgess and Gideon A. Rosen, *A Subject with No Object* (Oxford: Clarendon, 1997), 6–7, 205–37; John P. Burgess, 'Mathematics and *Bleak House*', *Philosophia Mathematica*, 12/1 (2004): 23–30; Gideon Rosen and John P. Burgess, 'Nominalism Reconsidered', in Stewart Shapiro (ed.), *The Oxford Handbook of Philosophy of Mathematics and Logic* (Oxford: OUP, 2005), 515–28.

[14] See, e.g. Charles S. Chihara, 'Nominalism', in Stewart Shapiro (ed.), *The Oxford Handbook of Philosophy of Mathematics and Logic* (Oxford: OUP, 2005), 506; Geoffrey Hellman, 'On Nominalism', *Philosophy and Phenomenological Research*, 62/3 (2001): 703.

[15] Yablo, 'Go Figure', 85, 87.

First, Yablo has presented extensive and, I think, very persuasive grounds for thinking that abstract object talk in general is figurative rather than literal. Burgess and Rosen do not respond to the many intriguing parallels that Yablo draws between figurative discourse and talk of Platonic objects. Instead, they respond to three subsidiary arguments in Yablo's work, not all of which are really arguments for figuralism.

First, they take Yablo's claim that figuralism best explains the failure of overly easy existence proofs to be a version of an argument for anti-realism from the *lightheartedness* with which mathematicians introduce novel mathematical entities. The idea is that mathematicians, unlike natural scientists, are carefree about postulating previously unknown entities because they do not consider themselves to be making a genuine addition to the world's ontology. Burgess and Rosen claim that the phenomenon of lightheartedness admits of other explanations. For example, mathematicians' willingness to switch back and forth between affirming 'There are *n* *F*s' and 'The number of *F*s is *n*' is because, for whatever reason, 'mathematicians don't regard the existence of numbers as problematic'.[16] But this cannot be right. For suppose the reason mathematicians take existential affirmations about numbers to be unproblematic is because they are not realists. Then the question will be what best explains their insouciance about Platonistic discourse, and in light of the parallels Yablo adduces, the answer could well be figuralism. Burgess and Rosen need to show that, for whatever reason, mathematicians do not find the Platonistic existence of numbers to be problematic and are therefore lighthearted about their existence assertions. Ironically, Burgess and Rosen themselves observe that number claims are not generally interpreted by mathematicians as ontologically committing to numbers, but are interpreted structurally, so that numbers are replaced by characterless positions in a mathematical structure. Moreover, Burgess and Rosen fail to take cognizance of the fact that Yablo's claim about overly easy existence proofs is not limited to mathematics but, as we have seen, concerns a wide and varied range of so-called Platonic objects, some of which are concrete. Even if mathematicians are insouciant about overly easy existence proofs because they are, in fact, closet Platonists, such an explanation cannot

---

[16] Rosen and Burgess, 'Nominalism Reconsidered', 531.

account for the full range of examples Yablo adduces. Yablo's contention that figurative speech is a pervasive feature of natural language is surely correct and removes any presumption of literalness.[17]

A second argument for figuralism, to which Burgess and Rosen respond, has to do with what number statements are about. Yablo points out that someone who is concerned about the number of starving people in the world is concerned about people, not some mathematical object. Burgess and Rosen respond that intuitions of aboutness are unstable and context-dependent. For example, suppose someone says, 'The number of cats in the yard is two.' If we point out to him that his statement implies that the number of cats in the yard is a prime number, he would agree that this latter claim is about a number. Now if we return to his original statement and ask if it was not also about a number, Burgess and Rosen maintain, 'it seems well within reason that he will now report that his original claim was in part about the number 2, and not just about the cats'.[18] I find it difficult to take such a reply seriously. Not only is it highly implausible that an ordinary language user would admit that he was originally concerned about or talking about a number, but, more importantly, if intuitions of aboutness claims are shifting and context-dependent, that underscores the fact that one may be talking about people or cats in one context and then talking about a number in another context. Of course, we can talk about mathematical objects, but that goes no distance towards undermining the claim that in many contexts in which we employ number words, we are not talking about numbers but, plausibly, are using figurative speech to communicate a truth about something else.

The third argument for figuralism that Burgess and Rosen consider is the anti-realist claim that, since working mathematicians would be utterly unfazed if the Oracle of Philosophy (or God?) were to reveal

---

[17] The literary figure C. S. Lewis similarly claims that the greater part of our language is metaphorical rather than literal. Lewis was an anti-realist about mathematical discourse, taking it to be metaphorical and its objects unreal. Lewis thinks that mathematicians themselves realize that their discourse is not literal, but metaphorical. Lewis was apparently also an anti-realist about other abstract objects, such as universals. Indeed, it is likely that he took the whole Platonic host to be creatures of metaphor, for he writes, 'open your Plato, and you will find yourself among the great creators of metaphor, and therefore among the masters of meaning'. C. S. Lewis, 'Bluspels and Flalansferes: A Semantic Nightmare', in Walter Hooper (ed.), *Selected Literary Essays* (Cambridge: CUP, 1979), 265; see all of pp. 260–5. Lewis is thus an example of a theistic figuralist.

[18] Rosen and Burgess, 'Nominalism Reconsidered', 532.

that mathematical objects do not, in fact, exist, they must not be committed to the literal truth of mathematical theorems postulating the existence of mathematical objects. This third argument is not really an argument for figuralism per se, but rather is an argument for thinking that mathematicians do not generally take their existence theorems Platonistically. Burgess and Rosen respond to this argument by saying that, were such a revelation to be made, perhaps mathematicians would just refuse to believe it or perhaps they would adjust to the realization that they were wrong, so long as they were assured that mathematical theorizing could go on successfully under the pretence that such objects exist. Again, such a response seems frivolous. The point is that if mathematicians really took themselves to be describing an independently existing, Platonic realm, just as natural scientists are engaged in describing the independent, physical world, then if it were revealed that no such realm actually exists, they would be quite upset. Whether they could be so convinced or whether they could adjust to such a revelation is simply irrelevant. The point is that if mathematicians really thought themselves to be metaphysicians, then of course they would be initially shaken by the revelation that all their theorizing was empty. The fact that working mathematicians would not so react provides some reason to think that they do not take themselves to be doing metaphysics.

In addition to responding to these three arguments for figuralism, Burgess and Rosen also present an objection against figuralism, namely, the lack of direct evidence for it. They complain that we lack the best kind of direct evidence that the practice of mathematics and science involves something less than belief in the existence theorems of mathematics, namely, efforts to disavow such belief, warning students against believing them, and so on. But it seems to me that such insouciance on the part of mathematicians is consistent with an attitude of indifference towards such metaphysical conundrums—'We'll leave that question to the philosophers!'—or with the conviction that such theorems can be true without making ontological commitments. Since it just does not matter to mathematical or scientific practice whether mathematical objects exist, practitioners simply have no incentive to be bothered about them—unless, of course, they have taken a class in the philosophy of mathematics, in which case, well-informed practitioners may well be sceptical about either the literal truth of the existence theorems or else the ontological commitments of such truths. We would need a sociological study to tell.

Burgess and Rosen protest:

> Certainly in all *clear* cases of figurative language—and it is worth stressing that the boundary between figurative and literal is as fuzzy as can be—the non-literal character of the linguistic performance will be *perfectly obvious* as soon as the speaker is forced to turn attention to the question of whether the remark was meant literally.
> We further submit that mathematical discourse fails this test for non-literalness.[19]

They offer no evidence in favour of their claim that mathematical discourse fails the test, but never mind. The more important point is that this objection, if sound, at best proves that mathematical discourse is not a *clear* case of figurative language, a hardly surprising result. What does not follow is that mathematical discourse does not lie somewhere in that fuzzy area between clearly figurative and clearly literal expressions, just as Yablo claims.[20]

All this concerns my first point, that Yablo has, in fact, presented extensive and pretty persuasive reasons for his hermeneutic claim that abstract object talk in general is figurative rather than literal. But my second and more important point about figuralism is that, while Yablo espouses it as a hermeneutic thesis, there is no reason the anti-realist has to present it as such. Like most anti-realists, the figuralist can, in the absence of linguistic and sociological studies of the mathematical and scientific community, remain agnostic about hermeneutical questions and present the figurative interpretation as one reasonable way of understanding abstract object talk without commitment to abstract objects. If such a figurative interpretation is, indeed, reasonable, as it seems to be, then the Indispensability Argument has been defeated.

CONCLUDING REMARKS

A key plank in the Indispensability Argument for the existence of abstract objects is the claim that sentences quantifying over or

---

[19] Ibid., 533.
[20] Burgess and Rosen themselves explain that on Yablo's view, 'an existence theorem is ambiguous between a literal and a figurative sense' (ibid., 528). I am not sure how seriously they take this ambiguity.

containing singular terms referring to abstract objects are not merely true, but are literally true. Unlike neo-Meinongians, neutralists, and free logicians, the figuralist is willing to concede that the literal truth of mathematical statements would be ontologically committing to abstract objects. We therein see revealed the figuralist's tacit agreement with the neo-Quinean criterion of ontological commitment embodied in the first premiss of the Indispensability Argument. But in contradiction to the argument's second premiss, the figuralist sees no reason to take abstract discourse to be literally true. That does not imply that such statements are false, as the fictionalist claims. Rather, such statements are figuratively true.

Figuralism strikes me as a perfectly reasonable interpretation of abstract discourse. The parallels between figurative speech and Platonistic discourse are striking and many. Figuralism also does a good job of explaining why overly easy existence proofs fail. So long as one eschews a hermeneutic claim about how most mathematicians understand their discourse and offers a figurative interpretation as one reasonable way of construing such discourse, it seems to me that anti-realist figuralism cannot be gainsaid.

Figuralism therefore presents itself as a different, viable alternative for the classical theist concerned to meet the challenge of Platonism to divine aseity. One may accept the criterion of ontological commitment assumed by realists but deny that the truth of sentences quantifying over or containing singular terms referring to abstract objects commits us to the reality of said objects because such sentences may be understood to be, not literally, but figuratively true.

10

Make-Believe

Closely related to fictionalism and figuralism about abstract discourse is what we may call pretence theory. According to this view, abstract discourse is a kind of fictional discourse and thus analysable in terms of theories of fiction. In that sense, it is more aptly called 'fictionalism' than is fictionalism! Like fictionalists and figuralists, pretence theorists do not challenge the neo-Quinean meta-ontological theses that come to expression in premiss (I) of the Indispensability Argument, but instead challenge premiss (II). Pretence theory differs from fictionalism in that it does not claim that sentences involving quantification over or reference to abstract objects are untrue. But neither does it affirm with figuralism that such discourse is often true. Pretence theory is just neutral about the truth value of such discourse.

The pretence theorist's essential point, rather, is that, whether or not such sentences are true, we are invited to *pretend* that they are true. The pretence theorist agrees with the figuralist against the fictionalist that abstract discourse ought not, or need not, be taken literally; but he differs from the figuralist in attributing non-literality, not to the figures of speech employed, but to the fictional nature of such discourse. Thus, abstract discourse, being fictional, does not commit us to the reality of abstract objects. If we have good reason, as the theist does, to think that such objects do not exist, the objects of such discourse may be taken to be mere pretence and nothing more.

WALTON'S THEORY OF FICTION

Contemporary theories of fiction draw much of their inspiration from the brilliant, pioneering work of University of Michigan professor of philosophy Kendall Walton.¹ Walton takes the practice of 'make-believe' to lie at the heart of fiction. 'The central idea of the make-believe approach', says Walton, 'is...that what seem to be commitments, by speakers of theories, to non-existent entities are to be understood in a spirit of pretence or make-believe.'² He thinks that the activities which produce representational works of art, like literature, painting, film, and so forth, are best seen as continuous with children's games of make-believe. In support of his viewpoint, Walton makes the interesting observation:

> Children devote enormous quantities of time and effort to make-believe activities. And this preoccupation seems to be nearly universal, not peculiar to any particular cultures or social groups. The urge to engage in make-believe and the needs such activities address would seem to be very fundamental ones. If they are, one would not expect children simply to outgrow them when they grow up; it would be surprising if make-believe disappeared without a trace at the onset of adulthood.³

In Walton's view, artistic activities such as those mentioned are themselves games of make-believe. Such games are a type of imaginative activity. Walton gives examples to illustrate this familiar activity: Fred imagines himself to be rich, Jennifer imagines herself coming across a bear in the forest, and so on.

Prescribed imagining lies at the heart of Walton's theory of fiction. Fictional propositions are propositions which in certain contexts we are to imagine to be true.⁴ Walton recognizes that some propositions which are fictional may not, strictly speaking, be prescribed because they are trivial or distracting (for example, that Hamlet had a heart); nonetheless, they are prescribed to be imagined *should the question arise*. Games of make-believe involve certain explicit or implicit understandings (what Walton calls principles of generation) as to what someone playing the game is to imagine to be true. These principles of generation may or may not be explicit. Walton thinks

---

[1] Kendall L. Walton, *Mimesis as Make-Believe: On the Foundations of the Representational Arts* (Cambridge, MA: Harvard University Press, 1990).

[2] Kendall Walton, 'Existence as Metaphor', in Anthony Everett and Thomas Hofweber (eds), *Empty Names, Fiction, and the Puzzles of Non-Existence* (Stanford, CA: Center for the Study of Language and Information, 2000), 70–1.

[3] Walton, *Mimesis as Make-Believe*, 11–12.

[4] Ibid., 39. 'Fictional propositions are propositions that are *to be* imagined—whether or not they are in fact imagined.'

that some principles of generation, 'including most involving works of art, are never explicitly agreed on or even formulated, and imaginers may be unaware of them, at least in the sense of being able to spell them out'.[5] But those who play the game correctly have an implicit understanding of what is to be imagined, though in some cases uncertainty and disagreement may persist.

Walton emphasizes that truth and fictionality are not mutually exclusive. Some of the propositions prescribed to be imagined (by a historical fiction like *War and Peace*, for example) may be true. Even if all the sentences in a novel about the future like Orwell's *1984* turned out to be true, that novel still remains fiction—similarly, in the case of a novel whose sentences accurately describe events on some unknown planet in the universe.[6] What is essential to fictionality is not falsehood, but a prescription to be imagined.

This cursory sketch of Walton's theory of fiction does not do justice to its fascinating richness, but it does serve to draw our attention to some of the salient features of pretence theory when it is applied to abstract discourse: the centrality of make-believe, the importance of prescribed imagining, the neutrality of fiction with regard to the truth value of propositions which are to be imagined, the absence of any challenge to the neo-Quinean view of quantification and reference—all are elements adapted by pretence theorists in dealing with discourse about abstract objects.

LENG'S PRETENCE THEORETICAL PHILOSOPHY OF MATHEMATICS

Mary Leng is an anti-realist philosopher of mathematics who embraces Walton's theory of fiction in order to deal with the alleged commitments of our best scientific theories to mathematical objects. She does not appeal to pretence theory when dealing with the sentences of pure mathematics. In Leng's view, the practice of pure mathematics consists primarily in formulating various mathematical concepts and then inquiring into their consequences.[7] So she treats

---

[5] Ibid.   [6] Ibid., 74.
[7] Mary Leng, *Mathematics and Reality* (Oxford: OUP, 2010), 83.

the statements of pure mathematics as disguised conditionals, for example, 'If there were numbers, then it would be the case that 2 + 2 = 4.' This part of Leng's philosophy of mathematics is thus quasi-deductivist rather than pretence theoretical and forms a relatively tiny part of her defence of anti-realism.

Her central concern, rather, is the applied mathematics found in empirically successful scientific theories. She proposes to treat the applied mathematical sentences of scientific theories as fictional, prescribed to be imagined true. Leng regards the mathematical objects appearing in our scientific theories as merely useful fictions. She explains:

> it is reasonable to view the assumption that there are mathematical objects that are related to non-mathematical objects in various ways as generative of a *fiction*, which provides us with a means, indirectly, to represent non-mathematical objects and their relations. Merely *pretending* that there are mathematical objects satisfying the axioms of a given mathematical theory provides us with a means to represent non-mathematical objects (as being related to these mathematical objects in certain ways) ... *all* that is confirmed by our empirical successes is that these hypotheses are indeed fictional ..., that is, that they are correct in their representation of the non-mathematical objects they concern.[8]

The echoes of Walton's theory of fiction are unmistakable: the notions of pretence, principles of generation, fiction, representation, statements' being fictional all trace back to Walton's work.

In support of the plausibility of her view, Leng provides two non-mathematical examples of the use of fictions in scientific theorizing: idealizations and theoretical entities. These two cases illustrate the point that, even in our best scientific theories, a reason to speak *as if* an object existed is not always a reason to believe that that object exists.

With respect to scientific idealizations, Leng notes that scientists sometimes make use of idealizations which are explicitly contradicted by theoretical assumptions made elsewhere.[9] For example, textbooks on fluid dynamics treat fluids as continuous (composed of points), in order to be able to say that they have a density, velocity, and temperature defined at a certain point. No real fluid is composed of points. But given the approximation of ideal fluids to actual fluids, it can be useful to adopt such literally false theories in

[8] Ibid., 9–10.   [9] Ibid., 111.

making predictions about real fluids. Obviously, the empirical confirmation of such a theory does not extend to the literal truth of its idealizations.

A second example of the scientific use of fictions to which Leng appeals is theoretical entities towards which scientists have an attitude of agnosticism. There are cases in which our theories indispensably posit objects of a certain sort, and yet scientists refrain from saying that these objects exist until they have direct evidence of their reality. Leng has particularly in mind theories of particle physics, which will often posit certain fundamental particles (like the Higgs boson), even as scientists look for evidence of their actual existence. This case differs from the case of scientific idealizations because in this case we have no good reason for taking the fictional content of the theory to be false. The postulated theoretical entities in this case might well exist and will be believed to exist if direct evidence of their existence emerges. This circumstance nicely illustrates the point that fictional statements may well be true. We are to imagine that certain objects exist, and therefore it is fictional that such objects exist, even if it should turn out that they actually do exist.

So in line with Walton's theory of fiction, Leng does not take the fact that the mathematical sentences in our best scientific theories are fictional to imply their falsity or untruth. She explains:

> If Walton is right, then ... in viewing our mathematically stated empirical theories as merely fictional, the mathematical fictionalist need take no stand on the question of the actual, metaphysical existence of a realm of objects satisfying the mathematical utterances of our empirical theories. Viewing the mathematical objects posited by our empirical theories as *mere* fictions requires us only to view our theories as prescribing us to *imagine* that there are such objects, and as prescribing imaginings concerning their nature (including their relations to real non-mathematical objects), rather than attempting to answer to the true nature of *actual* mathematical objects.[10]

Leng claims that nothing in our current, best scientific world view gives us good reason to believe in mathematical objects as anything more than useful fictions. Hence, we have no reason to think that such objects exist.

[10] Ibid., 206–7.

OBJECTIONS TO PRETENCE THEORY IN MATHEMATICS

The Obvious Truth of Mathematics

A common objection to fictionalism, as we have seen, is that some mathematical statements, like '2+2=4,' are obviously true. This objection to fictionalism might seem irrelevant to pretence theory, since the latter view does not imply that mathematical sentences, in virtue of being fictional, are also false or untrue. Pretence theory, unlike fictionalism, is thus compatible with Platonism and serves merely as a way of defeating the Indispensability Argument for Platonism by showing that quantification and singular reference are not ontologically committing when occurring in a fictional context.

That being said, however, it remains the case that the pretence theorist who is a classical theist is committed to the falsehood or untruth of fictional sentences supposedly quantifying over or involving reference to various abstract objects. For since he denies the existence of uncreated abstract objects, he cannot remain merely agnostic about the truth of sentences taken to be fictional due to their unwanted ontological commitments. Such fictional sentences cannot, unbeknownst to us, be in fact true, for, given the pretence theorist's assumption of the neo-Quinean criterion of ontological commitment, that would involve us in commitments incompatible with divine aseity. Therefore, given pretence theory's neo-Quinean assumptions, we cannot find in pretence theory a solution to the challenge facing us unless we are willing to regard fictional sentences involving apparent quantification over or reference to mathematical objects as literally false. So the classical theist who embraces pretence theory must address the challenge posed by the obvious truth of elementary mathematical statements.

In our assessment of fictionalism, we saw that how one assesses the objection from the obviousness of mathematics is apt to hinge upon one's attitude towards the neo-Quinean criterion of ontological commitment. If we accept the neo-Quinean criterion for ontological commitment, then we shall find upon reflection that the sentences of elementary arithmetic are anything but obvious. On the other hand, if we find that the statements of elementary mathematics force themselves upon us as true, then the classical theist should simply reject the criterion which would saddle us with such strange and unwelcome ontological commitments as sets and other mathematical objects. Even if we are neutralists about ordinary language, we may on occasion be forced to resort to metaphysically heavyweight discourse in order to make our ontological commitments clear. The pretence theorist who is a classical theist will agree with the fictionalist that statements like 'There are odd as well as even numbers' are false in a metaphysically heavyweight sense. So what advantage over fictionalism does pretence theory in the end enjoy? The gain to be had from pretence theory, it seems to me, is that, like figuralism, it offers a plausible, positive account of why mathematical and other abstract sentences should not be taken to be ontologically committing to abstract objects. Because mathematical sentences are merely to be imagined as true, mathematical objects are just matters of make-believe.

Mathematics and Fiction

An important objection to interpreting mathematics as make-believe is that mathematics is not of the genre of fiction. In particular, mathematics is not to all appearances a matter of make-believe. Mathematicians and scientists take mathematics to be a body of knowledge and a realm of discovery, not invention. To regard mathematical statements as fictional is to distort the nature of this discipline.

In weighing this objection, we need to keep in mind that the pretence theorist is not defending a hermeneutical claim about how professional mathematicians or scientists in fact understand mathematical sentences. In order to undercut the Indispensability Argument for Platonism, the pretence theorist need show only that mathematical sentences *can* be reasonably taken to be fictional. So, we may ask, are the differences between fiction and mathematics so great that mathematical sentences, whether pure or applied, cannot be reasonably regarded as fictional? Remember that the truth of a sentence is not incompatible with that sentence's being fictional, so the supposed truth of mathematical sentences is not grounds for denying their status as fictional. Rather, the objection must be that mathematics is not reasonably construed to be a matter of make-believe.

But why not? Why can we not reasonably take mathematical statements as prescribed to be imagined to be true rather than believed to be true? It might be said that mathematical theories are altogether lacking such prescriptions to imagine. But the absence of such prescriptions is of little significance, since, as Walton notes, representational works of art typically lack such explicit prescriptions.[11] Indeed, literary fictions not infrequently present themselves as genuine historical records, such as a ship's log or a personal journal. The prescription to imagine them to be historical records is anything but explicit. Mathematics, being a collective enterprise, even lacks any author's intent to guide us in our interpretation. Perhaps mathematics is in that respect like mythology, which people may take either literally or fictionally.

In fact, there are some features of mathematics that make it seem a prime candidate for a fictional interpretation. I shall mention three such features.

Axiomatizaton

In the first place, axiomatization of mathematical theories naturally invites a pretence theoretical interpretation. For example, the axioms of standard set theory are plausibly taken as prescribed to be imagined. University of California philosopher of mathematics Penelope Maddy distinguishes between *believing* the axioms of standard set theory and *defending* the axioms of standard set theory.[12] Although such an apologetic concern seems at first blush to assume that the axioms are true and that it is the truth of the axioms that is to be defended, what Maddy is in fact talking about is defending *the use* of the axioms, regardless of their truth. Indeed, her aim is to 'shift attention away from... elusive matters of truth and existence'.[13] In Maddy's view, what justifies the use of set-theoretical axioms is fruitfulness: axioms

---

[11] Recall that Walton points out that not all principles of generation are established by explicit stipulation. 'Some, including most involving works of art, are never explicitly agreed on or even formulated, and imaginers may be unaware of them, at least in the sense of being unable to spell them out': *Mimesis as Make-Believe*, 38.

[12] See Penelope Maddy, 'Believing the Axioms. I', *Journal of Symbolic Logic*, 53/2 (1988): 481–511; Maddy, 'Believing the Axioms. II', *Journal of Symbolic Logic*, 53/3 (1988): 736–64; Maddy, *Defending the Axioms: On the Philosophical Foundations of Set Theory* (Oxford: OUP, 2011). The question is whether the intrinsic and extrinsic justifications she surveys really provide grounds for believing the axioms to be true rather than for entertaining or accepting the axioms without believing them.

[13] Maddy, *Defending the Axioms*, 1.

Make-Believe

are properly adopted which are rich in mathematical consequences, or what Maddy calls 'mathematical depth'.[14] In short, we do not have to believe the axioms in order to use the axioms.

Consider the axioms of standard set theory.[15] The following is a representative statement of those axioms:[16]

1. Axiom of Extensionality: Two sets are identical if they have the same members.

2. Axiom of Foundation: If any set x has a member, then there is a set y which is a member of x and which has no common member with x.

3. Axiom Schema of Restricted Comprehension or Separation: Letting Φ be any property which the members of any set z may have, there is a subset of z which contains just those members of z which have that property.

4. Axiom of Pairs: For any given sets x and y, there is a set having only x and y as members.

5. Axiom of Union: For any given set x, there is a set y containing exactly the members of all the members of x.

6. Axiom Schema of Replacement: If Φ is a formula in the language of standard set theory which relates each set x uniquely to a set y, then for a given set w a new set v can be constructed by collecting all the sets to which the members of w are uniquely related by Φ.

7. Axiom of Infinity: There exists a set x having the empty set $\emptyset$ as a member, and for any member y of x, the union of y and $\{y\}$ is also a member of x.

8. Axiom of Power Set: For any set x, there is a set y containing all the subsets of x.

9. Axiom of Choice: For any set z of disjoint, non-empty sets, there is a set w containing exactly one member from each set in z.

---

[14] Ibid., 82.

[15] For a nice discussion of the standard set theoretical axioms, see Penelope Maddy, *Naturalism in Mathematics* (Oxford: Clarendon, 1997), ch. 3, 'The Standard Axioms'.

[16] Often the Empty Set Axiom, which asserts the existence of the empty set, will be included in the list. But this axiom is not independent of the others, being entailed by the Axiom of Infinity, and is therefore superfluous.

It is striking that, with the exception of the Axiom of Infinity, these axioms are all universally quantified statements devoid of any existential implications. They explicitly have the conditional logical form attributed to them by a deductivist like Leng. One advantage of pretence theory over deductivism is that we need not reconstrue the Axiom of Infinity to have any other logical form than its apparent form. Rather, one takes the Axiom of Infinity as something we are prescribed to imagine. We are to make-believe that there is an infinity of these things called sets and then are free to explore the fictional world of our imagination. This will certainly be a journey of discovery, which will issue in a great deal of knowledge of the mathematical world determined by the axioms. Such an attitude towards the axioms of set theory is not uncommon among mathematicians and philosophers of mathematics. For example, postulationalism, which treats the axioms of competing theories as postulates whose consequences may be explored, invites us, in effect, to make-believe that the axioms are true without committing ourselves to their objective truth.[17]

But is it plausible to take the Axiom of Infinity as something prescribed to be imagined rather than as a straightforward metaphysical assertion? I think the answer is obviously affirmative. It is universally admitted that the Axiom of Infinity is not intuitively obvious. Its lack of intuitive warrant was one of the heavy stones that helped to sink logicism, an early twentieth-century attempt to derive set theory from logic alone. Since the axiom lacks intuitive warrant, the Axiom of Infinity is adopted by contemporary mathematicians for reasons that are variously called 'pragmatic' or 'regressive' or 'extrinsic', reasons which do not justify its truth, but its mathematical utility. Moreover, as Michael Potter points out, there are multiple versions of the Axiom of Infinity which postulate different sets. A defence of the axiom on pragmatic grounds 'does not directly give us a ground for preferring one sort of axiom of infinity over another', he says,

---

[17] See Michael Potter, *Set Theory and its Philosophy* (Oxford: OUP, 2004), 6–11. Since Potter takes postulationism to be a species of formalism rather than realism (or so-called full-blooded or plenitudinous Platonism), it is plausibly interpreted as an expression of pretence theory. One imagines certain objects to exist as prescribed by the axioms, and then one explores what is (unconditionally) fictional in that world. It is the fictionality of the theorems that enables them to be unconditionally asserted without ontological commitment, in contrast to full-blooded Platonism. Eliminative structuralism can be a postulationism, it seems to me, if one imagines a structure of a certain sort to exist.

since any of them will work.[18] As a result, says Potter, Platonists 'have frustratingly little they can say' by way of justification for their preferred version of the axiom.[19] As a serious assertion of ontology, the Axiom of Infinity is a breathtaking assertion that utterly outstrips our intuitions.

If any conception of sets had a claim to be intuitive, it would be the conception of nineteenth-century naïve set theory, which turned out to be riddled with logical paradoxes. The pioneers of set theory, Richard Dedekind, Georg Cantor, and Gottlob Frege, all embraced a principle of universal comprehension, according to which any property serves to determine a set of things having that property. That they were blind to the incoherence implicit in this assumption is testimony to the strength of the intuition motivating the naïve conception of sets.[20] Set theorists Abraham Fraenkel and Yehoshua Bar-Hillel believe that, were it not for the paradoxes of naïve set theory, Platonists would most naturally adopt a theory whose main feature is an Axiom Schema of Unrestricted Comprehension, such that for any property there is a set of things having that property.[21]

Axiomatization was an ad hoc fix aimed at precluding the paradoxes inherent in naïve set theory.[22] The Axiom of Infinity postulates the existence of sets governed now by (3) the Axiom Schema of Restricted Comprehension, which is an ad hoc fix of naïve set theory aimed at avoiding the paradoxes. If we take the axioms of standard set theory merely as prescribing what we are to imagine, such

---

[18] Potter, *Set Theory*, 70.   [19] Ibid., 72.
[20] Fraenkel and Bar-Hillel call the paradox discovered by Bertrand Russell 'a glaring contradiction, derived from the most plausible assumptions by a chain of seemingly unquestionable inferences'. Abraham A. Fraenkel and Yehoshua Bar-Hillel, *Foundations of Set Theory* (Amsterdam: North-Holland, 1958), 6. Russell originally formulated the paradox in terms of properties, showing that the property of being impredicative is impredicative if and only if it is not impredicative. Bertrand Russell, 'Letter to Frege' (1902), in Jean van Heijenoort (ed.), *From Frege to Gödel: A Source Book in Mathematical Logic, 1879–1931* (Cambridge, MA: Harvard University Press, 1967), 125.
[21] Fraenkel and Bar-Hillel, *Foundations of Set Theory*, 333.
[22] See Ernst Zermelo, 'Investigations in the Foundations of Set Theory I' (1908), repr. in *From Frege to Gödel*, 200; John von Neumann, 'An Axiomatization of Set Theory' (1925), in *From Frege to Gödel*, 396. K. Kuratowski and A. Mostowski observe: 'In the course of the polemic which arose over the antinomies it became obvious that different mathematicians had different concept [*sic*] of sets. As a result it became impossible to base set theory on intuition . . . it became clear that there is no unique intuitive notion of a set': *Set Theory: With an Introduction to Descriptive Set Theory* (Amsterdam: North-Holland, 1976), 5, 54.

stipulations are unobjectionable; but if we take them as serious ontological assertions about the existence of mind-independent objects, we have left behind any intuitive support for the existence of such things.[23]

Indeed, as a result of the axiomatization of set theory and the concomitant abandonment, not just of the naïve conception of what a set is, but of any definition of 'set' at all, we really do not know what we are talking about in the theory of sets.[24] One might, in line with David Hilbert's axiomatic approach to geometry in his *Foundations of Geometry* (1899), take the set-theoretical axioms to offer an implicit definition of 'set'; but then, as Frege rightly protested, we have sacrificed any intuitive warrant for taking the axioms to be *true*.[25] I could not help but smile at Frege's indignant comparison of Hilbert's axiomatic existence assertions with the ontological argument for the existence of God—as if one could simply define things into existence![26] Such a comparison is not altogether fair to Hilbert, it must be said, since he understood mathematical existence in a very lightweight sense, amounting to nothing more than consistency relative to a system of axioms;[27] but if we take the Axiom of Infinity to be a piece of serious metaphysics, then to treat its terms as implicitly

---

[23] See Goodman and Quine's poignant comment: 'What seems to be the most natural principle for abstracting classes or properties leads to paradoxes. Escape from these paradoxes can apparently be effected only by recourse to alternative rules whose artificiality and arbitrariness arouse suspicion that we are lost in a world of make-believe.' Nelson Goodman and W. V. Quine, 'Steps toward a Constructive Nominalism', *Journal of Symbolic Logic*, 12/4 (1947): 105. The failure of their own constructive nominalism should only reinforce this suspicion. See further W. V. O. Quine, 'On What There Is', *Review of Metaphysics*, 2/5 (1948): 18: the antinomies of set theory 'had to be obviated by unintuitive, *ad hoc* devices; our mathematical myth-making became deliberate and evident to all'.

[24] One recalls Russell's quip that 'Mathematics may be defined as the subject in which we never know what we are talking about, nor whether what we are saying is true.' Bertrand Russell, 'Recent Work on the Principles of Mathematics', *International Monthly*, 4 (1901): 84, cited by Mary Leng, 'Revolutionary Fictionalism: A Call to Arms', *Philosophia Mathematica*, 13/3 (2005): 277–93.

[25] Gottlob Frege, 'The Frege-Hilbert Correspondence', tr. Hans Kaal, in Gottfried Gabriel et al. (eds), *Philosophical and Mathematical Correspondence* (Chicago: University of Chicago Press, 1980), 34–51.

[26] Frege to Hilbert, 6 Jan. 1900, IV/5 [xv/5], in *Philosophical and Mathematical Correspondence*, 46.

[27] Hilbert to Frege, 29 Dec. 1899, IV/4 [xv/4], in *Philosophical and Mathematical Correspondence*, 38–9; cf. Hilbert, 'On the Foundations of Logic and Arithmetic' (1904), in *From Frege to Gödel*, 134, and 'On the Infinite' (1925), in *From Frege to Gödel*, 370.

defined by the other axioms leaves us in perplexity as to whether such things as sets really do exist. On the other hand, if we simply make-believe that they exist, then, Frege notwithstanding, we cannot be accused of trying to define things into existence.

Moreover, it deserves to be said that, wholly apart from principles of comprehension, sets, even naïvely conceived, are such strange entities that if we take set theory to be a serious piece of ontology, certain intuitive questions arise that would otherwise be obtuse. Consider, for example, the Axiom of Extensionality. According to George Boolos, the Axiom of Extensionality is the central axiom of standard set theory.[28] It requires that sets have their members essentially. But is that true? How do we know that sets do not have their members contingently? Intuitively, the set of living US Presidents loses and gains members over time. Intuitively, if Ronald Reagan were still alive, he would be a member of the set of living US Presidents. Intuitively, in a possible world in which Jimmy Carter and Bill Clinton lose their respective presidential races, they are not members of the set of living US Presidents, but others are. If I did not eat lunch today, then the Axiom of Extensionality requires that the set of things I ate for lunch is identical to the set of unicorns, namely, the empty set, which is intuitively bizarre. Indeed, the idea of an empty set is itself intuitively strange, for how can there be a collection if there is nothing to be collected? What is it a set of? Why not think that in such a case there simply is no set rather than that there is a set and it has nothing in it?[29] Why think that the Axiom of Extensionality is true?

Such questions will strike the set theorist as maladroit: sets are simply stipulated to be such that they are identical if they have the same members. Boolos takes the Axiom of Extensionality to be analytically true; any justification for it will look like justification for

---

[28] George Boolos, 'The Iterative Conception of Set', *Journal of Philosophy*, 68 (1971): 215–31, repr. in Paul Benacerraf and Hilary Putnam (eds), *Philosophy of Mathematics: Selected Readings*, 2nd edn, (Cambridge: CUP, 1983), 501.

[29] See comments by Bertrand Russell, *Introduction to Mathematical Philosophy* [1919] (London: George Allen & Unwin, 1985), 183, who accordingly takes classes to be 'symbolic fictions', about whose existence we may remain agnostic. For Fraenkel, the Null Set Axiom should not be thought of as a factual statement which may be true or false, but as a definition or convention adopted for convenience's sake: Abraham A. Fraenkel, *Abstract Set Theory* (Amsterdam: North-Holland, 1953), 23–4. Potter observes that, apart from arguments of convenience, it is rare to find arguments given for the empty set. But convenience, he emphasizes, is hardly sufficient to constitute an argument for the *truth* of the Null Set Axiom (*Set Theory*, 58–60).

sentences like 'All bachelors are unmarried.' Anyone who says that there are distinct sets with the same members is just not talking about sets.[30]

This sort of stipulation is unobjectionable so long as the Axiom of Extensionality merely prescribes what we are to imagine. But if, as Platonists believe, the axiom is an accurate description of objective reality, then why think that there are any such things as sets?[31] If such questions as these seem outrageously inept, I suspect that that is because we are not taking the axioms to be sober descriptions of mind-independent reality, but just stipulations of what sets are like.

And what about the Axiom of Foundation? It is this axiom which precludes any set's being a member of itself, thus determining the hierarchy of sets. But while such a conception of sets might make good sense on a constructivist view of sets, according to which an ideal mind constructs a hierarchy of sets, it seems an ad hoc and even counter-intuitive manoeuvre given Platonism. For why should there not be sets which are members of themselves? For example, the set of all things mentioned in this book is itself mentioned in this book. Standard axiomatic set theory banishes such sets by sheer fiat.

It is noteworthy that in his classic defence of the so-called 'iterative concept of set', Boolos's approach is undisguised constructivism:

---

[30] According to Maddy, 'most writers seem to echo the opinion of Boolos, ... the Axiom of Extensionality should be counted as analytic' ('Believing the Axioms. I', 484). She notes that Fraenkel, Bar-Hillel, and Levy also offer extrinsic reasons for its adoption, arguing that an extensional notion of set is simpler, clearer, and more convenient, unique (as opposed to the many different ways intensional collections could be individuated), and capable of simulating intensional notions when the need arises. This is all she has to offer on behalf of Extensionality, none of which justifies our belief that any actually existing entities have the relevant property.

[31] I take the suggestion of the early Maddy, now abandoned, that 'We perceive sets of physical objects much as we perceive the objects themselves' to be absurd. Maddy, 'The Roots of Contemporary Platonism', *Journal of Symbolic Logic*, 54/4 (1989): 1140. Even if we concede that we do perceive collections of objects, it is patently false, in view of the many peculiar properties of sets, that we perceive these collections to be *sets*. My teaching assistant tells me: 'I had one or two classes with Pen Maddy at UCI, and I recall one instance during a seminar in which she remarked with incredulity that someone as well-regarded as so-and-so could have held some view or other—a view that she happened to think not just false, but obviously so. At this point, one of her colleagues who sat in from time to time on the seminar stopped her, saying that she should not regard it as so remarkable that a distinguished philosopher could hold an absurd view. And he then proceeded to give her a good-natured ribbing over the fact that he knew of a philosopher who had once plumped for the unbelievable view that sets are in fact sense perceptible. She acknowledged with a sheepish grin, and everyone had a good laugh. She was a good sport about it.'

a set will include itself as a subset; but how can it contain itself as a member? This idea is paradoxical not in the sense that it is contradictory that some set is a member of itself, ... but that if one understands '∈' as meaning 'is a member of,' it is very, very peculiar to suppose it is true. For when one is told that a set is a collection into a whole of definite elements of our thought, one thinks: Here are some things. Now we bind them up into a whole. *Now* we have a set. We don't suppose that what we came up with after combining some elements into a whole could have been one of the very things we combined.[32]

Boolos even describes the formation of the hierarchy of sets as proceeding in a sequence of stages ordered by relations like 'earlier than' and 'immediately after'. At stage 0, we begin by forming collections of individuals. If there are no individuals, only one collection is formed, the null set (how or why this is a collection, rather than there being no collection at all, is not explained). One of the collections formed will be the set of all individuals, no matter how many. Then at stage 1 are formed all sets composed of individuals and stage 0 sets; at stage 2, one forms all sets composed of individuals and stages 0 and 1 sets, and so on through all the natural numbers. 'Immediately after' stages 0, 1, 2, 3, ..., there is a stage ω, which is succeeded by stage $\omega + 1$, and so on.[33] As Charles Parsons observes, the language employed here suggests that the iterative conception of set is analogous to the concepts of constructive mathematics, according to which an idealized mind forms the sequence of stages over time, a view which is 'flatly incompatible' with a Platonistic theory of sets.[34] While the iterative conception of set makes good sense on a constructivist view, it is gratuitous on a Platonist view to think that sets obey the Axiom of Foundation so as to form such a hierarchy.[35]

---

[32] Boolos, 'Iterative Conception of Set', 490–1.

[33] Again, this 'immediately after' is very counter-intuitive, since ω has no immediate predecessor, and so there is no level immediately below level ω in the hierarchy. But if there is no such level, it is mysterious how the collections at level ω can gather together all the sets on the previous levels.

[34] Charles Parsons, 'What is the Iterative Conception of Set?', in *Philosophy of Mathematics*, 507.

[35] On Maddy's account, the common attitude among mathematicians is that restricting one's attention to 'ordinary' sets is just a good working procedure, since 'no field of set theory or mathematics is in any general need of sets which are not well-founded' (Maddy, 'Believing the Axioms. I', 484). Notice that in this case, the Axiom of Foundation is actually false with respect to all the sets there really are; one just ignores the non-well-founded sets!

Or consider the Axiom of Choice. Not included among Zermelo's original axioms of set theory, it is today widely regarded as intuitively obvious for a finite family of sets but far from intuitively obvious for an infinite family of sets.[36] Though once the subject of considerable controversy, the axiom has become virtually universally accepted today—not because of its evident truth, but because of its utility and fecundity. Reflecting on the controversy, Fraenkel and Bar-Hillel muse that mathematicians' initial acceptance or rejection of the axiom was 'far more strongly influenced by emotional or practical reasons than by arguments of principle'.[37] Use of the Axiom of Choice, they advise, is to be justified by analysing concepts, methods, and proofs actually found in mathematics rather than in an intuitive manner. Even so, they opine, we should not ask whether the Axiom of Choice is true, but what additional parts of mathematics can be obtained by means of the axiom, while at the same time examining what results can be obtained without it. They recognize that such an attitude is incompatible with Platonism; but it makes perfect sense on the view that we are invited to imagine the Axiom of Choice to be true or false and to explore the respective consequences, just as the pretence theorist advocates.

In sum, axiomatic set theory seems to be a perfect candidate for a pretence theoretical approach. The philosopher of mathematics Stewart Shapiro observes: 'The strongest versions of working realism are no more than claims that mathematics can (or should) be practiced *as if* the subject matter were a realm of independently existing, abstract, eternal entities.'[38] This characterization would make working realists into pretence theorists! We are invited to imagine the axioms are true and then are free to explore the fictional world established by such prescriptions. Indeed, many mathematicians do, in fact, so understand the axioms.

---

[36] Potter e.g. states that 'it is far from clear that the axiom of choice is correctly regarded as a set-theoretical principle at all' (*Set Theory*, 4).

[37] Fraenkel and Bar-Hillel, *Foundations of Set Theory*, 74.

[38] Stewart Shapiro, *Philosophy of Mathematics: Structure and Ontology* (Oxford: OUP, 1997), 7. One recalls 19th-century philosopher Hans Vaihinger's anti-realist philosophy of *as if*.

Creative Freedom

A second respect in which set theory seems particularly apt for a fictional interpretation concerns the creative freedom enjoyed by mathematicians. Just as authors of literary fiction are free to shape their characters as they wish, without concern for correspondence with reality, so mathematicians are at liberty to craft and explore different axiomatic systems without worrying that they are misrepresenting reality in doing so. Abraham Fraenkel has spoken eloquently of abstract set theory as showing 'that possibility of *free creation* in mathematics which is not equaled in any other science. It is no accident that at the birth of the theory of sets, there was coined the sentence: the very essence of mathematics is its freedom.'[39] The freedom of 'the creative mathematician' is, he says, restricted only by 'the postulate of consistency, of logical non-contradiction'.[40] In Fraenkel's view, sets are 'logical fictions', that is to say, 'abstract concept[s]' which are the result of 'an intellectual act' of collecting things into an aggregate.[41] He notes that taking sets as logical fictions is no impediment to mathematical practice: 'The logical character of the objects called "sets" is of no importance to the mathematical theory of sets—in the same way as the results of arithmetical calculating are independent of what may be, in the view of the calculator, the logical or psychological meaning of number.'[42]

So set theorists have felt free to formulate quite a variety of set theories, some with different ontologies. For example, von Neumann-Bernays-Gödel set theory (NBG) includes, in addition to sets, mathematical objects called classes, which are governed by a universal principle of comprehension.[43] NBG thus has a fundamentally different ontology

---

[39] Fraenkel, *Abstract Set Theory*, 3–4. He attributes this sentence to set theory's founder Georg Cantor, 'Über unendliche, lineare Punktmannigfaltigkeiten', *Mathematische Annalen*, 21/4 (1883): 564.
[40] Fraenkel, *Abstract Set Theory*, 4–5.
[41] Ibid., 6, 8. Cf. Russell's remark: 'numbers do not have being—they are, in fact, what are called "logical fictions"' (*Introduction to Mathematical Philosophy*, 138). Fraenkel considers set theory to be the branch of mathematics 'most genuinely originating from the free creation of the human mind' (*Abstract Set Theory*, 331).
[42] *Abstract Set Theory*, 331.
[43] Von Neumann, 'Axiomatization of Set Theory' 394–413; Kurt Gödel, *The Consistency of the Axiom of Choice and of the Generalized Continuum Hypothesis with the Axioms of Set Theory* (Princeton: Princeton University Press, 1940). Kunen notes as well Morse-Kelley class theory, which strengthens NBG. J. L. Kelley, *General*

than standard set theory. Potter lists four variable features of the 'enormously varied' potpourri of set theories: (1) whether there are individuals or just pure sets; (2) how many levels there are in the hierarchy of sets; (3) how rich a conception there is, once a level is given, of the level that follows it in the hierarchy; and (4) whether there are classes as well as sets.[44]

Theorists working with the axioms of standard set theory are at liberty to bracket certain axioms which are independent of the others and to explore the consequences. Zermelo-Fraenkel set theory without the Axiom of Choice is probably the most familiar example, but one might omit instead the Axiom of Foundation. This will have the consequence of allowing sets which are not well founded, that is, sets exhibiting an infinite descent or circle of membership rather than ascent.[45] Such sets subvert the iterative hierarchy of sets founded on the empty set $\emptyset$. According to set theorist Kenneth Kunen, the Axiom of Foundation 'is never used in mathematics, but it leads to a much clearer picture of the set theoretic universe'.[46] In this case, the Platonist cannot even justify use of the Axiom of Foundation on the grounds of its fruitfulness; its adoption appears to be mere convenience. But then why should we think that the set-theoretical hierarchy really exists?

On the other hand, one might freely add axioms to standard set theory.[47] Adding an Axiom of Constructibility will ensure that the universe of constructible sets L is identical to the entire realm of sets V. On the other hand, we can compel moving beyond V = L by replacing the Axiom of Choice with a so-called Axiom of

---

Topology (New York: Van Nostrand Reinholdt, 1955), appendix. Kenneth Kunen comments, 'None of the three theories, ZF, NBG, and MK can claim to be the "right" one': *Set Theory: An Introduction to Independence Proofs* (Amsterdam: North-Holland, 1980), 36.

[44] Potter, *Set Theory*, 312.

[45] See Fraenkel and Bar-Hillel, *Foundations of Set Theory*, 91. A set having a single element which is the set itself $a = \{a\}$, or a descending sequence of sets, $a_1 = \{a_2\}$, $a_2 = \{a_3\}, \ldots$ subverts the iterative hierarchy of sets founded on $\emptyset$.

[46] Kunen, *Set Theory*, p. xi. Kunen adds, 'our adopting the Axiom of Foundation does not comment on whether there are *really* (whatever that means) any x such that $x = \{x\}$; we are simply refraining from considering such x' (95). 'This axiom,' he says, 'like the Axiom of Extensionality, has the effect of restricting the domain of discourse to those sets where mathematics actually takes place' (94). I can make sense of Kunen's remarks only if we take set theory as something prescribed to be imagined.

[47] Many of these are the subject of the second part of Maddy's article, 'Believing the Axioms. I', 501–11; Maddy, 'Believing the Axioms. II', 736–57.

Determinacy. In the absence of an Axiom of Constructibility, the mathematician's imagination may soar boundlessly through inaccessible cardinals, Mahlo cardinals, and indescribable cardinals, to partition cardinals, measurable cardinals, and so on.[48] Pretence theory makes far better sense of this remarkable freedom than does Platonism. For within the bounds of logical consistency, we are free to make-believe that there are mathematical entities of every imaginable sort and to explore the consequences without concern that we are thereby misdescribing reality.

Maddy observes that mathematicians employ 'maximizing principles of a sort quite unlike anything that turns up in the practice of natural science: crudely, the scientist posits only those entities without which she cannot account for our observations, while the set theorist posits as many entities as she can, short of inconsistency'.[49] Such a modus operandi seems objectionable given realism. If the set-theoretical universe, like the physical universe, were an independently existing reality, then caution would be the word of the day, not freedom. Hence, 'Quine counsels us to economize, like good natural scientists, and thus to prefer $V = L$, while actual set theorists reject $V = L$ for its miserliness.'[50] Why so? Plausibly because the set theorist does not take himself to be ontologically committed to the sets he studies. He can reap the mathematical benefits of his postulates while remaining indifferent to ontological questions.

Maddy imagines a set theorist recommending an extension of standard set theory, according to which $V \neq L$ on the grounds of its mathematical attractiveness. She then imagines how the realist might respond.

> From the realist's point of view, it would seem fully rational to respond, 'Yes, I agree with you that [it] is a very nice theory, but if all sets are

---

[48] See Frank R. Drake, *Set Theory: An Introduction to Large Cardinals* (Amsterdam: North-Holland, 1974), esp. the summarizing chart on p. 317; Kuratowski and Mostowski, *Set Theory*, ch. 10.

[49] Maddy, *Naturalism in Mathematics*, 131. In Maddy, 'Believing the Axioms. I', she identifies quite a few of these 'rules of thumb' followed by set theorists in choosing their axioms and constructing their theories, such as *maximize, richness, diversity, one step back from disaster*, etc. It is evident that reality is under no obligation whatsoever to conform to these rules of thumb. Indeed, as the example of empirical science shows, in trying to determine what actually exists, one ought to avoid such rules of thumb. By contrast, such rules make sense if we take them as prescriptions in a game of make-believe.

[50] Maddy, *Naturalism in Mathematics*, 131.

constructible, this theory is false, despite its niceness.' From this point of view, the set theorist owes evidence, not that the theory has many virtues, but that it is actually true in the real world of sets... Yet—and here's the problem—this reply to the set theorist's argument... seemed to me out of place, out of step with the actual practice of set theory.[51]

The significance of Maddy's point needs to be appreciated. Realism, if taken seriously, would be a positive impediment to mathematical practice and progress. The maximizing principles she mentions are unobjectionable on a pretence theoretical approach, since we are at liberty to make-believe as we choose. But such freedom is hard to reconcile with Platonic realism. Platonism cannot accept such principles, since we have not only an abundance of nice, rival theories, but more fundamentally, no warrant to think that 'niceness' coincides with reality in the first place.

Set theory is typically regarded as foundational for the rest of mathematics, since the whole of mathematics can be reductively analysed in terms of pure sets. Maddy comments:

> The astounding achievement of the foundational studies of the late nineteenth and early twentieth centuries was the discovery that these fundamental assumptions could themselves be proved from a standpoint more fundamental still, that of the theory of sets. The idea is simple: the objects of any branch of classical mathematics—numbers, functions, spaces, algebraic structures—can be modeled as sets, and resulting versions of the standard theorems can be proved in set theory. So the most fundamental of the fundamental assumptions of mathematics, the only such assumptions that truly cannot be proved, are the axioms of the theory of sets itself.
>
> In this sense, then, our much-valued mathematical knowledge rests on two supports: inexorable deductive logic, the stuff of proof, and the set theoretic axioms.[52]

Such a reductive analysis makes sense on a pretence theoretical approach. We imagine that there are objects such as are characterized by the set-theoretical axioms and allow them to stand in for all other mathematical objects. As Maddy explains, the mathematical benefits of such a procedure are impressive in terms of exposing inconsistencies, organizing knowledge, leading to theories of greater power and

---

[51] Ibid., 131–2.   [52] Ibid., 1; see further ch. 2, 'Set Theory as a Foundation'.

fruitfulness, and so on. But these benefits do not depend on set-theoretical foundations' providing any sort of metaphysical insight. A realist ought to be sceptical of such reductive analyses, since the ability to represent, for example, numbers as sets in no way proves that numbers are sets. Indeed, such a claim seems intuitively bizarre, for we do not normally take numbers, for example, to have members, as sets do. Moreover, different set-theoretical reductions of mathematical objects are available and equally tenable. Is the number 3 to be identified with $\{\{\{\emptyset\}\}\}$, as Zermelo suggested, or with $\{\emptyset, \{\emptyset\}, \{\emptyset, \{\emptyset\}\}\}$, as von Neumann held?[53] The Platonist must hold that there is an objective truth about this matter, yet any answer seems equally good. The Platonist might rightly say that our inability to discern the truth about the ontology of numbers is not a good argument for thinking that there is no such objective truth. But our concern here is not to offer a rebutting defeater of Platonism, but simply to inquire whether a pretence theoretical perspective is not just as plausible as Platonism. The answer to that question seems evidently, 'Yes.' We can make-believe that numbers are the sets defined by Zermelo or we can make-believe that numbers are von Neumann's sets, and it will make no difference to mathematical practice.[54]

Incompleteness of Mathematical Entities

Finally, a third respect in virtue of which set theory is especially amenable to a pretence theoretical interpretation is the incompleteness of mathematical entities. One of the most striking features of fictional characters is their incompleteness. It is not merely unknown whether, for example, Hamlet was left-handed or Sherlock Holmes

---

[53] Zermelo, 'Investigations in the Foundations of Set Theory I', 199–215; John von Neumann, 'On the Introduction of Transfinite Numbers' (1923), in *From Frege to Gödel*, 346–54.

[54] In recent decades, many philosophers of mathematics have embraced the view that numbers are ontologically nothing more than intrinsically similar positions in a relational structure having the properties of a progression. The Platonist takes structures to be mind-independent, abstract objects, so that structures simply take the place of numbers in the Platonic heaven. A pretence theoretical perspective, which takes structures merely as something prescribed to be imagined, is surely an equally plausible interpretation. On this sort of eliminative structuralism, we are invited to make-believe that an abstract ordinal structure exists and that the empty positions in this structure are what are called numbers; then we are free to explore what else is fictional about such a structure.

wore a size nine shoe; rather, there is no fact of the matter at all about such things because there are no fictional truths concerning such matters. It is neither fictional that Hamlet was left-handed nor fictional that Hamlet was right-handed. It is for that reason that many philosophers think that Hamlet could not possibly exist. For real objects are complete, at least if they are concrete, and there is nothing that would make a left-handed 'Hamlet' rather than a right-handed 'Hamlet' really be Hamlet.

The mathematical objects of infinite set theory are incomplete in a number of significant ways. The most celebrated example is the Continuum Hypothesis (CH), that the number of real numbers is $\aleph_1$, the successor to $\aleph_0$, which is the number of natural numbers. Paul Cohen demonstrated in 1963 that CH is independent of the standard set-theoretical axioms.[55] The pretence theorist plausibly maintains that CH is neither fictional nor not fictional in the game prescribed by those axioms. Of course, the mathematician is free to play a different game using different principles of generation, and in some of these CH may be fictional. For example, if we imagine certain inaccessible cardinals to exist, then CH follows. The Platonist will say that some such system of higher mathematics is true, so that CH has an absolute truth value. But none of these stronger systems, which permit virtually any answer to the question of the size of the continuum, has any intuitive warrant. The pretence theorist may surely be excused if he is sceptical about the objectivity of such conjectural systems.

There are quite a number of other mathematical hypotheses which are independent of the axioms of standard set theory, notably the Axiom of Constructibility that V = L. While the Platonist may insist that there is some objective truth about such matters, it seems equally plausible to maintain that the mathematical entities imagined to exist in such cases are, like fictional characters, simply incomplete in the standard set-theoretical story. Other stories can be told, for example, those postulating certain inaccessible cardinals, in which some of these hypotheses are fictional; but there is no reason to think that those stories are any less prescriptive of what we are to imagine.

A prescient von Neumann, discussing the question of the categoricity of set theory, that is to say, whether the axioms uniquely determine the system they describe, voiced a pessimistic conclusion:

---

[55] Paul J. Cohen, *Set Theory and the Continuum Hypothesis* (New York: W. A. Benjamin, 1966), ch. 4.

The consequence of all this is that no categorical axiomatization of set theory seems to exist at all; for probably no axiomatization will be able to avoid the difficulty connected with the axiom of restriction and the 'higher' systems. And since there is no axiom system for mathematics, geometry, and so forth that does not presuppose set theory, there probably cannot be any categorically axiomatized infinite systems at all.[56]

'This circumstance', he mused, 'seems to me to be an argument for intuitionism.'[57] That is to say, the Law of Excluded Middle fails for statements such as the Continuum Hypothesis: neither CH nor not-CH is true. Such a view fits well with the intuitionists' view of mathematics as the product of human intellectual construction; but it sits ill with Platonism. Intuitionism is not one's only choice, however: it is equally plausible to take set theory to be a realm of the human imagination, a fictional world of make-believe entities. In such a world, it is neither fictional that CH nor fictional that not-CH.

In summary, we have seen three features of set theory which make it especially amenable to a pretence theoretical interpretation: (i) the axiomatization of conflicting set theories that outstrip any intuitions that may have undergirded naïve set theory, (ii) the creative freedom of the mathematician to extend the mathematical realm as far as consistency allows, and (iii) the incompleteness of the mathematical objects referred to in mathematical theories. These seem to make a pretence theoretical approach to such objects at least as plausible as Platonism.

CONCLUDING REMARKS

Since mathematics is the last bastion of Platonism, the viability of a pretence theoretical approach to set-theoretical discourse is a devastating blow to realism. Without challenging the Platonist's assumed neo-Quinean criterion of ontological commitment, the pretence theorist undercuts the Indispensability Argument by giving a plausible account of mathematics that is not committed to its literal truth.

---

[56] Von Neumann, 'Axiomatization of Set Theory', 412.   [57] Ibid.

It is this positive account of mathematical discourse that makes pretence theory superior to the flat assertion of standard fictionalism that mathematical sentences involving quantification over or reference to abstract objects are untrue. Although the pretence theorist who is also a classical theist will agree with the fictionalist that such statements, given the neo-Quinean criterion of ontological commitment, are untrue, still, he gives a plausible account of why such sentences should not be taken to be true, namely, they are prescribed to be imagined. Therefore, their supposed ontological commitments are just make-believe.

Pretence theory's treatment of axiomatic set theory as fictional also makes pretence theory even more credible, I think, than figuralism. For while figuralism plausibly claims that the real content of many mathematical truths is purely logical, the same cannot be said of mathematical existence axioms such as the Axiom of Infinity. The lesson of logicism's failure is that infinite set theory cannot be reduced to purely logical truths about collectings, for the Axiom of Infinity is an existence assertion that has non-logical content.[58] Better to view this axiom as prescribed to be imagined, and then the consequences logically deduced.

Figuralist Stephen Yablo in fact sometimes characterizes figuralism as a sort of pretence theoretical fictionalism,[59] which shows just how blurred the lines of demarcation between these three views can become. His mature view seems to be that figurative language is not a matter of make-believe (which he, unlike Walton, takes to be a conscious activity), but of simulating belief (which he takes to be unconscious). Someone is simulating belief that S if, although things are as if that person believed that S, he finds upon reflection that he really either disbelieves or is agnostic about S taken literally or feels that the propriety of his stance does not depend upon believing

---

[58] Similarly, the first of the Peano axioms for arithmetic asserts the existence of a natural number, typically 0, which is a non-logical claim.

[59] Stephen Yablo, 'Does Ontology Rest on a Mistake?', *Proceedings of the Aristotelian Society* (Supplement), 72 (1998): 232, 243–7; Yablo, 'Go Figure: A Path through Fictionalism', in Peter A. French and Howard K. Wettstein (eds), *Figurative Language* (Oxford: Blackwell, 2001), 74, 90; Yablo, 'A Paradox of Existence', in Anthony Everett and Thomas Hofweber (eds), *Empty Names, Fiction, and the Puzzles of Non-Existence* (Stanford, CA: Center for the Study of Language and Information, 2000), 290, 295, 302–4; Yablo, 'The Myth of the Seven', in Mark Eli Kalderon (ed.), *Fictionalism in Metaphysics* (Oxford: Clarendon Press, 2005), 111.

S taken literally. Such a view of figurative discourse remains pretence theoretical at heart.

In short, pretence theory is a tenable and, I should say, attractive option for theists seeking to meet Platonism's challenge to God's status as the sole ultimate reality. For that status is not threatened by the spectre of make-believe bogeymen.

11

God Over All

When I commenced my study of divine aseity over a dozen years ago, I anticipated that I would be defending the historic Christian position with respect to abstract objects, namely, divine conceptualism. Platonism was ruled out theologically, and I was keenly aware of the bootstrapping problem that attended absolute creationism. I was not, however, aware of the difficulties confronting divine conceptualism. More than that, I had little acquaintance with the wide range of antirealist alternatives that are available to the theist. It now seems to me that both absolute creationism and divine conceptualism concede far too much to the realist.

My study of the New Testament materials and of the Church Fathers, not to mention considerations of philosophical theology, have cemented my conviction that God is to be conceived as the sole ultimate reality, the Creator of all things apart from Himself. While I now think that the absolute creationist can escape the bootstrapping objection, he can do so only by abandoning the Platonistic ontological assay of things and holding that logically prior to His creation of *abstracta* God can be as He is without exemplifying properties or propositions' being true. But then the nerve of realism has been cut, for if God can be, for example, omnipotent without exemplifying the property of *omnipotence*, we may as well forgo the postulation of properties at all. In any case, even if the bootstrapping problem can be solved, absolute creationism is still saddled with the existence of necessary and eternal objects other than God, which, as I have explained, attenuates either God's freedom or the scope of creation. There is no good reason to take on board these problems in formulating one's doctrine of divine aseity.

While divine conceptualism remains for me a fallback position, its difficulties—in particular, the ill-suitedness of divine thoughts to play the roles attributed to various abstract objects—make it a much less attractive option than it at first appeared to be. It is noteworthy, moreover, that Church Fathers who apparently espoused conceptualism did not always attribute a substantial existence to the divine thoughts standing in for abstract objects. Many of them, I suspect, were actually closer to anti-realism than to a sort of divine psychologism.

The overriding point, however, is that there is just no compelling reason to be a realist. The Indispensability Argument, which is the centrepiece of contemporary Platonism, is, in my studied opinion, a hopeless argument. Both its premisses are plausibly false. But for the purposes of our study, so bold an opinion need not be defended. In order to defeat the Indispensability Argument, one need not rebut either of its premisses, but simply undercut the warrant for one of its premisses. Given how controversial the debate over contemporary Platonism is, no view can plausibly commend itself philosophically to the exclusion of all others. (Recall that even our reason for rejecting Platonism is not philosophical but theological.) As I have tried to show, there is a plethora of philosophically defensible anti-realist alternatives to Platonism on offer today. In order to undercut the Indispensability Argument, the theist need not defend any one of these views, but can recognize the viability of a plurality of viewpoints.

For my part, I find a combinatorial approach to abstract objects to be most plausible. To begin with, I think that neutralists are right that first-order logical quantification and use of singular terms are not ontologically committing. The first-order quantifiers simply facilitate logical inferences and should not be taken as devices of ontological commitment. A deflationary theory of reference affords us the option of construing reference, not as a word–world relation, but as an intentional activity of persons. As such, given the pervasiveness of terms used to refer to socially constructed realities, most of the things we successfully refer to do not exist. A deflationary theory of truth, according to which the truth predicate is simply a device of semantic ascent, naturally and plausibly accompanies a deflationary theory of reference.

Of course, often we will find it convenient to speak of things like properties, propositions, numbers, and possible worlds. Such talk may be viewed as proceeding within an adopted linguistic framework in which we speak without making metaphysically heavyweight commitments. We can view the expressions of such a language as figurative or involving pretence. As I have argued, set theory seems to me a very plausible example of make-believe, whose affirmations carry no metaphysical weight. Ordinary English seems to be just such a metaphysically lightweight language.

Now on occasion we shall be forced to assume a perspective external to the linguistic framework in order to make our metaphysical commitments (or lack thereof!) clear. We shall want to say, for example, 'There are no uncreated abstract objects.' In this case, we are using the first-order quantifier in a metaphysically heavyweight sense. We are then speaking Ontologese, not the lightweight language of the framework. We can make this clear by rhetorical devices or modifying phrases such as 'There *really* are no uncreated abstract objects', or 'There are no uncreated abstract objects in a metaphysically heavyweight sense of "there are"'.

Ontologese is the language spoken by the fictionalist when he says that abstract object statements are untrue. But given a deflationary theory of reference, we need not go so far as the fictionalist in treating singular terms as devices of ontological commitment, even in Ontologese. Rather, with the positive free logician and with Quine himself, we may take only the logical quantifiers of Ontologese to be ontologically committing. We can still affirm the truth of predications involving singular terms for things like numbers and properties, for example, '2 + 2 = 4' and '*Wisdom* is exemplified by Socrates', without implying 'There is something which is identical to 4' or 'There is something which is exemplified by Socrates', since in free logic the rules of Existential Generalization and Universal Instantiation apply only to things of which metaphysically heavyweight existence has been truly predicated, and we have not agreed or asserted that 2 + 2 exists or that *Wisdom* exists. Thus, one need not with the fictionalist deny the truth of such predications.

Such a combinatorial approach makes good sense of the many insights of the diversity of anti-realisms. Almost all of them offer valuable insights, and we may glean from them the best of the lot.

I conclude that the challenge posed by Platonism to the doctrine of divine aseity can be met successfully. The doctrine that God is the sole ultimate reality is eminently reasonable. We may affirm without hesitation or mental reservation Paul's doxology: 'God who is over all be blessed for ever. Amen' (Rom. 9: 5).

Glossary

a se: Latin expression for self-existence; lit., by itself

absolute creationism: the view that God has created all abstract objects

abstract objects: immaterial entities which are essentially causally powerless

abstracta: Latin word for abstract objects

alethicity: being truth-apt; capable of being true or false

analytic philosophy: a method of philosophizing, dominant in Anglophone philosophy, that places a high value on clear definitions, analysis of concepts, logical rigour, and careful argumentation

analytic truth: a statement which is true simply in virtue of the meaning of its terms

anti-Platonism: the view that abstract objects do not exist

anti-realism: the view with respect to a certain thing that the thing does not exist

applicability of mathematics: mathematics' utility in describing the physical world

arché: Greek word for beginning or ultimate source

arealism: the view that there is no fact of the matter concerning something's existence

Arianism: a third-century heresy which held that God the Father is alone uncreated and therefore Christ is not God, but a created thing

aseity: self-existence

aspectual shape: the particular way in which propositional content is grasped, e.g. from a first-person or third-person perspective

asymmetric: not symmetric

axiomatization: a method of avoiding the paradoxes of naïve set theory by postulating a series of axioms, while leaving 'set' undefined; more generally, stating a mathematical theory in terms of basic axioms from which theorems may be derived

axioms of mathematics: basic postulates of a mathematical theory

bare particular: a thing logically prior to its exemplifying any properties

biblical theology: exegetical theology aimed at determining the view of the biblical author

bootstrapping objection: an objection alleging a vicious circularity class: a mathematical set-like object which is even more comprehensive than a set

composite: made up of more fundamental parts

conceptual: pertaining to the intellect, to ideas

conceptualism: the view that supposedly abstract objects are really concrete thoughts of God

concrete objects: objects which have causal powers, such as minds and material objects

conservation: God's preserving things in being moment by moment

constant: a logical term which stands for an individual, typically, 'a', 'b', 'c', etc.; constants may be substituted for variables, typically 'x', 'y', 'z', in order to form statements about specific individuals

contingent: possible but not necessary

contingentism: the view that some things exist contingently

conventionalism: the view that answers to metaphysical questions are wholly arbitrary, having no truth value

counterfactuals: conditional statements in the subjunctive mood; e.g. 'If I were rich, I would buy a Mercedes.'

creatio ex nihilo: Latin expression for creation without a material cause (lit., creation out of nothing)

criterion of ontological commitment: a criterion revealing to us just what existential commitments our assertions have; it tells us what we have to believe exists in order to hold to the truth of our assertion

deductivism: the view that mathematical statements have the (disguised) logical form of conditional statements; also called If-thenism

deflationary: minimalist; reducing one's ontological commitments; opposite of inflationary

demiurge: in Plato's dialogue *Timaeus*, a god-like being who looks to the Forms as his model for creating the sensible world

denote: a term's singling out some object which has the properties predicated by the statement in which the term occurs; the object is the denotation of the term

domain of quantification: in logic, the class of things over which one is quantifying; one says something about either all the members of the domain or some of the members of the domain

doxastic attitudes: attitudes towards some propositional content, such as belief, doubt, hope, expectation

doxasticity: capable of being the object of doxastic attitudes

dual domain semantics: in free logic, a semantics featuring two domains, one over which the quantifiers range and the other containing the referents of singular terms which fail to refer to things in the first domain

eliminative structuralism: anti-realist view of mathematical structures

emanationism: the view that things proceed from the being of God independent of His will

entity: a thing; a being; an object

epistemic: cognitive; knowledge related

essential: belonging to a thing's very nature

eternal: having neither beginning nor end in time; permanent

eternalism: a view of time as tenseless

ex nihilo: see *creatio ex nihilo*

exemplification: a relation between a thing and a property which the thing has; e.g. Fido exemplifies the property of *brownness*

exemplify: to have (a property)

Existential Generalization: a logical rule permitting us to infer from '*a* is *F*' that 'There is something that is *F*' (or, 'Something is *F*')

existential quantifier: a logical operator which makes a statement an existentially quantified statement. Ordinary language expressions like 'there is/are', 'some', 'at least one', and so forth, are informal quantifiers; in formal or symbolic logic, the operator '∃' is a formal quantifier symbolizing such informal expressions

existential sentence: an existentially quantified sentence

existentially loaded: carrying ontological commitment

existentially quantified statement: an assertion about some of the members of a class, usually indicated by words like 'some', 'there is/are', 'at least one', and so forth

extensional context: sentence phrases which have two characteristics: (i) singular terms referring to the same entity can be switched without affecting the sentence's truth value; (ii) one can quantify into such contexts from the outside

external questions: questions posed in a language not used in an adopted linguistic framework

fictionalism: the view that abstract object discourse is false or untrue

fictionally true: prescribed to be imagined as true

figuralism: the view that abstract object discourse is figurative language

figurative language: non-literal language, e.g. metaphorical language

Form: for Plato, transcendent, abstract objects on which God patterns the sensible world; for Aristotle, immaterial entities which imbue matter to make it into some specific thing, such as a rock or a horse

free logic: a logic which holds that the quantifiers of first-order logic are ontologically committing but denies that singular terms are devices of ontological commitment

genus and species: ancient categories for classifying things into kinds

heavyweight Platonism: the view that abstract objects are fundamental features of reality

Hellenistic Judaism: Judaism which bore the imprint of Greek thinking and culture. Though it is sometimes distinguished from Palestinian Judaism, in fact, Greek influence was strong in the Jewish homeland.

hermeneutic nominalism: the view that mathematicians themselves do not take their mathematical sentences to be ontologically committing to mathematical objects

ideal: non-physical, conceptual

idealization: a fictitious entity in a scientific theory which real objects approximate, e.g. ideal gases or ideal fluids

impredicative: pertaining to something's being a member or constituent of itself

indispensability of mathematics: the necessity of using mathematical terms in describing the physical world

instantiation: the relation between a thing and its essence, whereby the essence is particularized; the thing is an instance of its essence; e.g. Paul and John instantiate or are instances of *humanity*

instrumental: not descriptive of reality, but nevertheless useful for various practical purposes, such as making predictions

instrumentalism: the view that a certain type of discourse is not to be taken as descriptive of reality, but merely as useful for various purposes

intellective activity: thinking

intelligible realm/world: in ancient Platonism, the realm of the Ideas; a static, conceptual realm

intensional context: a non-extensional context (*see* extensional context)

intentional attitude: an object-directed attitude; an attitude *about* something

intentionality: about-ness; object-directedness; being *of* something; 'intentional' must not be confused with 'intensional'

internal questions: questions posed in the language of an adopted linguistic framework

Glossary

intransitive: not transitive

intuitionism: the view that mathematics is a construction of human minds; it denies the Law of Excluded Middle: p or not-p

Law of Excluded Middle: for any proposition p, either p or not-p is true

lightweight Platonism: the view that abstract objects merely serve as the semantic referents of certain terms and as values of the variables of quantification

linguistic framework: an object language involving terms for certain kinds of objects to which one is not ontologically committed when speaking from a standpoint outside the framework

literally true: true; not metaphorically true

logically prior: prior in the order of explanation

logicians: persons who specialize in the study of logic

logicism: an early twentieth-century attempt to derive set theory from logic alone

LXX: the Septuagint, an ancient Greek translation of the Old Testament

mereological nihilism: the view that there are no composite objects

mereological universalism: the view that any plurality whatsoever compose an object

mereology: area of metaphysics which studies parts and wholes

metalanguage: language used to talk about a lower level language

meta-ontological anti-realism: the view that there are no objective answers to certain ontological questions

meta-ontology: a higher level philosophical discipline about how to settle questions of ontology

metaphysical: pertaining to metaphysics; beyond the physical world; what is ultimately real

metaphysical necessity/possibility: what must be actual/what could be actual

metaphysics: a branch of philosophy exploring reality in its various aspects

Middle Platonism: a school of philosophical thought which evolved from classical Platonism and flourished from the first century BC until the third century; Middle Platonists identified Plato's Ideas with God's thoughts

mind-independent: not products of human thinking or imagination; objectively existing

modal: having to do with something's possibility or necessity

modal operator: a logical prefix which serves to give a modal status to a statement, like 'Necessarily, . . .' or 'Possibly, . . .'

nature: the essence of a thing, or those properties without which the thing would not exist

necessary: having to be certain way; being impossible to be otherwise

necessitism: the view that everything that exists exists necessarily

neo-Meinongianism: the view deriving from Alexius Meinong that there are (in a neutral sense) nonexistent objects bearing properties

neo-Quinean: deriving from the view of the influential American philosopher W. V. O. Quine

neutralism: the view that existential quantification and use of singular terms are not ontologically committing

nominalism: in medieval debates, the view that universals do not exist; in the contemporary debate, the view either that abstract objects do not exist or that objects of a certain sort normally taken to be abstract, such as mathematical objects, do not exist

nominalistic content: the non-Platonistic contents of scientific theories

nominalistic scientific realism: the view that the nominalistic content of scientific theories is mostly true, while its Platonistic content is untrue

nominalization: finding a noun or noun phrase to express a notion; gerunds are often used for this purpose

object language: ground level language about the objects in one's quantificational domain

objectual semantics for quantificational logic: a theory of quantification according to which the variables which lie within the scope of the quantifiers range over a specified domain of objects to pick out various objects in the domain

occurrent: present in consciousness

Ockham's Razor: the principle that, all things being equal, simpler explanations are to be preferred; causes should not be multiplied unnecessarily

One over Many: an ancient philosophical problem of explaining the resemblance of particular objects to each other; what is the one thing that they have in common that accounts for their resemblance?

ontically relevant: carrying ontological implications

onticity: ontological reality

ontological: pertaining to being or existence

ontological assay: an account of the metaphysical constituents of a thing

ontological commitment: something that one must regard as real or existent

ontological dependence: dependence in being (regardless of temporal beginning) ontological dispute: a disagreement over what exists or is real

ontologically inflationary: carrying gratuitous ontological commitments

ontologists: philosophers who study ontology

ontology: the study of what exists; an account of what exists

ontology, constituent: an ontology which takes things to be metaphysically composed of other entities; e.g. a substratum and its properties

ontology, relational: an ontology which takes things to be metaphysically simple, i.e. lacking any metaphysical constituents

paradigms: representative examples

paraphrastic strategies: anti-realist strategies for paraphrasing sentences involving quantification over, or singular terms referring to, abstract objects, so that their ontological commitments are eliminated

particular quantifier: an ontologically neutral existential quantifier

patristic: pertaining to the Church Fathers

personification: the portrayal of some property or aspect of a thing as a person, e.g. Lady Luck

Platonism: the view that there exist abstract objects

possible worlds: ways reality might have been; maximal states of affairs

postulationalism: the view which treats the axioms of competing mathematical theories as postulates whose consequences may be explored

presentism: the view that the present is ontologically privileged; the past and future do not exist

pretence theory: a theory of fiction according to which statements of fiction are prescribed to be imagined true

principle of universal comprehension: the principle according to which any property serves to determine a set of things having that property

property: a universal quality which is exemplified by particulars

property instance: the particular exemplification of a property, as the redness of this rose; property instances are particulars, not universals

proposition: the information content expressed by sentences

quantification: *see* existentially quantified statement, universally quantified statement

quantifier: *see* existential quantifier, universal quantifier

quantify over (something): to take (something) as the value of the variable lying within the scope of the quantifier

realism: the view with respect to a certain thing that that thing exists

referent: what one refers to

referentialism: the doctrine that singular terms successfully refer only if there are mind-independent objects in the world which are the denotations or referents of the terms

reify: to construe something as a thing by nominalizing an expression for it; e.g. if one hunts deer, one might say that one is engaged in deer-hunting

revolutionary nominalism: the view that mathematics needs to be revised in such a way that its sentences are not ontologically committing to abstract objects

Second Temple period: the time when King Herod's temple in Jerusalem was still standing

self-existent: existing independently of anything else

semantic ascent: talking *about* a claim rather than simply *making* the claim itself

semantic descent: simply *making* a claim rather than talking *about* the claim

semantic theory: theory concerning the meaning of linguistic expressions

sensible realm/world: in ancient Platonism, the realm of temporal becoming and concrete objects

simple: having no parts; uncomposed

simplicity: the property of being simple

single domain semantics: in free logic, a semantics featuring a single domain, typically everything that exists

singular term: a word (or words) which serves to pick out a specific individual, typically proper names like 'John' or 'USS Constitution', definite descriptions like 'the coin in my pocket' or 'your left arm', and demonstratives like 'this' and 'that'

socially constructed reality: objects dependent upon social conventions

sole ultimate reality: the only self-existent, uncreated thing

Sophia: a female personification of God's wisdom in Jewish Wisdom literature

sovereignty: God's control over all things

speaker's reference: what the person using certain terms intends to refer to

special composition question: a question in mereology as to what conditions have to be met in order for a plurality to compose an object

Stoicism: an ancient Greco-Roman philosophy originating in the third century BC that included an impersonal *logos* principle which supplied the world with rational structure

structuralism: the view which takes numbers to be no more than positions in a certain kind of structure or pattern

substances: things which exist in their own right and not as modifications of something else

substitutional semantics for quantified logic: a theory of quantification according to which the variables within the scope of the quantifier serve as dummy letters which may be replaced by linguistic expressions in order to form sentences

symmetric: a relation > is symmetric just in case A > B, and B > A

systematic theology: reflection upon the data of Scripture using philosophical and other tools

temporal: located in time

tense operator: a logical prefix which serves to give a tenseless statement a tense, like 'It was the case that . . .' or 'It will be the case that . . .'

tensed theory of time: a view of time which holds that the tense of moments or events in time is objective and so the distinction between past, present, and future is an objective feature of the world

tenseless: lacking any relation to the present and so neither past, present, nor future

tenseless theory of time: a view of time which implies that all moments or events in time are equally real and the distinction between past, present, and future is merely a subjective feature of consciousness

theistic activism: the view that modality is at least partly grounded in God's free will

theorems of mathematics: statements deducible from the axioms of a mathematical theory

theoretical entity: an unobservable object which may or may not exist but is posited by a scientific theory for its value in modelling physical phenomena

transcendent: beyond space and time, or beyond the physical universe

transitive: a relation > is transitive just in case if A > B, and B > C, then A > C

truth value: the property of being true/false

universal (*n.*): a property; it is what particular objects have in common that explains their resemblance to one another; e.g. a British pillar box and a fire engine both share the universal *redness*

Universal Instantiation: a logical rule permitting us to infer from 'Everything is F' that 'a is F'

universal quantifier: a logical operator which makes a statement a universally quantified statement. Ordinary language expressions like 'all', 'every', 'any', and so forth, are informal quantifiers; in formal or symbolic logic, the operator '$\forall$' is a formal quantifier symbolizing such informal expressions. The symbol for the formal quantifier is often omitted for simplicity's sake.

For example, instead of $(\forall x)\ (Fx \to Gx)$, one might write $(x)\ (Fx \to Gx)$, to be read 'For any x, if x is F, then x is G'

universally quantified statement: an assertion about all the members of a class, usually indicated by words like 'all', 'every', 'any', and so forth

univocal: having a single meaning; not equivocal

value: in logic, the thing that replaces the variable in a sentence like $(\exists x)\ (x$ is an $F)$; e.g. in 'a is F', the thing a stands for is the value of x

variable: in first-order logic, the universal and existential quantifiers '$\forall$' and '$\exists$' are said to bind or have within their scope variables (like x, y, z) which may be replaced by certain constants (like a, b, c) to make statements about certain individuals in the domain of objects. E.g. in $(\forall x)\ (Fx \to Gx)$, x is a variable which may be replaced by the constant a to make the statement $Fa \to Ga$

verificationism: the view that meaningful sentences must be, in principle, capable of being verified empirically

voluntarism: any view that privileges God's free will over His nature

Wisdom literature: ancient Jewish literature which especially emphasized the role of God's wisdom in creation

YHWH: abbreviation for the Hebrew name of God *Yahweh*, or the LORD

Zermelo-Fraenkel set theory: standard set theory whose axioms were laid by Ernst Zermelo and Abraham Fraenkel

ZFC: Zermelo-Fraenkel set theory plus the Axiom of Choice

Works Cited

Adams, Robert. 'The Metaphysical Lightness of Being.' Paper presented to the Philosophy Department colloquium at the University of Notre Dame, 7 Apr. 2011.
Armstrong, D. M. *Universals and Scientific Realism: Nominalism and Realism*, vol. i. Cambridge: Cambridge University Press, 1978.
Armstrong, D. M. *Universals: An Opinionated Introduction*. Boulder, CO: Westview Press, 1989.
Azzouni, Jody. *Deflating Existential Consequence: A Case for Nominalism*. Oxford: Oxford University Press, 2004.
Azzouni, Jody. 'Ontological Commitment in the Vernacular.' *Noûs*, 41/2 (2007): 204–26.
Azzouni, Jody. 'Ontology and the Word "Exist": Uneasy Relations.' *Philosophia Mathematica*, 18/1 (2010): 74–101.
Azzouni, Jody. *Talking about Nothing: Numbers, Hallucinations, and Fictions*. Oxford: Oxford University Press, 2010.
Azzouni, Jody. 'Singular Thoughts (Objects-Directed Thoughts).' *Proceedings of the Aristotelian Society Supplementary Volume*, 85/1 (2011): 45–61.
Azzouni, Jody. 'A New Characterization of Scientific Theories.' *Synthèse*, 191/13 (2014): 2993–3008.
Baker, Lynne Rudder. *The Metaphysics of Everyday Life: An Essay in Practical Realism*. Cambridge: Cambridge University Press, 2007.
Balaguer, Mark. *Platonism and Anti-Platonism in Mathematics*. New York: Oxford University Press, 1998.
Balaguer, Mark. 'Platonism in Metaphysics.' In *The Stanford Encyclopedia of Philosophy*, Summer 2009 edn. Article published 21 June 2009. <http://plato.stanford.edu/archives/sum2009/entries/platonism>.
Balaguer, Mark. 'Fictionalism in the Philosophy of Mathematics.' In *The Stanford Encyclopedia of Philosophy*, Fall 2013 edn. Article published 21 Sept. 2013. <http://plato.stanford.edu/archives/fall2013/entries/fictionalism-mathematics>.
Bauckham, Richard. 'Biblical Theology and the Problems of Monotheism.' In *Jesus and the God of Israel: God Crucified and Other Studies on the New Testament's Christology of Divine Identity*, 60–106. Grand Rapids, MI: William B. Eerdmans, 2008.
Bauckham, Richard. 'God Crucified.' In *Jesus and the God of Israel: God Crucified and Other Studies on the New Testament's Christology of Divine Identity*, 1–59. Grand Rapids, MI: William B. Eerdmans, 2008.
Båve, Arvid. 'A Deflationary Theory of Reference.' *Synthèse*, 169/1 (2009): 51–73.

Bergmann, Michael, and Jeffrey E. Brower. 'A Theistic Argument Against Platonism (and in Support of Truthmakers and Divine Simplicity).' In Dean Zimmerman (ed.), *Oxford Studies in Metaphysics*, ii. 357–86. Oxford: Oxford University Press, 2006.

Boolos, George. 'The Iterative Conception of Set.' In Paul Benacerraf and Hilary Putnam (eds), *Philosophy of Mathematics: Selected Readings*, 2nd edn, 486–502. Cambridge: Cambridge University Press, 1983.

Boolos, George, and Richard Jeffrey. *Computability and Logic*. Cambridge: Cambridge University Press, 1974.

Brentano, Franz. 'The Distinction between Mental and Physical Phenomena.' Tr. D. B. Terrell. In Roderick M. Chisholm (ed.), *Realism and the Background of Phenomenology*, 39–61. Atascadero, CA: Ridgeview, 1960.

Brentano, Franz. 'Genuine and Fictitious Objects.' Tr. D. B. Terrell. In Roderick M. Chisholm (ed.), *Realism and the Background of Phenomenology*, 71–5. Atascadero, CA: Ridgeview, 1960.

Burgess, John P. 'Why I Am Not a Nominalist.' *Notre Dame Journal of Formal Logic*, 24/1 (1983): 93–105.

Burgess, John P. 'Mathematics and *Bleak House*.' *Philosophia Mathematica*, 12/1 (2004): 18–36.

Burgess, John P., and Gideon A. Rosen. *A Subject with No Object: Strategies for Nominalistic Interpretation of Mathematics*. Oxford: Clarendon, 1997.

Cantor, Georg. 'Über unendliche, lineare Punktmannigfaltigkeiten.' *Mathematische Annalen*, 21/4 (1883): 545–91.

Carnap, Rudolf. *Meaning and Necessity: A Study in Semantics and Modal Logic*. Chicago: University of Chicago Press, 1956.

Chalmers, David J. 'Ontological Anti-Realism.' In David J. Chalmers, David Manley, and Ryan Wasserman (eds), *Metametaphysics: New Essays on the Foundations of Ontology*, 77–129. Oxford: Clarendon, 2009.

Chihara, Charles S. 'Nominalism.' In Stewart Shapiro (ed.), *The Oxford Handbook of Philosophy of Mathematics and Logic*, 483–514. Oxford: Oxford University Press, 2005.

Clouser, Roy A. *The Myth of Religious Neutrality: An Essay on the Hidden Role of Religious Belief in Theories*, rev. edn. Notre Dame, IN: University of Notre Dame Press, 2005.

Cohen, Paul J. *Set Theory and the Continuum Hypothesis*. New York: W. A. Benjamin, 1966.

Copan, Paul, and William Lane Craig. *Creation Out of Nothing: A Biblical, Philosophical, and Scientific Exploration*. Grand Rapids, MI: Baker Academic, 2004.

Craig, William Lane. *Divine Foreknowledge and Human Freedom: The Coherence of Theism: Omniscience*. Studies in Intellectual History. Leiden: E. J. Brill, 1990.

Craig, William Lane. *The Tensed Theory of Time: A Critical Examination.* Synthèse Library. Dordrecht: Kluwer Academic Publishers, 2000.
Craig, William Lane. *The Tenseless Theory of Time: A Critical Examination.* Synthèse Library. Dordrecht: Kluwer Academic Publishers, 2000.
Craig, William Lane. 'Critical Notice of Alvin Plantinga, *Where the Conflict Really Lies: Science, Religion, and Naturalism.*' *Philosophia Christi,* 14 (2012): 473–7.
Craig, William Lane. 'Response to Greg Welty.' In Paul M. Gould (ed.), *Beyond the Control of God? Six Views on the Problem of God and Abstract Objects,* 100–2. London: Bloomsbury, 2014.
Craig, William Lane. 'God and Abstract Objects.' *Philosophia Christi,* 17/2 (2015): 269–76.
Craig, William Lane. 'Response to Bridges and van Inwagen.' *Philosophia Christi,* 17/2 (2015): 291–7.
Craig, William Lane. *God and Abstract Objects.* Berlin: Springer Verlag, forthcoming.
Crane, Tim. 'Intentionality.' In Edward Craig (ed.), *The Routledge Encyclopedia of Philosophy,* 2nd edn. London: Routledge, 1998.
Crane, Tim. 'Intentionality as the Mark of the Mental.' In Anthony O'Hear (ed.), *Current Issues in Philosophy of Mind,* 229–52. Cambridge: Cambridge University Press, 1998.
Crane, Tim. *Elements of Mind: An Introduction to the Philosophy of Mind.* Oxford: Oxford University Press, 2001.
Devitt, Michael. '"Ostrich Nominalism" or "Mirage Realism"?' *Pacific Philosophical Quarterly,* 61/4 (1980): 433–9.
Drake, Frank R. *Set Theory: An Introduction to Large Cardinals.* Studies in Logic and the Foundations of Mathematics. Amsterdam: North-Holland, 1974.
Dummett, Michael. 'Nominalism.' In *Truth and Other Enigmas,* 38–49. Cambridge, MA: Harvard University Press, 1978.
Dummett, Michael. *Frege: Philosophy of Mathematics.* Cambridge, MA: Harvard University Press, 1991.
Dunn, James D. G. *Romans 9–16.* Word Biblical Commentary. Dallas, TX: Thomas Nelson, 1988.
Field, Hartry. *Realism, Mathematics, and Modality.* Oxford: Basil Blackwell, 1989.
Field, Hartry H. *Science without Numbers: A Defence of Nominalism.* Princeton: Princeton University Press, 1980.
Findlay, J. N. *Meinong's Theory of Objects and Values,* 2nd edn. Oxford: Clarendon, 1963.
Fraenkel, Abraham A. *Abstract Set Theory.* Studies in Logic and the Foundations of Mathematics. Amsterdam: North-Holland, 1953.
Fraenkel, Abraham A., and Yehoshua Bar-Hillel. *Foundations of Set Theory.* Studies in Logic and the Foundations of Mathematics. Amsterdam: North-Holland, 1958.

Frege, Gottlob, and David Hilbert. 'The Frege-Hilbert Correspondence.' Tr. Hans Kaal. In Gottfried Gabriel, Hans Hermes, Friedrich Kambartel, Christian Thiel, Albert Veraart, and Brian McGuiness (eds), *Philosophical and Mathematical Correspondence.*, 33–51. Chicago: University of Chicago Press, 1980.

Gödel, Kurt. *The Consistency of the Axiom of Choice and of the Generalized Continuum Hypothesis with the Axioms of Set Theory.* Annals of Mathematical Studies. Princeton: Princeton University Press, 1940.

Goodman, Nelson, and W. V. Quine. 'Steps toward a Constructive Nominalism.' *Journal of Symbolic Logic*, 12/4 (1947): 105–22.

Gottlieb, Dale. *Ontological Economy: Substitutional Quantification and Mathematics.* Oxford: Oxford University Press, 1980.

Gould, Paul M., and Richard Brian Davis. 'Response to Critics.' In Paul M. Gould (ed.), *Beyond the Control of God? Six Views on the Problem of God and Abstract Objects*, 75–80. London: Bloomsbury, 2014.

Gould, Paul M., and Richard Brian Davis. 'Response to Greg Welty.' In Paul M. Gould (ed.), *Beyond the Control of God? Six Views on the Problem of God and Abstract Objects*, , 99–100. London: Bloomsbury, 2014.

Gould, Paul M., and Richard Brian Davis. 'Response to Keith Yandell.' In Paul M. Gould (ed.), *Beyond the Control of God? Six Views on the Problem of God and Abstract Objects*, 36–7. London: Bloomsbury, 2014.

Hale, Bob. *Abstract Objects*. Philosophical Theory. Oxford: Basil Blackwell, 1987.

Hellman, Geoffrey. 'On Nominalism.' *Philosophy and Phenomenological Research*, 62/3 (2001): 691–705.

Hersh, Reuben. 'Mainstream Before the Crisis.' In *What is Mathematics, Really?*, 91–118. New York: Oxford University Press, 1997.

Hilbert, David. 'On the Foundations of Logic and Arithmetic.' In Jean van Heijenoort (ed.), *From Frege to Gödel: A Source Book in Mathematical Logic, 1879–1931*, 129–38. Cambridge, MA: Harvard University Press, 1967.

Hilbert, David. 'On the Infinite.' In Jean van Heijenoort (ed.), *From Frege to Gödel: A Source Book in Mathematical Logic, 1879–1931*, 367–92. Cambridge, MA: Harvard University Press, 1967.

Hofweber, Thomas. 'Ontology and Objectivity.' Ph.D. dissertation, Stanford University, 1999.

Horsley, Richard A. 'Gnosis in Corinth: I Corinthians 8.1–6.' *New Testament Studies*, 27/1 (1980): 32–51.

Horwich, Paul. *Meaning*. Oxford: Clarendon, 1998.

Hudson, Hud. 'Confining Composition.' *Journal of Philosophy*, 103/12 (2006): 631–51.

Husserl, Edmund. *Logical Investigations*, 2 vols. Tr. J. M. Findlay. New York: Humanities Press, 1970.

Inman, Ross. 'On Christian Theism and Unrestricted Composition.' Paper presented at the annual meeting of the Evangelical Philosophical Society, Milwaukee, WI, Nov. 2012.

Jacquette, Dale. 'Meditations on Meinong's Golden Mountain.' In Nicholas Griffin and Dale Jacquette (eds), *Russell vs. Meinong: The Legacy of 'On Denoting'*, 169–203. London: Routledge, 2009.

Jones, Roger Miller. 'The Ideas as the Thoughts of God.' *Classical Philology*, 21/4 (1926): 317–26.

Keener, Craig S. *The Gospel of John: A Commentary*, i. Peabody, MA: Hendrickson Publishers, 2003.

Kelley, J. L. *General Topology*. New York: Van Nostrand Reinholdt, 1955.

Kripke, Saul A. 'Is There a Problem about Substitutional Quantification?' In Gareth Evans and John McDowell (eds), *Truth and Meaning: Essays in Semantics*, 324–419. Oxford: Clarendon, 1976.

Kripke, Saul A. 'Speaker's Reference and Semantic Reference.' In Peter A. French, Theodore E. Uehling, Jr, and Howard K. Wettstein (eds), *Contemporary Perspectives in the Philosophy of Language*, 6–27. Minneapolis: University of Minnesota Press, 1979.

Kunen, Kenneth. *Set Theory: An Introduction to Independence Proofs*. Studies in Logic and the Foundations of Mathematics. Amsterdam: North-Holland, 1980.

Kuratowski, Kazimierz, and Andrzej Mostowski. *Set Theory: With an Introduction to Descriptive Set Theory*. Studies in Logic and the Foundations of Mathematics. Amsterdam: North-Holland, 1976.

Lamarque, Peter, and Stein Haugom Olsen. *Truth, Fiction, and Literature: A Philosophical Perspective*. Oxford: Clarendon, 1994.

Lambert, Karel. 'Existential Import Revisited.' *Notre Dame Journal of Formal Logic*, 4/4 (1963): 288–92.

Lambert, Karel. *Meinong and the Principle of Independence*. Cambridge: Cambridge University Press, 1983.

Lambert, Karel. 'The Nature of Free Logic.' In Karel Lambert (ed.), *Philosophical Applications of Free Logic*, 3–14. Oxford: Oxford University Press, 1991.

Lambert, Karel. *Free Logic: Selected Essays*. Cambridge: Cambridge University Press, 2003.

Leftow, Brian. 'Is God an Abstract Object?' *Noûs*, 24/4 (1990): 581–98.

Leftow, Brian. 'God and the Problem of Universals.' In Dean Zimmerman (ed.), *Oxford Studies in Metaphysics*, ii. 325–56. Oxford: Oxford University Press, 2006.

Leftow, Brian. *God and Necessity*. Oxford: Oxford University Press, 2012.

Leng, Mary. 'Revolutionary Fictionalism: A Call to Arms.' *Philosophia Mathematica*, 13/3 (2005): 277–93.

Leng, Mary. *Mathematics and Reality*. Oxford: Oxford University Press, 2010.

Works Cited

Leonard, Henry S. 'Essences, Attributes, and Predicates.' *Proceedings and Addresses of the American Philosophical Association*, 37 (1963): 25–51.

Leonhardt-Balzer, Jutta. 'Der Logos und die Schöpfung: Streiflichter bei Philo (Op 20-25) und im Johannesprolog (Joh 1, 1-18).' In Jörg Frey and Udo Schnelle (eds), *Kontexte des Johannesevangeliums*, 295–320. Tübingen: Mohr Siebeck, 2004.

Lewis, C. S. 'Bluspels and Flalansferes: A Semantic Nightmare.' In Walter Hooper (ed.), *Selected Literary Essays*, 251–65. Cambridge: Cambridge University Press, 1979.

Lewis, David K. *Parts of Classes*. Oxford: Basil Blackwell, 1991.

Lewis, David K. 'Tensed Quantifiers.' In Dean Zimmerman (ed.), *Oxford Studies in Metaphysics*, i. 3–14. Oxford: Oxford University Press, 2004.

Lewis, David K., and Stephanie Lewis. 'Holes.' *Australasian Journal of Philosophy*, 48/2 (1970): 206–12.

Linnebo, Øystein. 'Platonism in the Philosophy of Mathematics.' In *The Stanford Encyclopedia of Philosophy*, Fall 2009 edn. Article published 21 Sept. 2009. <http://plato.stanford.edu/archives/fall2009/entries/platonism-mathematics>.

Loewer, Barry. 'A Guide to Naturalizing Semantics.' In Bob Hale and Crispin Wright (eds), *A Companion to the Philosophy of Language*, 108–26. Oxford: Wiley-Blackwell, 1997.

Loux, Michael J. 'Ontology.' In C. F. Delaney (ed.), *The Synoptic Vision: Essays on the Philosophy of Wilfrid Sellars*, 43–72. Notre Dame, IN: University of Notre Dame Press, 1977.

Loux, Michael J. 'Rules, Roles, and Ontological Commitment: An Examination of Sellars' Analysis of Abstract Reference.' In Joseph C. Pitt (ed.), *The Philosophy of Wilfrid Sellars: Queries and Extensions*, 229–56. Dordrecht: D. Reidel, 1978.

McCann, Hugh J. *Creation and the Sovereignty of God*. Bloomington, IN: Indiana University Press, 2012.

Maddy, Penelope. 'Believing the Axioms. I.' *Journal of Symbolic Logic*, 53/2 (1988): 481–511.

Maddy, Penelope. 'Believing the Axioms. II.' *Journal of Symbolic Logic*, 53/3 (1988): 736–64.

Maddy, Penelope. 'The Roots of Contemporary Platonism.' *Journal of Symbolic Logic*, 54/4 (1989): 1121–44.

Maddy, Penelope. *Naturalism in Mathematics*. Oxford: Clarendon, 1997.

Maddy, Penelope. *Defending the Axioms: On the Philosophical Foundations of Set Theory*. Oxford: Oxford University Press, 2011.

Mag Uidhir, Christy. 'Introduction: Art, Metaphysics, and the Paradox of Standards.' In Christy Mag Uidhir (ed.), *Art and Abstract Objects*, 1–26. Oxford: Oxford University Press, 2012.

Marcus, Ruth Barcan. 'Quantification and Ontology.' *Noûs*, 6/3 (1972): 240–50.
Margolis, Joseph. 'Reference as Relational: *Pro* and *Contra*.' In Rudolf Haller (ed.), *Non-Existence and Predication*, 327–58. Amsterdam: Rodopi, 1986.
Maudlin, Tim. 'On the Foundations of Physics.' Article published 5 July 2013. <http://www.3ammagazine.com/3am/philosophy-of-physic>
Meinong, Alexius. 'The Theory of Objects' ('*Über Gegenstandstheorie*', 1904). Tr. Isaac Levi, D. B. Terrell, and Roderick M. Chisholm. In Roderick M. Chisholm (ed.), *Realism and the Background of Phenomenology*, 76–117. Atascadero, CA: Ridgeview, 1960.
Menzel, Christopher. 'God and Mathematical Objects.' In Russell W. Howell and W. James Bradley (eds), *Mathematics in a Postmodern Age*, 65–97. Grand Rapids, MI: William B. Eerdmans, 2001.
Menzel, Christopher. 'Problems with the Bootstrapping Objection: A Response to Craig's "God and Abstract Objects".' Paper presented at the Central Division meeting of the American Philosophical Association, Chicago, IL, 27 Feb. 2014.
Merricks, Trenton. *Truth and Ontology*. Oxford: Clarendon Press, 2007.
Meyer, Ulrich. 'The Presentist's Dilemma.' *Philosophical Studies*, 122/3 (2005): 213–25.
Moltmann, Friederike. *Abstract Objects and the Semantics of Natural Language*. Oxford: Oxford University Press, 2013.
Moo, Douglas J. *The Epistle to the Romans*. New International Commentary on the New Testament. Grand Rapids, MI: Wm. B. Eerdmans, 1996.
Moreland, J. P. *Universals*. Central Problems of Philosophy. Chesham, Bucks.: Acumen, 2001.
Morris, Thomas V. 'On God and Mann: A View of Divine Simplicity.' *Religious Studies*, 21/3 (1985): 299–318.
Morris, Thomas V. *Anselmian Explorations: Essays in Philosophical Theology*. Notre Dame, IN: University of Notre Dame Press, 1987.
Morris, Thomas V. 'Metaphysical Dependence, Independence, and Perfection.' In Scott MacDonald (ed.), *Being and Goodness: The Concept of the Good in Metaphysics and Philosophical Theology*, 278–98. Ithaca, NY: Cornell University Press, 1991.
Morris, Thomas V., and Christopher Menzel. 'Absolute Creation.' *American Philosophical Quarterly*, 23/4 (1986): 353–62.
Naylor, Margery Bedford. 'A Note on David Lewis's Realism about Possible Worlds.' *Analysis*, 46/1 (1986): 28–9.
Nicomachus of Gerasa. *Introduction to Arithmetic*. Tr. Martin Luther D'Ooge. New York: Macmillan Co., 1926.
Nolt, John. 'Free Logics.' In Dale Jacquette (ed.), *Handbook of the Philosophy of Science*, v. *Philosophy of Logic*, 1023–60. Amsterdam: Elsevier, 2006.

Nolt, John. 'Free Logic.' In *The Stanford Encyclopedia of Philosophy*, Summer 2010 edn. Article published 21 June 2010. <http://plato.stanford.edu/archives/sum2010/entries/logic-free>.

O'Brien, Peter T. *Colossians, Philemon*. Word Biblical Commentary. Nashville, TN: Thomas Nelson, 2000.

Ogden, C. K. *Bentham's Theory of Fictions*. New York: Harcourt, Brace, & Co., 1932.

Oppy, Graham. 'Response to Greg Welty.' In Paul M. Gould (ed.), *Beyond the Control of God? Six Views on the Problem of God and Abstract Objects*, 104–6. London: Bloomsbury, 2014.

Orenstein, Alex. 'Is Existence What Existential Quantification Expresses?' In Robert B. Barrett and Roger F. Gibson (eds), *Perspectives on Quine*, 245–70. Oxford: Basil Blackwell, 1990.

Origen. *On First Principles [De Principiis]*. Tr. G. W. Butterworth. Gloucester, MA: Peter Smith, 1973.

Parsons, Charles. 'What is the Iterative Conception of Set?' In Paul Benacerraf and Hilary Putnam (eds), *Philosophy of Mathematics: Selected Readings*, 2nd edn, 503–29. Cambridge: Cambridge University Press, 1983.

Plantinga, Alvin. *Does God Have a Nature?* Milwaukee, WI: Marquette University Press, 1980.

Plantinga, Alvin. *Warrant and Proper Function*. Oxford: Oxford University Press, 1993.

Plantinga, Alvin. *Warranted Christian Belief*. Oxford: Oxford University Press, 2000.

Plantinga, Alvin. 'Against Materialism.' *Faith and Philosophy*, 23/1 (2006): 3–32.

Plantinga, Alvin. *Where the Conflict Really Lies: Science, Religion, and Naturalism*. Oxford: Oxford University Press, 2011.

Plantinga, Alvin. 'Response to William Lane Craig's Review of *Where the Conflict Really Lies*.' *Philosophia Christi*, 15/1 (2013): 175–82.

Posy, Carl. 'Intuitionism and Philosophy.' In Stewart Shapiro (ed.), *The Oxford Handbook of Philosophy of Mathematics and Logic*, 318–55. Oxford: Oxford University Press, 2005.

Potter, Michael. *Set Theory and its Philosophy: A Critical Introduction*. Oxford: Oxford University Press, 2004.

Prestige, George L. *God in Patristic Thought*. London: SPCK, 1964.

Priest, Graham. *Towards Non-Being: The Logic and Metaphysics of Intentionality*. Oxford: Clarendon, 2005.

Proudfoot, Diane, and B. Jack Copeland. 'Wittgenstein's Deflationary Account of Reference.' *Language and Communication*, 22/3 (2002): 331–51.

Quine, W. V. O. 'On What There Is.' *Review of Metaphysics*, 2/5 (1948): 21–38.

Quine, W. V. O. 'Logic and the Reification of Universals.' In *From a Logical Point of View*, 102–29. Cambridge, MA: Harvard University Press, 1953.
Quine, W. V. O. *Word and Object*. Cambridge, MA: MIT Press, 1960.
Quine, W. V. O. *The Roots of Reference*. LaSalle, IL: Open Court, 1973.
Quine, W. V. O. 'Responses.' In *Theories and Things*, 173–86. Cambridge, MA: Harvard University Press, 1981.
Quine, W. V. O. *Philosophy of Logic*, 2nd edn. Cambridge, MA: Harvard University Press, 1986.
Reimer, Marga. 'Reference.' In *The Stanford Encyclopedia of Philosophy*, Spring 2003 edn. Article published 21 Mar. 2003. <http://plato.stanford.edu/archives/spr2003/entries/reference>.
Resnik, Michael D. *Frege and the Philosophy of Mathematics*. Ithaca, NY: Cornell University Press, 1980.
Rich, Audrey N. M. 'The Platonic Ideas as the Thoughts of God.' *Mnemosyne*, 7/2 (1954): 123–33.
Rodriguez-Pereyra, Gonzalo. 'Nominalism in Metaphysics.' In *The Stanford Encyclopedia of Philosophy*, Fall 2011 edn. Article published 21 Sept. 2011. <http://plato.stanford.edu/archives/fall2011/entries/nominalism-metaphysics>.
Rosen, Gideon. 'What is Constructive Empiricism?' *Philosophical Studies*, 74/2 (1994): 143–78.
Rosen, Gideon. 'Problems in the History of Fictionalism.' In Mark Eli Kalderon (ed.), *Fictionalism in Metaphysics*, 14–64. Oxford: Clarendon Press, 2005.
Rosen, Gideon, and John P. Burgess. 'Nominalism Reconsidered.' In Stewart Shapiro (ed.), *The Oxford Handbook of Philosophy of Mathematics and Logic*, 515–35. Oxford: Oxford University Press, 2005.
Rosenberg, Alex. *The Atheist's Guide to Reality: Enjoying Life without Illusions*. New York: W. W. Norton & Co., 2011.
Routley, Richard. *Exploring Meinong's Jungle and Beyond: An Investigation of Noneism and the Theory of Items*. Canberra: Australian National University Research School of Social Sciences, 1979.
Runia, David T. *Philo of Alexandria and the 'Timaeus' of Plato*. Amsterdam: Free University of Amsterdam, 1983.
Russell, Bertrand. 'Recent Work on the Principles of Mathematics.' *International Monthly*, 4 (1901): 83–101.
Russell, Bertrand. 'Letter to Frege.' In Jean van Heijenoort (ed.), *From Frege to Gödel: A Source Book in Mathematical Logic, 1879–1931*, 124–5. Cambridge, MA: Harvard University Press, 1967.
Russell, Bertrand. *Introduction to Mathematical Philosophy*. London: George Allen & Unwin, 1985.
Sainsbury, R. M. *Reference without Referents*. Oxford: Clarendon, 2005.

Schock, Rolf. *Logics without Existence Assumptions*. Stockholm: Almqvist & Wiksell, 1968.
Searle, John R. *Speech Acts: An Essay in the Philosophy of Language*. Cambridge: Cambridge University Press, 1969.
Searle, John R. *Expression and Meaning: Studies in the Theory of Speech Acts*. Cambridge: Cambridge University Press, 1979.
Searle, John R. *Intentionality: An Essay in the Philosophy of Mind*. Cambridge: Cambridge University Press, 1983.
Searle, John R. *The Construction of Social Reality*. New York: Free Press, 1995.
Sellars, Wilfrid. 'Realism and the New Way of Words.' *Philosophy and Phenomenological Research*, 8/4 (1948): 601–34.
Shapiro, Stewart. *Philosophy of Mathematics: Structure and Ontology*. Oxford: Oxford University Press, 1997.
Shapiro, Stewart. 'Philosophy of Mathematics and Its Logic: Introduction.' In Stewart Shapiro (ed.), *The Oxford Handbook of Philosophy of Mathematics and Logic*, 3–27. Oxford: Oxford University Press, 2005.
Sider, Theodore. 'Presentism and Ontological Commitment.' *Journal of Philosophy*, 96/7 (1999): 325–47.
Sider, Theodore. 'Quantifiers and Temporal Ontology.' *Mind*, 115/457 (2006): 75–97.
Sider, Theodore. 'Introduction.' In Theodore Sider, John Hawthorne, and Dean W. Zimmerman (eds), *Contemporary Debates in Metaphysics*, 1–8. Oxford: Blackwell, 2008.
Sider, Theodore. *Writing the Book of the World*. Oxford: Clarendon, 2011.
Smith, R. Scott. *Naturalism and Our Knowledge of Reality: Testing Religious Truth-Claims*. Farnham: Ashgate, 2012.
Steiner, Mark. *Mathematical Knowledge*. Ithaca, NY: Cornell University Press, 1975.
Steiner, Mark. *The Applicability of Mathematics as a Philosophical Problem*. Cambridge, MA: Harvard University Press, 1998.
Sterling, Gregory E. '"Day One": Platonizing Exegetical Traditions of Genesis 1: 1–5 in John and Jewish Authors.' Paper presented at the Philo section of the Society of Biblical Literature, San Antonio, TX, 20 Nov. 2004.
Tilling, Chris. 'Problems with Ehrman's Interpretive Categories.' In Michael F. Bird (ed.), *How God Became Jesus: The Real Origins of Belief in Jesus' Divine Nature*, 117–33. Grand Rapids, MI: Zondervan, 2014.
Vaihinger, Hans. *The Philosophy of 'As If'* (1911), 2nd edn. Tr. C. K. Ogden. International Library of Psychology, Philosophy, and Scientific Method. London: Routledge & Kegan Paul, 1949.
van Inwagen, Peter. 'Creatures of Fiction.' *American Philosophical Quarterly*, 14/4 (1977): 299–308.

van Inwagen, Peter. 'The Doctrine of Arbitrary Undetached Parts.' *Pacific Philosophical Quarterly*, 62 (1981): 123–37.
van Inwagen, Peter. 'Fiction and Metaphysics.' *Philosophy and Literature*, 7/1 (1983): 67–77.
van Inwagen, Peter. *Material Beings*. Ithaca, NY: Cornell University Press, 1990.
van Inwagen, Peter. 'Quantification and Fictional Discourse.' In Anthony Everett and Thomas Hofweber (eds), *Empty Names, Fiction, and the Puzzles of Non-Existence*, 235–46. Stanford, CA: Center for the Study of Language and Information, 2000.
van Inwagen, Peter. 'Meta-ontology.' In *Ontology, Identity, and Modality: Essays in Metaphysics*, 13–31. Cambridge: Cambridge University Press, 2001.
van Inwagen, Peter. *Ontology, Identity, and Modality: Essays in Metaphysics*. Cambridge: Cambridge University Press, 2001.
van Inwagen, Peter. 'A Theory of Properties.' In Dean Zimmerman (ed.), *Oxford Studies in Metaphysics*, i. 107–38. Oxford: Clarendon, 2004.
van Inwagen, Peter. 'Being, Existence, and Ontological Commitment.' In David J. Chalmers, David Manley, and Ryan Wasserman (eds), *Metametaphysics: New Essays on the Foundations of Ontology*, 472–506. Oxford: Clarendon, 2009.
van Inwagen, Peter. 'God and Other Uncreated Things.' In Kevin Timpe (ed.), *Metaphysics and God: Essays in Honor of Eleonore Stump*, 3–20. London: Routledge, 2009.
van Inwagen, Peter. *Metaphysics*, 3rd edn. Boulder, CO: Westview, 2009.
van Inwagen, Peter. 'Relational vs. Constituent Ontologies.' *Philosophical Perspectives*, 25/1 (2011): 389–405.
van Inwagen, Peter. 'Dispensing with Ontological Levels: An Illustration.' LanCog Lectures in Metaphysics 2013, *Disputatio*, 6/38 (2014): 25–43.
van Inwagen, Peter. 'Did God Create Shapes?' *Philosophia Christi*, 17/2 (2015): 285–90.
Varzi, Achille C. 'Words and Objects.' In Andrea Bottani, Massimiliano Carrara, and Pierdaniele Giaretta (eds), *Individuals, Essence and Identity: Themes of Analytic Metaphysics*, 49–75. Dordrecht: Kluwer Academic Publishers, 2002.
Vision, Gerald. 'Reference and the Ghost of Parmenides.' In Rudolf Haller (ed.), *Non-Existence and Predication*, 297–326. Amsterdam: Rodopi, 1986.
von Neumann, John. 'An Axiomatization of Set Theory.' In Jean van Heijenoort (ed.), *From Frege to Gödel: A Source Book in Mathematical Logic, 1879–1931*, 394–413. Cambridge, MA: Harvard University Press, 1967.
von Neumann, John. 'On the Introduction of Transfinite Numbers.' In Jean van Heijenoort (ed.), *From Frege to Gödel: A Source Book in Mathematical Logic, 1879–1931*, 346–54. Cambridge, MA: Harvard University Press, 1967.

Walton, Kendall L. *Mimesis as Make-Believe: On the Foundations of the Representational Arts.* Cambridge, MA: Harvard University Press, 1990.

Walton, Kendall L. 'Existence as Metaphor.' In Anthony Everett and Thomas Hofweber (eds), *Empty Names, Fiction, and the Puzzles of Non-Existence,* 69–94. Stanford, CA: Center for the Study of Language and Information, 2000.

Welty, Greg. 'Theistic Conceptual Realism: The Case for Interpreting Abstract Objects as Divine Ideas.' D.Phil. thesis, University of Oxford, 2006.

Welty, Greg. 'Response to Critics.' In Paul M. Gould (ed.), *Beyond the Control of God? Six Views on the Problem of God and Abstract Objects,* 107–12. London: Bloomsbury, 2014.

Welty, Greg. 'Theistic Conceptual Realism.' In Paul M. Gould (ed.), *Beyond the Control of God? Six Views on the Problem of God and Abstract Objects,* 81–96. London: Bloomsbury, 2014.

Wigner, Eugene P. 'The Unreasonable Effectiveness of Mathematics in the Natural Sciences.' *Communications on Pure and Applied Mathematics,* 13/1 (1960): 1–14.

Willard, Dallas. 'Knowledge and Naturalism.' In William Lane Craig and J. P. Moreland (eds), *Naturalism: A Critical Analysis,* 24–48. London: Routledge, 2000.

Williamson, Timothy. 'Reference.' In Donald Borchert (ed.), *Encyclopedia of Philosophy,* 2nd edn. New York: Thomson-Gale, 2006.

Williamson, Timothy. *Modal Logic as Metaphysics.* Oxford: Oxford University Press, 2013.

Wolfson, Harry A. 'Plato's Pre-existent Matter in Patristic Philosophy.' In Luitpold Wallach (ed.), *The Classical Tradition: Literary and Historical Studies in Honor of Harry Caplan,* 409–20. Ithaca, NY: Cornell University Press, 1966.

Wolfson, Harry A. 'The Logos and Platonic Ideas.' In *Philosophy of the Church Fathers: Faith, Trinity, Incarnation,* 3rd edn rev. Cambridge, MA: Harvard University Press, 1970.

Yablo, Stephen. 'Does Ontology Rest on a Mistake?' *Proceedings of the Aristotelian Society* (Supplement), 72 (1998): 229–61.

Yablo, Stephen. 'A Paradox of Existence.' In Anthony Everett and Thomas Hofweber (eds), *Empty Names, Fiction, and the Puzzles of Non-Existence,* 275–312. Stanford, CA: Center for the Study of Language and Information, 2000.

Yablo, Stephen. 'Go Figure: A Path through Fictionalism.' In Peter A. French and Howard K. Wettstein (eds), *Figurative Language,* Midwest Studies in Philosophy, 25: 72–102. Oxford: Blackwell, 2001.

Yablo, Stephen. 'Abstract Objects: A Case Study.' In Ernest Sosa and Enrique Villanueva (eds), *Realism and Relativism,* 220–40. Boston: Blackwell, 2002.

Yablo, Stephen. 'The Myth of the Seven.' In Mark Eli Kalderon (ed.), *Fictionalism in Metaphysics*, 88–115. Oxford: Clarendon Press, 2005.

Yagisawa, Takashi. 'Beyond Possible Worlds.' *Philosophical Studies*, 53/2 (1988): 175–204.

Yagisawa, Takashi. 'Critical Notice of *Modal Logic as Metaphysics*, by Timothy Williamson.' *Notre Dame Philosophical Reviews*. Article published 15 Oct. 2013. <http://ndpr.nd.edu/news/43612-modal-logic-as-metaphysics>.

Yandell, Keith. 'God and Propositions.' In Paul M. Gould (ed.), *Beyond the Control of God? Six Views on the Problem of God and Abstract Objects*, 21–35. London: Bloomsbury, 2014.

Zermelo, Ernst. 'Investigations in the Foundations of Set Theory I.' In Jean van Heijenoort (ed.), *From Frege to Gödel: A Source Book in Mathematical Logic, 1879–1931*, 199–215. Cambridge, MA: Harvard University Press, 1967.

General Index

aboutness 75, 77, 126, 129–30, 138; *see also* intentional; intentionality; reference
absolute creationism 50, 54–7, 66–8, 206
  and ontological commitment 70
  bootstrapping objection 60–3, 64, 68, 206
  heavyweight 68–71
  problems of scope and freedom in creation 56–8
abstract objects, *see* objects, abstract
Adams, Robert 112–13
agenētos/genētos 32–4, 37, 39; *see also agennētos/gennētos*; *ginomai*; Council of Nicea
agennētos/gennētos 32, 38; *see also agenētos/genētos*; Council of Nicea
ante-Nicene Fathers, *see* early Church Fathers
anti-Platonism 6–8, 173; *see also* Platonism
anti-realism 6–9, 11–12, 50, 82–3, 139, 151–2, 157–8
  argument from "lightheartedness" 176
  theistic 164, 206–8
  see also taxonomy of views on abstract objects
applicability of mathematics, *see* mathematical, structure of physical world
arealism 50, 51–3; *see also* taxonomy of views on abstract objects
Arianism 32–3
Aristotle 56
aseity 1, 12, 206
  and biblical theology, *see* biblical theology
  and perfect being theology 41
  as corollary of omnipotence 41, 43, 54–5
  early Church Fathers on 33–40
  as essential attribute 30–1, 53
  see also doctrine of aseity

Athanasius 32–3
atheism 11, 72 n.1
Athenagoras 35
attributes, *see* properties, aseity, as essential attribute
Augustinian tradition 73
axiomatization 188–97
  as fix for naïve set theory 191
axioms 42, 133, 145, 148, 162–3
  Peano 149, 162
  set theory, *see* set theory, axioms of
  Zermelo-Fraenkel set theory 174
  see also statements; mathematical
Azzouni, Jody 105–6, 108, 129–30, 134, 139, 152

Balaguer, Mark 45, 49, 52, 145–6, 163
Bar-Hillel, Yehoshua 191, 196
Bauckham, Richard 16, 34
Båve, Arvid 135–9
being, to come into 14–15, 18, 79; *see also ginomai*
being, uncreated 14, 15
begotten, Christ as, *see* Christ and Nicene statements on, *agennētos/gennētos*
Bentham, Jeremy 145
biblical theology 29–31; *see also* biblical; exegesis; systematic theology; theology
Boolos, George 193
bootstrapping objection, *see* absolute creationism, conceptualism, ontological assay
Brentano, Franz 136
Burgess, John 11, 113, 155, 174

Cantor, Georg 191
Carnap, Rudolf 51–3, 158
causal dependence 61–3, 78; *see also* logical dependence; ontological dependence
Christ 24
  and Nicene statements on 32; *see also agenētos*; Council of Nicea
  as Logos or agent of creation 25

Christian Platonism, see Platonism, Christian
"Christological monotheism" 18
Church Fathers, see early Church Fathers
classical theism 12, 43, 50, 56, 69, 74, 78, 144, 165, 180, 186–7, 204; see also theism
Cohen, Paul 202
combinatorial approach, see objects, abstract objects, combinatorial approach to
communicable attributes, see properties, communicable
conceptualism 51, 55, 72, 206
   and bootstrapping objection 78–9
   and God's first-person beliefs, see God, first-person beliefs of
   problem of thoughts as concrete objects; see also objects; concrete; as God's thoughts 84–5, 92–4
   see also taxonomy of views on abstract objects; theistic conceptual realism
concrete objects, see objects, concrete
concretism 50–1
constructivism 194–5
contingent 6, 30, 34; see also metaphysical contingency
Continuum Hypothesis 174, 202–3
conventionalism 51–3; see also taxonomy of views on abstract objects
Council of Nicea 31, 34–5, 39; see also Nicene Creed
counterfactuals 160
counting, see numbers, experience of counting
creatio ex nihilo 26, 37, 173; see also doctrine, of creation
creation, the 57–8, 164; see also doctrine, of creation
Creator, see God

Davis, Richard 66 n.27, 78
Dedekind, Richard 191
deductivism 184, 190
deflationary theory, see reference, deflationary theory of; truth, deflationary theory of
demiurge 36 n.38, 43
discourse:
   figurative and literal, see figuralism

mathematical, see statements, mathematical
metaphysically heavyweight, see Ontologese
modal, see statements, modal
possible worlds, see statements, modal
divine aseity, see aseity
divine conceptualism, see conceptualism
divine omnipotence, see omnipotence
divine omniscience, see omniscience
divine simplicity, see simplicity
divine sovereignty, see sovereignty
doctrine:
   of aseity 3, 17, 81, 208
   of creation 3, 57
   of independence and eternality of matter 35
domain of quantification, see quantification; quantifiers
Dummett, Michael 9, 11, 131
Dunn, James D. G. 26

early Church Fathers 31–40
   and divine conceptualism 72, 207
   and use of quantifiers, see quantifiers
   views on numbers 34, 38
   views on properties 34–5, 37, 40
eternal and eternity 2, 3, 17; see also eternality; objects, abstract; temporal vs timeless
eternality 6, 34, 57
exegesis, biblical 17, 33; see also biblical theology
exemplification 43, 67–8, 80
existential metaphors 168
existential quantification, see quantification, existential
"exists" 49, 105–6, 112–13, 115–16, 120
   stipulated as heavyweight, see quantifiers, stipulated as heavyweight 208
existentially loaded quantifier, see ontological commitment, existentially loaded quantifier
extensional contexts 47–8, 74 n.8
external questions, see linguistic frameworks

fictionalism 51, 144–7, 153
   and linguistic frameworks 158–60
   and neo-Quinean criterion 148–51, 186, 208

and obviousness of
    arithmetic 147–51, 156
and utility of mathematics 153–7,
    161, 163
as self-defeating 158–60,
    162, 164
see also taxonomy of views on abstract
    objects
fictionally true 159–60; see also truth
Field, Hartry 8, 145–6, 161
figuralism 51, 144, 145, 165, 167
    arguments and replies 174–8
    explanatory benefits 173
    figurative discourse and Platonic
        object discourse 169
    figurative discourse vs literal
        discourse 167, 176–9
    see also taxonomy of views on abstract
        objects; anti-realism
first-order logic, see logic, first-order
formalism 190 n.17; see also taxonomy
    of views on abstract objects
Forms, Platonic 2
    as ideas in the mind of God 36, 38 n.41
    see also Platonism
Fraenkel, Abraham 191,
    196, 197
free logic, see logic, free; taxonomy of
    views on abstract objects
Frege, Gottlob 7, 72, 191, 192

ginomai 14; see also being, to come into;
    agenētos/genētos
God 1–6, 11, 177–8
    and "late creation", see "late creation"
    as beginningless 35
    as cause of everything other than
        Himself 4, 33, 41, 82
    concept of 1, 31
        from Stoic philosophers 24–6
    as creator 2, 4, 11–12, 14, 16, 24–5,
        30, 35, 57–8, 164
    of His own properties, see absolute
        creationism, bootstrapping
        objection
    first-person beliefs of 85–7
    the Father as source and goal of all
        things 24, 26
    goodness of 8 n.6, 19, 35
    as greatest conceivable being 31
    nature of 43, 43 n.47, 55,
        57, 64

objects existing "inside" vs "outside"
    Himself 80–3
ontological argument for, see
    ontological argument
self-existence of 1, 3, 9, 12; see also
    self-existence
as sole ultimate reality 2, 12,
    13–43, 206
as sole uncreated being 14, 16, 16 n.4,
    18, 23–4, 26, 31–4, 40
the Son as creator 26; see also Logos;
    Christ
thoughts as abstract objects 80–1,
    92–4; see also conceptualism
as transcendent 34
will of 57, 58
Word of 14–15, 17, 18, 39–40; see also
    Logos
see also perfect being theology
Gould, Paul 66 n.27, 78
great-making property, see properties,
    great-making

Hale, Bob 10
heavyweight, see metaphysically
    heavyweight; Platonism,
    heavyweight; absolute
    creationism
Hilbert, David 192
Hippolytus 33, 38–9
Horsley, Richard 25
Husserl, Edmund 136

ideal objects, see objects, abstract
identity statements, see logic, free; logic,
    standard
immaterial vs material objects, see
    objects, immaterial vs material
incommunicable attributes, see
    properties, incommunicable
Indispensability Arguments, see
    Platonism, arguments for
Inman, Ross 122 n.59
instrumentalism
    154–7
intelligible realm 20, 20 n.12, 21, 23, 25,
    35, 38, 39; see also *kosmos noētos*;
    sensible realm
intensional contexts 47–8, 74 n.8,
    114, 118
intentional statements, see statements,
    intentional

intentionality 74, 92, 137, 139
  derivative vs intrinsic 75-6, 134
  see also reference
internal questions, see linguistic
  frameworks
intuitionism 203
intuitive warrant 190, 191, 192, 202-3
"iterative concept of set" 194, 195

Jewish merism 26
Jewish monotheism 18, 30
John (biblical author) 13, 15, 17, 18
  Logos doctrine of 13-19, 27, 38-9
John's prologue 13-23, 38-9
  use of quantifiers in, see quantifiers
  uses of 'being' and 'becoming' 23-4
Judaism
  first-century 16-17
  Hellenistic 18, 24, 25, 38, 39

kosmos noētos 21, 25-6; see also
  intelligible realm
Kripke, Saul 110-11
Kunen, Kenneth 198

Lambert, Karel 140, 141
"late creation":
  and abstract objects 29
  and angels 29
  and souls 29
  models of 28-9
Leftow, Brian 2, 27-8, 30, 55, 82
Leng, Mary 148-51, 163, 183-6
Leonhardt-Balzer, Jutta 18-19, 20 n.10
Lewis, C. S. 177 n.17
Lewis, David 119, 122-3
lightweight, see metaphysically
  lightweight; Platonism, lightweight
linguistic frameworks 51-2
  and external questions 51, 159
  and internal questions 51-2, 158-9;
    see also fictionalism
  see also metalanguage
logic:
  existence assumptions of 140, 141
  first-order 49, 119
    semantics for 107-10
  free 51, 126, 127, 137, 153
    and dual domain semantics 128
    identity statements in 141-2
    positive 142, 166, 208
  see also taxonomy of views on abstract
    objects

standard 140 n.34
  identity statements in 141-2
logical dependence 61-2
logicism 190
Logos 25-6
  as Wisdom personified 36-7
  role causally prior to creation 20
  role in creation 18-21
  see also Christ; God, the Son as
    creator; God, Word of
Logos Christology 38-40

Maddy, Penelope 52, 153, 199
manifestation condition 154-6, 188
Marcus, Ruth Barcan 108
mathematical:
  depth 189
  discourse, see statements,
    mathematical
  fictional interpretation of, see set
    theory
  "maximizing principles", see
    Platonism, "maximizing
    principles"
  objects, see objects, mathematical
  philosophy of, see philosophy of
    mathematics
  structure of physical world 163-4
Maudlin, Tim 163
McCann, Hugh 56
Meinong, Alexius 104, 126-7,
  136-7
Menzel, Christopher 54
mereological nihilism 9 n.7,
  12 n.17, 30
mereological sums 122-4
mereological universalism 122
metalanguage 108-10, 159; see also
  linguistic frameworks
meta-ontology 49
  and neo-Quinean theses 97-8,
    100, 104
metaphysical contingency 5
metaphysically heavyweight 49, 120
metaphysically lightweight
  112-13, 208
metaphysical necessity 5, 5 n.4, 30,
  31, 35, 53; see also necessity;
  properties, essential;
  necessitism
Methodius 33, 37, 41
Middle Platonism, see Platonism, Middle
Moltmann, Friederike 68

General Index

Moo, Douglas 24, 26
Moreland, J. P. 63, 90–1
Morris, Thomas 31, 54

naturalism, explanatory resources of 164
necessitism 119, 121
necessity 3, 6, 30, 39, 57; *see also* metaphysical necessity; properties, essential
neo-Meinongianism 51, 104, 115–16, 125–7
   compared to neutralism 127
   see also taxonomy of views on
neo-Platonic emanationism 58
neutralism 51, 104–7, 110–12, 137, 142–3, 165, 207
   as collapsing into fictionalism 151–2
   compared to neo-Meinongian and neo-Quinean theses 127, 129–30, 141
   replies to 112–13, 115–16, 139
   see also taxonomy of views on abstract objects
Nicene Creed 31–2, *see also* Council of Nicea
Nicene Fathers, *see* early Church Fathers
Nicomachus of Gerasa 21
Nietzsche, Friedrich 11
Nolt, John 127–8
nominalism 7, 7 n.5, 8, 158
   hermeneutic vs revolutionary, *see* figuralism, arguments & replies
   vs anti-Platonism and anti-realism 7
non-existent objects, *see* objects, non-existent
numbers 34, 38, 42, 51–2, 57, 87–8, 92, 95, 130, 137, 149–50, 158
   experience of counting 150–1
   natural 42
   transfinite 42

objects:
   abstract 3–10, 12, 15–18, 21, 23, 26–7, 29, 32, 34, 40–1, 43
      combinatorial approach to 174, 207, 208
      examples of 3–5, 18
      as fictional entities 144; *see also* object, mathematical
      as mind-dependent 8, 20–4, 36, 79
      as mind-independent 15, 27, 72
      as referents 49–50
      role in a physical theory 16
      taxonomy of views on, *see* taxonomy of views on abstract objects
      temporal vs timeless 29 n.30, 57
abstract-concrete distinction 3–6, 16 n.3
   and social (or institutional) facts 131–2, 133 n.19, 207; *see also* socially constructed reality; Searle, John
concrete 3–9, 16 n.3, 18
   and immaterial objects 20 n.12
   as creations of God 23, 26–7
   as God's thoughts 80–1, 84; *see also* conceptualism
   as more substantial than abstract objects 35, 37
material vs immaterial 4, 20
mathematical 2–3, 7–8, 11, 27, 41, 50, 158
   as useful fictions 145, 157, 184–5, 190; *see also* fictionalism; pretence theory
   incompleteness of 201
non-existent 104, 126, 129, 136, 137, 139, 182; *see also* neo-Meinongianism
semantic 10, 12
spatiotemporal vs non-spatiotemporal 4, 5, 76, 91, 119; *see also* linguistic frameworks
omnipotence 1, 30, 41, 65; *see also* sovereignty
omniscience 86, 109
One over the Many, problem of 44
Ontologese 152–3, 152–3 n.22, 165, 207, 208
ontological argument 192
ontological assay 63, 64, 66–7, 68, 79, 206
ontological commitment 9, 12, 40, 165–6
   and beliefs of scientific community 155, 179
   and counterfactuals 160
   and existentially loaded quantifier 104–5, 116, 117–18, 119–21, 124, 126–7, 141, 143; *see also* quantifiers, particular
   and meta-ontological claims 49
   and set theory 199

ontological commitment (*cont.*)
    and truths of elementary
        arithmetic 148–51; *see also*
        statements, mathematical
    criterion of 46, 48, 69–70, 96–7,
        114, 118
    existential quantification as device
        of 48, 50, 51, 104, 107–10, 118,
        119, 159, 207
    neo-Quinean theses on 97–8, 116–17,
        118, 121, 142 n.38, 167, 186;
        see also meta-ontology
    as person-relative 106
    singular terms as devices of 46–8, 50,
        51, 125, 127, 140–3, 159, 207;
        see also heavyweight; lightweight
ontological dependence 57, 58
ontological pluralism 52
ontology:
    inflated 83
    relational vs constituent 69
    see also meta-ontology
Oppy, Graham 85–6
Origen 35–6

Paul (biblical author) 13, 24–7
paradox 158; *see also* fictionalism
paraphrasability 120, 169
paraphrases 10 n.13, 87–8, 97–8,
    101–3, 160
Parsons, Charles 195
particular quantifier, *see* quantifiers,
    particular; *see also* Routley,
    Richard
particulars 3, 4, 5, 7
perfect being theology 31, 41
Philo of Alexandria 18
    and Aristotle's four causes 19–20
    and provenance of John's views 23
    and provenance of Paul's
        expressions 25–6
    on creation 164
    Logos doctrine of 18–21
    view of ideal objects 23 n.16
philosophy of mathematics 7, 44–5,
    53–4, 72 n.1
Plantinga, Alvin 54–5, 73, 91, 92
Plato 2, 3, 3 n.3, 20, 34
Platonic Forms, *see* Platonic realm,
    Forms, Platonic
Platonic Ideas, *see* Platonic realm
Platonic realm 20–1, 145–6, 178

Platonism 2, 6–7, 8–12, 35, 41, 151, 203
    and anti-Platonism vs realism and
        anti-realism 7–8
    and Axiom Schema of Unrestricted
        Comprehension 191
    and uses of term "Platonism" 8–12
    arguments against, *see* taxonomy of
        views on abstract objects
    arguments for:
        Indispensability Arguments 45–6,
            49–53, 69, 70 n.37, 74, 96, 125,
            144, 186, 207
        see also taxonomy of views on abstract
            objects
    Christian 14, 15, 18, 26, 32, 43
    classical 3, 18
    contemporary 3, 5, 9, 12, 40
    heavyweight 8–9, 12, 16, 43, 151–2;
        see also heavyweight
    lightweight 9–10, 12, 69; *see also*
        lightweight
    "maximizing principles" 199–200
    Middle 18–19, 21
        and interpretation of Genesis 1, 20
        as reflected in John's Prologue 23
        as reflected in Paul's letters 24
        see also anti-Platonism; ontological
            commitment; taxonomy of views
            on abstract objects
positive free logic, *see* logic, free, positive
possible worlds 3, 18, 30–1, 74
Potter, Michael 190, 198
"prepositional metaphysics" 19, 24
prescribed imagining 182, 190; *see also*
    pretence theory
presentism 117–18, 119–20
Prestige, George 34
pretence theory 51, 93–4, 144, 165, 181,
    196, 203–5
    and make-believe 182, 187, 190–1
    vs fictionalism 187
    vs figuralism 204
    set theory as ideal candidate for
        200, 201
principle of universal
    comprehension 191, 197
principle of unrestricted mereological
    composition, *see* mereological
    sums
principles of generation 182–4, 202
problem of the One over the Many, *see*
    One over the Many, problem of

General Index 239

properties 1, 3–5, 7–9, 10 n.13, 29 n.30, 30–1, 34–5, 37, 40–1, 43, 59, 89–92, 206
and independent existence 34–5
communicable 1
created and uncreated 66
early Church Fathers' views, *see* early Church Fathers, views on properties
essential 61
great-making 31, 41
incommunicable 1
propositions 3–5, 7, 8, 18, 74, 76
aboutness of, *see* aboutness; intentionality
as objects of God's beliefs 84–5
psychologism 72
Pythagoras 34, 38

qualities, *see* properties
quantification:
and objectual semantics for, *see* logic, first-order, semantics for
and substitutional semantics for, *see* logic, first-order, semantics for
domain of 14, 15, 16, 26–7, 32–3, 40, 48, 107; *see also* quantifiers
existential:
as metaphysically heavyweight 49, 99, 151
vs universal 48–9
ontically irrelevant 105, 106
ontically neutral 106, 107; *see also* "exist"
quantifiers 17
existentially loaded, *see* ontological commitment, existentially loaded quantifier
objectual, *see* quantifiers, referential; logic, first-order, semantics for
particular 105
referential 110–11
stipulated as heavyweight 109, 110, 151, 152
as used by Church Fathers 32–3
as used in John's Prologue 15–16
as used in Paul's letters 26–7
see also quantification
quantifier-variable idiom 97, 100
quarantine (of a theory's implications) 154–5

Quine, W. V. O. 16, 45–6, 125, 208; *see also* meta-ontology; ontological commitment

realism 6–8, 11, 50, 80, 152, 196, 199
as impediment to mathematics 200
non-Platonic 72, 74
theistic 164, 207
see also anti-realism; arealism
reference 125–6
Azzouni's theory of 129–30, 134
deflationary theory of 135–9, 207
and empty singular terms 132
nature of 133–9
as a property 137
as a relation 130, 137
see also aboutness; *see also* intentionality
referentialism 126
resemblance 44–5; *see also* One over the Many, problem of; universals
Rosen, Gideon 155, 161–2, 174
Routley, Richard 104, 105, 114, 125–6
Runia, David 20

scientific use of fictions 184–5; *see also* objects, abstract; objects, mathematical
Searle, John 131–4, 138 n.30, 139 n.32; *see also* social (or institutional) facts
self-existence, *see* God, self-existence of
Sellars, Wilfrid 109
semantic ascent 162, 207
sensible realm 20–1, 35, 38, 39; *see also* intelligible realm
sets 3, 5, 8, 21, 42, 190, 193
and being well founded 198
as logical fictions 197
set-theoretical hierarchy 42, 195, 198
set theory 92–3, 162, 173–4, 200, 208
axioms 189, 192, 202
Axiom Schema of Restricted Comprehension 189, 191
of Choice 189, 196, 198
of Constructibility 189, 198–9, 202
of Determinacy 189, 199
of Extensionality 189, 193–4
of Foundation 189, 194–5, 198
of Infinity 189, 190–1, 192

set theory (cont.)
   as candidate for pretence theoretic approach 188, 196; see also set theory, reasons for fictional interpretation of
   naïve 191, 192
   other set theories 197–8
   reasons for fictional interpretation of 188–203
   axiomatization, see axiomatization
   creative freedom afforded by 197, 203
   incompleteness, see objects, mathematical, incompleteness of
   Zermelo-Fraenkel 174, 198
Sider, Theodore 10 n.13, 118, 152
simple sentences 46
simplicity 61–2, 64–6
singular terms, see ontological commitment, singular terms as devices of
empty, see reference
socially constructed reality, see objects, and social (or institutional) facts; Searle, John
"sole ultimate reality", see God, as sole ultimate reality
Sophia (personification of divine wisdom), see Logos
sovereignty:
   and theistic activism 55, 59, 71
   comparison to aseity debate in contemporary philosophy 54–5
   in Jewish monotheism 16
   see also omnipotence
spatiotemporal vs non-spatiotemporal objects, see objects, spatiotemporal vs non-spatiotemporal
special composition question, see statements, mereological; mereological nihilism; mereological sums; mereological universalism
statements:
   existentially quantified 45–6, 49–50
   as false but useful 98, 153–6, 161–2
   intentional 113–17
   mathematical 45–6, 50, 51, 96, 173
      axioms as truths 145, 148–9, 162, 174, 188
      obvious truth of 148–51
      truth of as indispensable in science 145–7, 153–6; see also Indispensability Arguments

   mereological 121–4
   modal 119–20
   tensed 117–18
   universally quantified 14, 15, 32, 49, 100, 108, 190
   see also simple sentences
static being vs temporal becoming, see Platonic realm
Steiner, Mark 16, 163
substances 37
systematic theology 31, 41; see also biblical theology; exegesis, biblical; theology

Tatian 35, 39
taxonomy of views on abstract objects:
   absolute creationism, see absolute creationism
   anti-realism, see anti-realism
   arealism, see arealism
   conceptualism, see conceptualism
   concretism, see concretism
   conventionalism, see concretism
   fictionalism, see fictionalism
   figuralism, see figuralism
   formalism, see formalism
   free logic, see logic, free
   neo-Meinongianism, see neo-Meinongianism
   neutralism, see neutralism
   Platonism, see Platonism
   pretence theory, see pretence theory
psychologism 72
temporal becoming 15, 57
tensed statements, see statements, tensed
terms, singular, see ontological commitment, singular terms as devices of tense 4
   as used in biblical creation accounts 27–9, 29 n.31
theism 14, 16, 43, 59, 79, 117, 163–4 n.38
   and tenable theories of abstract objects 165
   explanatory resources vs naturalism 164
   see also classical theism
theistic activism, see sovereignty, theistic activism
theistic conceptual realism 73, 78
   and violation of aseity 81

theology 59, 61; *see also* biblical theology; exegesis; systematic theology
theory of reference, *see* reference
"there is" and "there are", *see* "exists"
Timaeus 2 n.2, 43, 164
transcendence 34; *see also* God, as transcendent
truth 52, 97
  deflationary theory of 161–2, 207
  as entailing existence, *see* ontological commitment, logic, existence assumptions of
  logical 174
  quasi- 118
  trivial 141–2
truth conditions 109
truth value 4, 47, 49, 75, 143, 158; *see also* fictionally true

uncreatability 6
universals 3, 7
  problem of 44; *see also* One over the Many, problem of
  see also properties
"unreasonable effectiveness of mathematics" 163

unrestricted domain of quantification, *see* quantification, domain of

Vaihinger, Hans 145
Van Inwagen, Peter 9, 10 n.13, 69–71, 97–8, 112, 115
verisimilitude, *see* truth, quasi-
vicious circularity; *see also* bootstrapping objection 62
voluntarism 58
von Neumann, John 22, 202–3

Walton, Kendall 182–3
Walton's theory of fiction 182–3, 204
Welty, Greg 58, 73–7, 78, 80–1
Wigner, Eugene 163
Williamson, Timothy 119
will of God, *see* God, will of; voluntarism
Wisdom (personification of divine wisdom), *see* Logos
Wolfson, Harry Austryn 34
Word of God, *see* God, Word of; Logos

Yablo, Stephen 167, 172, 179, 204
Yahweh 17, 24
YHWH, *see* Yahweh

Index of Ancient Sources

Biblical
Genesis 1 20, 27
  1: 1 14, 19, 27
John 1: 1 27
  1: 1–3 39
  1: 1–5 13–14
  1: 3 27
  1: 3, 10 19, 20
Rom. 11: 36 24, 26
1 Cor. 8: 6 24, 25, 26
  11: 12 24
Col. 1: 15 27
  1: 15–16 24, 26
  1: 17b 29 n.31
Heb. 1: 3b 29 n.31

Athanasius
Defense of the Nicene Definition
  7.31–2 32–3
Discourses against the Arians 1.9.33–4 32–3
On the Councils of Ariminum and Seleucia 46–7 32

Athenagoras
Plea for the Christians 4 39 n.42
  15 35
  17 35
  24 35

Epiphanius
Panarion 33.7.6 33

Hippolytus
Against Noetus 10.1 33
  10–11 39–40
Refutation of All Heresies 4.43 38
  6.16 38
  6.18 38
  6.19 38
  10.28 33

Ireneaus
Against Heresies 4.38.3 33

Justin
Dialogue with Trypho, a Jew 5 33

Methodius
On Free Will 5 33

Origen
Commentary on the Gospel of John 1.22 36 n.38
On First Principles 1.2.2–3, 1.4.5 36
  1.4.5 37
  2.3.6 35–6

Philo of Alexandria
On the Cherubim 124–7 20
On the Creation of the World according to Moses 16–20, 24 22–3; 26–7; 19

Tatian
Address to the Greeks 4.10–14 35
  5.1–9 39

Tertullian
Against Praxeas 5.13–15 33

Theodoret
Letter of Eusebius of Nicomedia to Paulinus of Tyre, in *Ecclesiastical History* 1.5 33
Wisdom (or *Sirach*) 43:26 25

Printed and bound by CPI Group (UK) Ltd, Croydon, CR0 4YY